VACCINES AS TECHNOLOGY

The COVID-19 pandemic served as a powerful wake-up call, highlighting our collective need for the effective development and equitable distribution of new vaccines, in addition to widespread administration of existing ones. The current models of production and allocation of vaccines against emerging pathogens, which rely on predominantly market-driven mechanisms, are largely at odds with public health needs. This book explores the entire arc of vaccine development and distribution, from the decisions about allocation of vaccine R&D money to allocation and administration of vaccines resulting from the R&D process. It explains key concepts and problems in vaccine regulation, intellectual property, technology transfer, and international relations, making complex material accessible to a nonspecialist audience. Analyzing the impact of COVID-19, the book also covers several other vaccine races, as well as future directions in vaccine development and allocation.

Ana Santos Rutschman is outgoing Assistant Professor of Law, Saint Louis University and incoming Professor of Law at Villanova University. She was named a Health Law Scholar (2018) and a Bio Intellectual Property Scholar (2017) by the American Society of Law, Medicine & Ethics for her work on vaccine law and policy.

Vaccines as Technology

INNOVATION, BARRIERS, AND THE PUBLIC HEALTH

ANA SANTOS RUTSCHMAN

Saint Louis University School of Law

CAMBRIDGE
UNIVERSITY PRESS

University Printing House, Cambridge CB2 8BS, United Kingdom

One Liberty Plaza, 20th Floor, New York, NY 10006, USA

477 Williamstown Road, Port Melbourne, VIC 3207, Australia

314–321, 3rd Floor, Plot 3, Splendor Forum, Jasola District Centre,
New Delhi – 110025, India

103 Penang Road, #05–06/07, Visioncrest Commercial, Singapore 238467

Cambridge University Press is part of the University of Cambridge.

It furthers the University's mission by disseminating knowledge in the pursuit of
education, learning, and research at the highest international levels of excellence.

www.cambridge.org
Information on this title: www.cambridge.org/9781009123396
DOI: 10.1017/9781009129169

First published 2022

A catalogue record for this publication is available from the British Library.

ISBN 978-1-009-12339-6 Hardback
ISBN 978-1-009-12576-5 Paperback

Cambridge University Press has no responsibility for the persistence or accuracy of
URLs for external or third-party internet websites referred to in this publication
and does not guarantee that any content on such websites is, or will remain,
accurate or appropriate.

Contents

List of Figures   *page* ix

Acknowledgments   x

Introduction   1

   I.1   Vaccines as Instruments of Public Health   1
   I.2   Vaccine Races and Innovation Policy   3
   I.3   The Case for Considering Vaccines from a Technological Angle   5
   I.4   Limitations of the Book   7
   I.5   A Note on the Side Effects of Vaccines   9
   I.6   Structure of the Book   9

1   Vaccines as Instruments of Public Health   12

   1.1   The Spread of Infectious Diseases and the Role of Vaccines   12
      1.1.1   Infectious Disease Outbreaks: Epidemics and Pandemics in
              a Connected World   12
      1.1.2   The Road to Vaccines   16
   1.2   Benefits of Vaccination   18
      1.2.1   Public Health Value of Vaccination   18
      1.2.2   Economic and Other Societal Benefits   20
   1.3   Vaccines as a Form of Technology   22
      1.3.1   Different Types of Vaccine Technology   23

2   The Vaccine Development Ecosystem   26

   2.1   The Regulatory Framework Surrounding Vaccine Development   26
      2.1.1   The Dawn of Vaccine Regulation: The Case of the United
              States   27
      2.1.2   Vaccine Regulators: The Case of the FDA   28
      2.1.3   Vaccines as Biologics: The Applicable Legal Framework   29
      2.1.4   From the Lab to the Market: An Overview of the Standard
              Vaccine Regulatory Process   32

2.1.5   The Post-market: Continued Regulatory Oversight   35
2.2   The Centrality of Clinical Trials to Vaccine Development and
      Approval   37
      2.2.1   Vaccine Clinical Trials in Historical Context   38
      2.2.2   Persistent Shortcomings of Vaccine Clinical Trials: Racial
              and Ethnic Disparities   42
2.3   Other Players in Vaccine R&D   48
      2.3.1   The Public Sector   48
      2.3.2   The Case of Military R&D   51
      2.3.3   The Interplay between the Public and Private Sectors 53

3   Vaccine Development under Proprietary Paradigms   56
3.1   The Problem of the Commodification of Vaccines   56
      3.1.1   Characteristics of Vaccines That Render Them
              Unappealing for Market-Based R&D Approaches   57
      3.1.2   The Paradoxically Corrective Function of Public Health
              Crises   62
              3.1.2.1   The Zika Vaccine Race   62
              3.1.2.2   The Coronavirus Vaccine Races   64
      3.1.3   The Exceptionalism of Outbreak-Spiked Funding for
              Vaccine R&D   66
3.2   The Intellectual Property of Vaccines   66
      3.2.1   Intellectual Property   67
      3.2.2   The TRIPS Agreement and the Global Reach of Intellectual
              Property   69
      3.2.3   Proprietary Approaches to Vaccine R&D: Before Patents 71
      3.2.4   The Rise of the Vaccine Patent Culture   73
3.3   Intellectual Property as Incentives to R&D: Limitations of Current
      Models   79
      3.3.1   Insufficiencies of Market-Driven Incentives: R&D on Ebola
              Vaccines   79
      3.3.2   Insufficiencies at the Commercialization Stage: The Case of
              Lyme Disease Vaccines   81
      3.3.3   Instrumentalization of Intellectual Property in Tech
              Transfer: The Ebola Vaccine Race, Revisited   84
      3.3.4   R&D Attrition: The Problem of Exclusive Licensing in
              the Zika Vaccine Race   86
      3.3.5   Beyond Patents: Proprietary R&D through Secrecy   90

4   Access to Vaccine Technology   93
4.1   The Flipside of the Coin: Proprietary Rights and Pricing
      Considerations   93
      4.1.1   Uncertainty about Vaccine Affordability: The Zika
              Vaccine Race, Revisited   95

4.1.2   Vaccine Unaffordability and the Global South/North
        Divide: The Case of HPV Vaccines   97
4.2   Equity in Transnational Allocation of Vaccines   98
      4.2.1   The Problem of "Vaccine Nationalism"   99
      4.2.2   Vaccine Nationalism in the 2009 Swine Flu Pandemic   100
      4.2.3   Vaccine Nationalism in the COVID-19 Pandemic   102

5   Aligning Vaccine Innovation with Public Health Needs   106
    5.1   Addressing Commodification Problems through Non-IP Incentives
          Frameworks   106
          5.1.1   *Ex Ante* Incentives to Vaccine R&D: The Case of Grants   107
          5.1.2   *Ex Post* Incentives to Vaccine R&D: The Case of Prizes   108
          5.1.3   Industry-Specific Incentives Available to Vaccine R&D:
                  The Case of Regulatory Exclusivities and Insurance   110
          5.1.4   Limitations of Non-IP Incentives   113
    5.2   Collaborative Solutions within Intellectual Property Regimes:
          Patent Pools   114
          5.2.1   Patent Pools in Context   114
          5.2.2   Limitations of Patent Pools: The Case of the COVID-19
                  Technology Access Pool   117
          5.2.3   The Case for Vaccine Patent Pools   118
    5.3   Formalization of Soft Legal Approaches: The Case of Patent
          Pledges   121
          5.3.1   Pledges of Non-Assertion in Context   121
          5.3.2   Limitations of Pledges   122
          5.3.3   Formalizing Pledges: The Open COVID-19 Pledge   124
          5.3.4   The Case for a Vaccine Technology Pledge   127
    5.4   Reconsidering "Forced" Collaborations in Vaccine R&D   129
          5.4.1   Patent Waivers and Compulsory Licensing in Context   130
          5.4.2   The COVID-19 Vaccine Waiver   132
          5.4.3   The Case against Vaccine Patent Waivers   134
    5.5   The Expanding Role of Public–Private Partnerships   137
          5.5.1   Public–Private Partnerships in Context   138
          5.5.2   Shortcomings of (Over)Reliance on Public–Private
                  Partnerships   141
          5.5.3   The Role of Vaccine-Focused Public–Private Partnerships   143
                  5.5.3.1   The Coalition for Epidemic Preparedness
                            Innovations (CEPI)   144
                  5.5.3.2   The COVID-19 Vaccine Global Access Facility
                            (Covax)   148
          5.5.4   The Case for Expanding International Vaccine
                  Procurement   153

6   **Vaccines of the Future: Present and Emerging Challenges**   156

     6.1   (Re)Emerging Challenges to the Adoption of Vaccine
           Technology: Vaccine Misinformation and Disinformation   157
           6.1.1   Recent Events in the History of Vaccine Misinformation   158
           6.1.2   Vaccine Misinformation in the Online Environment:
                   The Role of Social Media   160
           6.1.3   The Automatization and Weaponization of Vaccine
                   Misinformation   161
           6.1.4   Responses to Vaccine Misinformation: Social Media
                   Self-Regulation   164
           6.1.5   Limitations of Current Modes of Self-Regulation   167
     6.2   Paving the Way for the Vaccines of the Future: Interdependency
           of Legal Regimes   173
           6.2.1   Expanding the Concept of Vaccine Technology: New
                   Frontiers in Vaccinology   174
           6.2.2   Tech on Tech: From 3D-Printed Vaccine Delivery to
                   Artificial Intelligence   177

     Conclusion: Broader Implications for Global Public Health   181

     C.1   Questioning the Desirability of Exclusionary Modes of
           Production of Health Goods   181
     C.2   Beyond Vaccines: Other Areas of Pharmaceutical R&D
           Faltering under Market-Driven Models   183
     C.3   A Fraught Relationship between Public Health and
           Sovereignty-Asserting Behaviors   185

Index   188

Figures

2.1 Funding for R&D on neglected versus non-neglected diseases   *page* 49
2.2 Main players involved in the development of the rVSV-ZEBOV
    vaccine during the 2014–2016 Ebola outbreak   55
3.1 FDA drug approvals 2000–2017   61
3.2 Number of worldwide first filings (1935–2009)   76
3.3 Granted patents covering active ingredients of human influenza
    vaccines   77

Acknowledgments

I owe a great deal to many colleagues and friends, conference and workshop attendees, and students in my vaccine-related seminars for the ideas expressed in this book. Either by providing direct feedback on the book or by engaging with my work on vaccines, these people have informed countless aspects of the book, and I am grateful for their support.

In particular, I wish to thank colleagues who read draft versions of chapters or sections of the book, providing invaluable comments: Maggie Chon, Jorge Contreras, Wendy Epstein, Irene Graham, Sam Halabi, Yaniv Heled, Sapna Kumar, Lisa Ouellette, Kevin Outterson, Nicholson Price, Sri Ragavan, Jerry Reichman, Judit Rius, Rachel Sachs, Josh Sarnoff, Liza Vertinsky, Sidney Watson, Lindsay Wiley, and Patti Zettler. Several others provided commentary on my work on vaccines that directly shaped many of the ideas I discuss here: Julie Barnes-Weise, Gian Luca Burci, Rochelle Cooper-Dreyfuss, Mirit Eyal-Cohen, Jesse Goldner, Irene Graham, Hank Greeley, Cynthia Ho, Dmitry Karshtedt, Mark Lemley, Doug Lichtman, Arti Rai, Jennifer Rothman, Bhaven Sampat, Tim Wiemken, Ruqaiijah Yearby, and Peter Yu.

My colleagues at Saint Louis University School of Law were especially supportive of my research for this project. I am indebted to my colleagues at the Center for Health Law Studies: Cheryl Cooper, Rob Gatter, Amy Sanders, Sidney Watson, and Ruqaiijah Yearby. Kathleen Casey and LeAnn Nolan were instrumental in the research for the book, unearthing the hardest sources to locate.

The book also benefited from feedback from participants at several dozen conferences and workshops. Parts of the book were presented or workshopped at the Health Law Policy, Bioethics and Biotechnology Workshop at Harvard Law School; the Bio Law Conference at Stanford Law School; the Innovation Policy Colloquium at New York University School of Law; the Texas A&M Law Workshop for Emerging Scholars in Intellectual Property and Technology; the Public Health Conference at the Javeriana University in Bogotá; a faculty workshop at the University of

Bournemouth; and the Intellectual Property and COVID-19 Conference at the Chinese University of Hong Kong (this one remotely, due to the pandemic).

Saint Louis University generously supported research on this book through the Beaumont Faculty Development Fund. Part of the initial research for this project was conducted during my time as the inaugural Jaharis Faculty Fellow in Health Law and Intellectual Property at DePaul University College of Law, where I received support from my colleagues at the Mary and Michael Jaharis Health Law Institute, as well as the Center for Intellectual Property Law & Information Technology.

Parts of the book drew on research performed in support of articles that have appeared in *UCLA Law Review, Arizona Law Review, Utah Law Review, Yale Law Journal Forum, University of Pennsylvania Journal of Law and Innovation, Washington University Journal of Law and Policy, Harvard Public Health Review, Michigan Law Review Online,* and *Current History.*

Finally, I am grateful beyond words to my family, especially Kirsten, to whom this book is dedicated.

Introduction

According to longstanding scientific consensus, vaccines are widely regarded as playing a fundamental role in public health. Therefore, one would reasonably expect that the dynamics of vaccine production and distribution would place a premium on incentivizing robust levels of investment in vaccine development, with the allocation of resulting vaccines occurring in ways that reflect public health priorities. Yet, that is often not the case. This book examines this disjunction from the viewpoint of the laws, policies, and other market-driven forces that shape the development and distribution of vaccines. Together, these mechanisms have long led to problems of under-investment in vaccine research and production, and inequitable allocation of limited vaccine supply in ways that recurrently disadvantage lower-income populations.

I.1 VACCINES AS INSTRUMENTS OF PUBLIC HEALTH

The use of vaccines is among the most effective and affordable ways of preventing disease or lessening its burden on the health of populations across the globe.[1] The development and use of many vaccines now labeled as "common" or "routine" has led to considerable decreases in morbidity and mortality.[2] Some potentially lethal diseases, such as polio, have been eradicated in many countries through broad vaccination campaigns.

Scientists Stanley Plotkin and Edward Mortimer, two leading figures in vaccinology, have highlighted the public health value of vaccination by stating that "the impact of vaccination on the health of the world's peoples is hard to exaggerate. With the exception of safe water, no other modality has had such a major effect on mortality reduction and population growth."[3]

---

[1] Mark Doherty et al., "Vaccine Impact: Benefits for Human Health" (2016) 34 *Vaccine* 6707–14 (calling vaccines "one of the cheapest and most effective forms of medical intervention").

[2] See e.g. US Centers for Disease Control and Prevention, "Routine Vaccines," (2019), wwwnc.cdc.gov /travel/page/routine-vaccines.

[3] Stanley A. Plotkin & Edward A. Mortimer, *Vaccines* (W. B. Saunders, 1988).

From a public health perspective, vaccines are thus instrumental in enabling medical interventions with overwhelmingly positive effects in both the lower- and higher-income countries:

> More children than ever before are being reached with immunization: over 100 million children a year in 2005–2007. And the benefits of immunization are increasingly being extended to adolescents and adults – providing protection against life-threatening diseases such as influenza, meningitis, and cancers that occur in adulthood.
>
> In developing countries, more vaccines are available and more lives are being saved. For the first time in documented history the number of children dying every year has fallen below 10 million – the result of improved access to clean water and sanitation, increased immunization coverage, and the integrated delivery of essential health interventions.[4]

In addition to their direct impact on the reduction of disease, disability, and death, the use of vaccines is known to generate several other welfare-enhancing benefits that stretch well beyond the confines of public health. Through their preventative and disease-mitigating functions, vaccines help generate important economic savings to health systems.[5] Their use also minimizes both temporary and permanent losses in the workforce and corresponding decreases in productivity, as well as in spending power by those foregoing wages. And, as illustrated by the COVID-19 pandemic, vaccination can help speed up the reopening of economies constrained by public health measures put in place to curb the uncontrolled spread of an infectious disease, or even avoid the adoption of these measures in the first place.

Robust levels of vaccination have also been linked to the lessening of inequalities between lower- and higher-income populations. The World Health Organization provides the following example:

> The burden of infectious, including vaccine-preventable, diseases falls disproportionately on the disadvantaged. Vaccines have clear benefits for the disadvantaged. Pneumococcal immunization programmes in the USA have at least temporarily removed racial and socioeconomic disparities in invasive pneumococcal disease incidence, while in Bangladesh, measles vaccination has enhanced equity between high- and low-socioeconomic groups.[6]

Relatedly, vaccination also contributes to the empowerment of women, especially in lower-income countries:

> The vaccination of children has a great impact on the lives of women in developing countries. Protecting the lives of children through vaccination and through other

---

[4] World Health Organization, UNICEF, World Bank. *State of the World's Vaccines and Immunization* (3rd ed., World Health Organization, 2009).

[5] Francis E. André et al., "Vaccination Greatly Reduces Disease, Disability, Death and Inequity Worldwide" (2008) 86 *Bulletin of the World Health Organization* 81–160.

[6] André et al., "Vaccination Greatly Reduces Disease," note 5.

PHC activities is a major strategy towards improving the lives of women. The opportunity and provision of vaccination empowers women to protect their own health and that of their children through their own actions, giving an added psychological feeling of control and empowerment in their lives.[7]

The continued and future success of local, regional, and global public health depends in considerable ways on the maintenance of robust levels of vaccination against known diseases. At the same time, new pathogens continue to emerge, posing renewed challenges to public health, as well as to those working to develop new vaccines against the backdrop of uncertainty as to which viruses or bacteria will cause the next outbreak. Coronaviruses like SARS-CoV-2, the pathogen that causes COVID-19, have long been part of an unfortunately long list of emerging pathogens identified by public health experts as likely to trigger severe public health crises in the near future.[8] These lurking threats to human health are a powerful reminder of our collective need for the development of new vaccines, in addition to widespread distribution of existing ones.

1.2 VACCINE RACES AND INNOVATION POLICY

The twentieth and twenty-first centuries have been interspersed with vaccine races. As seen in Chapter 3, the concept of vaccine races has become central to the way most modern vaccines come to market. In a temporal sense, vaccine races unfold whenever scientists attempt to develop new vaccine products against the backdrop of pressing public health crises, such as the recurring polio epidemics of the twentieth century or the recent COVID-19 pandemic.

Adding to the scientific and public health motivations behind vaccine races, there is a fear factor. Whether you choose to open David Oshinsky's 2006 monograph, *Polio: An American Story*, or to read Philip Roth's account of the widespread fear of polio during summers in mid-twentieth-century New Jersey in *Nemesis*, the extra-scientific impulses that have animated the quest for medicines addressing the outbreak of infectious diseases are palpable. Our more recent and quasi-global experience with COVID-19 has rekindled many of these sentiments, bringing vaccine races to the forefront of debates in public fora and around dinner tables, making them a touchstone of socioeconomic policies at the domestic and international level and stirring controversy about the adoption of emerging health goods – a type of controversy that is recurrent in the history of vaccines, and more broadly in the history of medicine, but that is often confined to very specific domains, from scientific scholarship and debate to segments of online discourse.

---

[7] A. E. Shearley, "The Societal Value of Vaccination in Developing Countries" (1999) 17(Suppl 3) *Vaccine* S109–12.

[8] World Health Organization, "An R&D Blueprint for Action to Prevent Epidemics" (2016), www.who.int/blueprint/about/r_d_blueprint_plan_of_action.pdf.

In addition to compressed timelines and motivating factors, there is yet another important dimension of vaccine races worth considering – one that attracted unusually strong levels of public attention during the COVID-19 pandemic. The concept of a vaccine race also speaks to the research and development (R&D) format that prevails in contemporary vaccine development, outside epidemic or pandemic contexts: Unless they are the sole sources of a vaccine, developers of vaccine technology compete with one another to be the first to market, in a process often structured around the prospect of obtaining intellectual property protection for their innovations. This protection, in the form of patents, contributes to R&D dynamics that emphasize expediency and secrecy as a norm over collaborative approaches to vaccine development. If R&D players succeed in obtaining one or more patents covering vaccine technology, the law grants them the ability to prevent others from commercializing or otherwise using those technologies for prolonged periods of time.

Intellectual property and adjacent areas of the law play therefore a key role in how the vaccine R&D ecosystem operates. These laws and policies were not designed or implemented with vaccines or other health goods in mind. Rather, they inform innovation processes in virtually all fields of science and technology, making no meaningful distinction between the underlying goods that R&D players are trying to invent, manufacture, and distribute. This, in turn, subjects vaccine races – and, more broadly, the development and distribution of vaccines – to market-driven modes of production and allocation that, as seen throughout the book, are largely inadequate in light of the specific characteristics of vaccines.

These inadequacies are compounded by barriers beyond intellectual property. Contracts and other general-purpose legal tools allow two or more parties to buy and sell vaccines with almost no restrictions. The law regulates the purchasing process by focusing on the obligations of the parties vis-à-vis one another, but leaves them free to allocate the existing vaccine supply as they see fit. As a result, countries and vaccine suppliers transact in vaccines in ways that are scarcely distinguishable from the transnational commerce of steel or computer chips – by allocating them first to the most competitive payers, who are invariably the wealthiest countries on Earth. As seen in Chapter 4, diverting the vaccine supply according to economic resources is bound to result in vaccine distribution patterns that hardly mirror transnational public health needs. This adds an additional layer to what the book calls "the commodification of vaccines," the coalescence of different strands of law, policy, and practices that make the production and distribution of vaccines predominantly driven by market forces, often to the detriment of public health.

Importantly, these practices are deemed consistent with current legal paradigms – both written domestic and international laws, and case law or other interpretive legal frameworks. If anything, laws have been consistently and deliberately engineered to preserve this status quo. The story told in this book is thus anchored on these sets of laws and the innovation policy precepts they help advance when applied to the production and distribution of goods as idiosyncratic as vaccines. The book employs the expression "innovation policy" to reference the interplay of legal and nonlegal mechanisms (such as economically motivated decisions or social norms) that shape how vaccines are produced and distributed.[9]

1.3 THE CASE FOR CONSIDERING VACCINES FROM A TECHNOLOGICAL ANGLE

The fact that vaccines are subject to many of the same market forces that regulate other types of technology warrants examining the vaccine ecosystem through the lens of technology-centered law and policies. The legal and policy frameworks referenced in the previous section were not created in the petri dishes of public health law and policy. Intellectual property as commonly understood today is largely a byproduct of the technological developments brought about by the Industrial Revolution and was implemented with the overarching utilitarian purpose of promoting innovation – which in the case of the patent system focuses specifically on scientific and technical innovation. Vaccines and other health goods join the ranks of innovations that qualify for patent protection, even though they are used in ways that are fundamentally different from other types of technologies.

Further back in time, contract law developed mechanisms to regulate the provision of goods. Unlike intellectual property, these early developments took place long before vaccines were created, as the Sumerians traded in cloth and the citizens of Ancient Rome transacted in glassware. Modern contractual mechanisms allow a country, or a restricted number of countries, to use contracts to exhaust the global supply of vaccines just as a wealthy Sumerian or Roman could appropriate all cloth or glassware. Yet, vaccines are markedly different from these commodities and used for non-commodifiable purposes. Even the emergence of international law, which regulates relationships between sovereign or quasi-sovereign actors, has yet to find a way to limit the exclusionary effects that contracts and patents combine to produce in vaccine markets. The book therefore interrogates these legal frameworks and the policies they generate and searches for solutions within the existing laws to mitigate long-lasting inequalities in vaccine production and distribution.

A second reason for the vaccines-as-technology approach adopted in the book relates to the nature of vaccines themselves: They are products of biotechnology, the engineering of a blend of living and nonliving materials with the goal of creating a product that does not exist in nature. As such, they are especially complex forms of technology. As seen in Chapters 1 and 3, modern vaccines consist of an

---

[9]   See e.g. Jakob Edler & Jan Fagerberg, "Innovation Policy: What, Why, and How" (2017) 33 *Oxford Review of Economic Policy* 2–23. See also European Parliament, "Innovation Policy" (defining innovation policy in general as "the interface between research and technological development policy and industrial policy and aims to create a conducive framework for bringing ideas to market"), www .europarl.europa.eu/factsheets/en/sheet/67/innovation-policy.

amalgamation of technologies, from the substance that prompts the body to trigger an immune response (the antigen) to stabilizers, to the delivery mechanism. Moreover, vaccines are a subset of pharmaceutical products known as biologics, which are known for being especially hard to replicate. The particular technological characteristics of vaccines set them apart from other goods – including several other health goods. This means that the process of bringing a new vaccine to market is subject to different regulations than those applicable to most other goods, as seen in Chapter 2. Their technological specificities also mean that some corrective interventions that are successful with regard to other technologies, and even other types of pharmaceutical products, might not work if a vaccine is at stake. For instance, if a less complex product is scarce, policymakers may direct competitors to make and distribute copies, even if the original manufacturer opposes the measure and refuses to collaborate. This policy may be successful if the product is a mask or structurally small drug, such as many of the drugs sold over the counter in a pill format. But if scarcity involves a vaccine – as it did during the COVID-19 pandemic – the same measure might not be enough to overcome the lack of cooperation from patent holders and to meet the heightened logistic standards required by vaccine manufacturing. A study of the specificities of vaccines as technologies is therefore necessary to inform innovation policy as applicable to vaccine R&D, manufacturing, and distribution.

A third reason for the book's technology-centric approach is tied to the fact that the discovery, development, and delivery of vaccines is becoming increasingly dependent on the application of technologies from fields that are not related to biotechnology or health. In providing a glimpse into the future of vaccines in Chapter 6, the book describes emerging uses of 3D printing technology and artificial intelligence in different areas of vaccinology. The ways in which exogenous technologies help push the boundaries of vaccine R&D and distribution have been hailed as promising. At the same time, their use makes the vaccine ecosystem to some extent dependent on innovation policies set in connection with non-vaccine technologies. For instance, if early-stage research using artificial intelligence incorporates racial or socioeconomic biases – as it often does in a myriad of non-vaccine contexts[10] – these biases are bound to affect the ultimate vaccine product, further tilting vaccine R&D and production in benefit of patients belonging to dominant racial and socioeconomic groups.

By introducing and using this vaccines-as-technology framework, the book makes three main contributions. First, it draws attention to the intertwining laws, policies, and other structures that determine and shape the development and distribution of vaccines. Second, the book shows that excessive reliance on market-driven forces – including but not limited to patent-centric modes of vaccine development – produces

---

[10] See e.g. Sharona Hoffman & Andy Podgurski, "Artificial Intelligence and Discrimination in Health Care" (2020) 19 *Yale Journal of Health Policy, Law & Ethics* 1–10; Cathy O'Neil, *Weapons of Math Destruction: How Big Data Increases Inequality and Threatens Democracy* (Crown, 2017).

results that are largely antithetical to public health and systemically disadvantage lower-income populations, especially those located in the Global South. And third, operating within the existing legal and policy tools, the book examines possible solutions to mitigate the most acute consequences of this reliance on markets instead of public health needs.

I.4 LIMITATIONS OF THE BOOK

The book focuses predominantly on vaccines against emerging pathogens. These pathogens have caused some of the greatest public health crises in history – including in recent history; consider the severe outbreaks of COVID-19, Zika, and Ebola that occurred in less than a decade (2014–2021, the time of writing). While there is great public health need for vaccines in other areas – for instance, cancer vaccines – vaccines against emerging pathogens fall prey to a particular paradox. When an outbreak takes place, scientists are often able to adapt existing technology and quickly create a new vaccine. Unlike cancer vaccinology, this is an area in which the underlying pathogens are simpler to understand, and innovation processes often work by adapting an existing vaccine targeting a similar pathogen. While relatively unencumbered from a scientific and technical perspective, work on vaccines targeting emerging pathogens remains chronically underfunded, compromising public health preparedness for pandemics and epidemics. The assessment of the World Health Organization on the R&D landscape before the large 2014–2016 Ebola outbreak was dire: "[T]here were no vaccines, no treatments, few diagnostics, and insufficient medical teams and trained responders."[11] Yet, as seen in Chapter 3, there was a successful vaccine candidate developed in the early 2000s, which was ready to enter clinical trials and start the admittedly time- and resource-consuming process of obtaining market approval from drug regulators. There was, however, no market interest in this vaccine before the outbreak. By the time it was rushed to clinical trials in 2014, the outbreak was beginning to wane. The vaccine eventually came to market in late 2019, with several other fatal outbreaks occurring in the meantime.

Many other vaccine-preventable diseases lack a commercially available vaccine. Data from 2015 revealed that there were forty-seven vaccine-preventable diseases and infections for which there were either no approved vaccines or only partially effective vaccines.[12] By contrast, there were only twenty-two vaccine-preventable diseases with "commonly used vaccines" and two (adenovirus types 4 and 7, and anthrax) for which there were "limited-use vaccines."

The book thus focuses on systemic problems that affect a large subset of vaccines – and one in which market-driven modes of production result in losses to public health preparedness.

---

[11] World Health Organization, "R&D Blueprint," note 8, at 6.
[12] See Stanley A. Plotkin et al., "Establishing a Global Vaccine-Development Fund" (2015) 373 *New England Journal of Medicine* 297–300.

Although one of the main themes of the book is the disparity in vaccine access by lower-income populations – including populations in the Global South as well as pockets of the Global North – a second limitation of the book is that it does not focus on vaccine development and production in countries of the Global South. Many of these countries are major players in the vaccine ecosystem. India, for instance, is home to the Serum Institute, which manufactures vaccines for 170 countries.[13] The book, however, focuses on how decisions made in the Global North, where the bulk of resources for vaccine R&D is concentrated, affect access to vaccines across the world. These decisions take the form of policies, laws, and market-driven behaviors that actors in the Global North control in disproportionate ways. The critiques offered by the book are thus aimed at this facet of the vaccine ecosystem.

Relatedly, several segments of the book are written with reference to the United States. For instance, when Chapter 2 describes the process used by drug regulators to evaluate new vaccines, it does so by using the Food & Drug Administration and US regulations as an example. Similarly, when explaining how the patent system works, Chapter 3 employs terminology derived from US law to illustrate how international intellectual property rules have been adopted at the domestic level. In these specific cases, the book takes this approach because both vaccine regulation and patents are regulated in largely similar ways throughout the world. National-level drug regulators make decisions based on scientific principles related to vaccine safety and efficacy and have similar processes for determining whether vaccines meet these criteria.[14] And because they derive from international law, modern domestic patent laws are said to be "harmonized," with the criteria for obtaining a patent being the same in virtually every country.[15] Of course, illustrative approaches are inherently limited and do not capture variability at the national level. Wherever possible – for instance, by providing data on vaccine-related patent applications across the world – the book provides information on relevant distinctions or country-level actions that are especially salient.

A final limitation of the book is that, although critical of strong market-driven models of vaccine R&D and distribution, it does not discuss at length solutions that would rely on alternative modes of production. Rather, it locates solutions available under current legal regimes, however imperfect they might be. In this sense, the book takes a pragmatic approach. As legal scholar Rochelle Cooper Dreyfuss put it when discussing how intellectual property systems often lead to the production of sub-optimal results, "intellectual property rights will not soon disappear" and therefore there is a need for corrective interventions within the sphere of intellectual property law itself.[16] The same can be said of overly permissive contractual

---

[13] Serum Institute, www.seruminstitute.com/about_us.php.

[14] World Health Organization, "Vaccine Regulation," www.who.int/immunization_standards/vacci ne_regulation/en/.

[15] See e.g. Peter K. Yu, "Currents and Crosscurrents in the International Intellectual Property Regime" (2004) 38 *Loyola Los Angeles Law Review* 323–444.

[16] Rochelle Cooper Dreyfuss, "Does IP Need IP? Accommodating Intellectual Production Outside the Intellectual Property Paradigm" (2010) 31 *Cardozo Law Review* 1437–73, 1439.

frameworks and the weak reach of international laws and policies affecting the allocation of vaccines. The prescriptive portion of the book therefore considers tools available under current legal frameworks. A discussion of solutions entailing a significant overhaul of current legal and economic regimes has an urgency of its own, but is outside the scope of this work.

1.5 A NOTE ON THE SIDE EFFECTS OF VACCINES

As with the use of pharmaceutical products in general, the use of vaccines presents some risks. In most cases, the side effects that may arise in connection with the administration of a vaccine are relatively minor.[17] Common effects include soreness or redness at the injection site and low fever. Sporadically, severe side effects do occur. An extensive body of scientific studies notes that the frequency of severe side effects is "extremely rare." To put this frequency in context, the US Department of Health and Human Services explains in its informational webpage on the side effects of vaccines that "if 1 million doses of a vaccine are given, 1 to 2 people may have a severe allergic reaction."[18] This does not render vaccines unsafe or particularly different from other pharmaceutical products. As seen in Chapter 2, scientific precepts and the laws that mirror them prevent drug regulators across the world from authorizing the commercialization of a given vaccine unless they determine that, according to the application of current scientific knowledge, it meets the regulatory standards for safety.

In a very limited number of cases, detrimental effects to the health of an individual do occur. This trade-off has long been regarded as tolerable from a public health and societal perspective, not just with regard to vaccines but health goods in general. Regulators and society have chosen to tolerate small amounts of risk – in this and many other areas – in exchange for the availability of technologies that, on balance, are overwhelmingly beneficial. While acknowledging the inherent risks posed by vaccines, the departing point of the book is informed by the scientific consensus that vaccines are welfare-enhancing, societally desirable instruments of public health.

1.6 STRUCTURE OF THE BOOK

The book is divided into six chapters. Chapter 1 provides background information on the spread of infectious diseases, emerging pathogens, and the history of vaccines. It also introduces the topic of technological heterogeneity in vaccinology, surveying different types of vaccine technology currently in use.

---

[17] US Centers for Disease Control and Prevention, "Possible Side Effects from Vaccines," (2020), www .cdc.gov/vaccines/vac-gen/side-effects.htm.
[18] US Department of Health and Human Services, "Vaccine Side Effects," (2021), www.hhs.gov/immun ization/basics/safety/side-effects/index.html.

Chapter 2 describes the regulatory processes in place to bring new vaccines to market and introduces the main players in the vaccine R&D ecosystem. In so doing, it highlights the centrality of clinical trials to the process of generating data used by drug regulators across the world to evaluate the safety and efficacy of vaccines, as well the shortcomings that affect the production of vaccine clinical trial data.

Chapter 3 shifts the narrative to the role of intellectual property in vaccine R&D, arguing that the race-to-patent format adopted in recent decades has contributed to an undesirable commodification of vaccines under market-driven dynamics. The chapter first theorizes the application of intellectual property to the development of vaccines against emerging pathogens and then provides several case studies on vaccine R&D.

Chapter 4 continues exploring the effects of the adoption of market-driven modes of vaccine production and distribution, now emphasizing the allocative imbalances that these modes are bound to create. It explains how contractual frameworks recurrently used in international transactions give rise to "vaccine nationalism" – the inequitable channeling of vaccine doses in situations of scarcity toward a restricted number of countries, irrespective of epidemiological factors.

Chapter 5 argues that policymakers and lawmakers should make greater use of existing mechanisms available under current domestic and international law to start remedying some of the problems diagnosed in the previous chapter. Each proposal made here is informed by notions of technology specificity, proactive adoption, permanency, and formalization – the idea that innovation policy affecting the production and distribution of vaccines requires ad hoc measures factoring in both the specific characteristics of vaccines and public health imperatives; that those measures should be negotiated and adopted before outbreaks occur, as opposed to the current practice of negotiating and creating mechanisms to promote vaccine R&D and distribution as public health crises unfold; that, as a consequence, these measures should lead to the creation of permanent agreements and structures; and that resulting collaborations between players in the vaccine ecosystem should be regulated by binding agreements, instead of relying on informal relationships and spur-of-the-moment collaborations.

Chapter 6 crosses the vaccines-as-technology idea with reflections on the growing number of non-health technologies that influence the vaccine ecosystem. It begins by exploring cases in which the use of technology contributes to hinder the reception of vaccine technology, by facilitating the propagation of vaccine misinformation and disinformation. It then turns to instances in which disparate technologies, such as 3D printing and artificial intelligence, are pushing vaccine R&D in new directions – with the implication that technology policy in non-vaccine domains is likely to become increasingly relevant for the vaccine ecosystem.

A brief conclusion links the topics explored throughout the book with larger questions, including the shortcomings of market-driven models of production of health goods; shared similarities between vaccines and other areas in public health also subject to these models, including rare diseases and antimicrobial resistance; and the ultimate incompatibility between nationalistic or otherwise sovereignty-asserting behaviors and the borderless nature of public health interventions.

1

Vaccines as Instruments of Public Health

1.1 THE SPREAD OF INFECTIOUS DISEASES AND THE ROLE OF VACCINES

1.1.1 *Infectious Disease Outbreaks: Epidemics and Pandemics in a Connected World*

Pathogens and humans have coexisted for a long time. Studies suggest that, even before recorded history, nomadic populations are likely to have suffered from a plethora of diseases, such as malaria and perhaps yellow fever.[1] The transition to a sedentary lifestyle anchored around small villages, and later on the establishment of large urban centers from Mesopotamia to the Indus Valley and what is modern-day China, paved the way for the increased spread and diversification of these pathogens. High population density, the comingling of humans and animals, and the proliferation of trade routes linking once-distant urban areas enabled viruses, bacteria, and other pathogens to propagate quickly and travel progressively farther. To this day, these dynamics set forth in antiquity continue to play out in similar ways in a world that has become more connected and densely populated.

The pathogens that thrived in the world's early cities would in a few centuries cause large-scale outbreaks, affecting vast numbers of people and spanning across geographical regions, in a phenomenon much later described as a pandemic, a word crafted in the mid-1600s by combining the Greek words *pan* (all) and *demos* (people). The first recorded infectious disease outbreak of pandemic proportions occurred in ancient Greece, with the plague of Athens in 430 BCE, which the historian Thucydides, having survived the disease, described in *The History of the Peloponnesian War*. Modern estimates calculate the death toll at between 75,000 and 100,000 people, almost a quarter of the besieged city's population.[2] There is still no unanimity among researchers as to what pathogen may have caused the outbreak,

---

[1] Andrew P. Dobson & E. Robin Carper, "Infectious Diseases and Human Population History: Throughout History the Establishment of Disease Has Been a Side Effect of the Growth of Civilization" (February 1996) 46(2) *BioScience* 115–26.

[2] Robert J. Littman, "The Plague of Athens: Epidemiology and Paleopathology" (October 2009) 76(5) *Mount Sinai Journal of Medicine* 456–67.

with smallpox, typhus, typhoid, and measles recurringly hypothesized as possible candidates.[3] The next recorded large event was the Antonine plague in 165 CE, which has been linked to the virus causing smallpox and appears to have originated in Mesopotamia, quickly extending throughout the Roman Empire.[4] The outbreak lasted until 180 CE and is regarded today as one of the contributing factors of the profound socioeconomic, agricultural, and military changes that swept the Roman Empire toward the end of the second century.[5]

Following these two events, spaced centuries apart, the record of outbreaks of diseases affecting relatively large communities – and sometimes spilling over national and regional borders – has expanded both geographically and in frequency. Although the pathogens at the root of these outbreaks are richly diverse and operate in markedly different ways, the diseases they are capable of producing are often addressed under the conceptual umbrella of "infectious diseases," which the World Health Organization (WHO) characterizes as illnesses "caused by pathogenic microorganisms, such as bacteria, viruses, parasites, or fungi; the diseases can be spread, directly or indirectly, from one person to another."[6]

Even though advances in science and public health interventions have helped control, and in some cases eradicate, the spread of many infectious diseases, old and new pathogens continue to circulate among animal and human communities. History and predictive models have taught us to both expect and prepare for a certain amount of disease: consider the flu, which typically makes a comeback during fall and winter seasons across the globe. When there is a spike in disease case counts beyond what would be normally expected, public health experts talk about the onset of an epidemic. The Centers for Disease Control and Prevention (CDC) in the United States define an epidemic as "an increase, often sudden, in the number of cases of a disease above what is normally expected in that population in [a given] area."[7] The CDC also notes that, although the terms "epidemic" and "outbreak" are definitionally equivalent, the latter tends to be reserved in practice to events occurring in more geographically limited areas.

Occasionally, outbreaks of infectious diseases acquire extraordinarily large proportions. This was, for instance, the case of the Athens and Antonine plagues; the bubonic plague or "Black Death" of the mid-1300s, which has been estimated to

[3] Burke A. Cunha, "The Cause of the Plague of Athens: Plague, Typhoid, Typhus, Smallpox, or Measles?" (March 2004) 18(1) *Infectious Disease Clinics of North America* 29–43; Littman, "The Plague of Athens," note 2.

[4] Robert J. Littman & M. L. Littman, "Galen and the Antonine Plague" (Autumn 1973) 94(3) *American Journal of Philology* 243–55.

[5] Sergio Sabbatani & Sirio Fiorino, "La peste antonina e il declino dell'Impero Romano" [The Antonine Plague and the Decline of the Roman Empire] (December 2009) 17(4) *Le Infezioni in Medicina* 261–75.

[6] World Health Organization, "Infectious Diseases," (2021), www.emro.who.int/health-topics/infectious-diseases/index.html.

[7] US Centers for Disease Control and Prevention, "Introduction to Epidemiology," (2014), www.cdc.gov/training/publichealth101/documents/introduction-to-epidemiology.pdf .

have killed 150 million people out of a global population projected to be at 450 million;[8] and, most recently, COVID-19. These extreme public health crises, during which an epidemic spreads across multiple countries or continents, are considered pandemics. The CDC also notes that, as a general rule, pandemics tend to affect considerably larger numbers of people than epidemics.

In addition to pathogens known to have been in circulation for centuries or even millennia, some of the more recent outbreaks of infectious diseases have been linked to newly discovered or otherwise emerging or reemerging pathogens. In the mid-1990s, virologist Stephen Morse coined the term "emerging viruses" to refer to pathogens at the root of "infections that have newly appeared in the population or are rapidly increasing their incidence or geographic range."[9] Diseases triggered by these pathogens have caused some of the largest public health crises in recent decades.[10] For instance, HIV/AIDS, which remains at epidemic levels in both high-income countries like the United States and lower-income countries (many of which are located in Africa), belongs to this group. The pathogens that caused some of the major transnational public health crises of the twenty-first century similarly belong to this group, as was the case of Ebola in 2014–2016[11] and Zika in 2015–2016.[12] Influenza viruses,[13] as well as viruses capable of producing severe respiratory disease also fall into this category. That is the case of the coronaviruses linked to the severe acute respiratory syndrome (SARS) outbreak of 2002–2004, the multiple outbreaks of Middle East respiratory syndrome (MERS) throughout the 2010s, and the COVID-19 pandemic.[14]

The universe of emerging pathogens is in flux, and existing categorizations may vary slightly among institutions, particularly in the ways they hierarchize these pathogens.[15] In 2016, the WHO published a list of "priority" emerging pathogens, in which priority was assessed from the perspective of insufficient research and

---

[8]   Michaela Harbeck et al., "Yersinia pestis DNA from Skeletal Remains from the 6th Century AD Reveals Insights into Justinianic Plague" (May 2, 2013) 9(4) *PLOS Pathogens* e1003349.

[9]   Stephen S. Morse, "Factors in the Emergence of Infectious Diseases" (1995) 1 *Emerging Infectious Diseases* 7–15; Stephen S. Morse, *Emerging Viruses* (Oxford University Press, 1996).

[10]   National Institute of Allergy & Infectious Diseases, "NIAID Emerging Infectious Diseases/Pathogens" (2018), www.niaid.nih.gov/research/emerging-infectious-diseases-pathogens.

[11]   See generally World Health Organization, "Ebola Virus Disease," www.who.int/health-topics/ebola/.

[12]   See generally World Health Organization, "Zika Virus: Key Facts" (July 20, 2018), www.who.int/en/news-room/fact-sheets/detail/zika-virus.

[13]   See Centers for Disease Control & Prevention, "Understanding Influenza Viruses" (2019), www.cdc.gov/flu/about/viruses/index.htm.

[14]   See generally Centers for Disease Control & Prevention, "Severe Acute Respiratory Syndrome (SARS)" (2017), www.cdc.gov/sars/index.html. See generally World Health Organization, "Middle East Respiratory Syndrome Coronavirus (MERS-CoV): Key Facts" (March 11, 2019), www.who.int/en/news-room/fact-sheets/detail/middle-east-respiratory-syndrome-coronavirus-(mers-cov); Centers for Disease Control & Prevention, "COVID-19" (2021), www.cdc.gov/coronavirus/2019-ncov/index.html.

[15]   See NIAID, note 10; Johns Hopkins, "Emerging Infectious Diseases," www.hopkinsmedicine.org/health/conditions-and-diseases/emerging-infectious-diseases.

development (R&D). Under this approach, pathogens causing respiratory diseases (coronaviruses) and hemorrhagic fevers (including Ebola viruses and several other pathogens across viral families) were deemed priority pathogens and occupied most of the seven slots reserved for "diseases to be urgently addressed."[16] By contrast, the 2018 list of emerging infectious diseases and pathogens published by the US National Institute of Allergy and Infectious Diseases ranked pathogens across three categories based on the threat they posed to national security and public health, with a focus on how easily these pathogens can spread if purposefully deployed for bioterrorism goals.[17] Category A encompassed pathogens posing the "highest risk" and included all of the pathogens causing viral hemorrhagic fevers that appeared in the WHO list, as well as several additional ones, including anthrax, the bacteria that cause plague, and the virus that causes smallpox. Category B, the "second highest priority," covered over thirty pathogens, including several mosquito-borne pathogens (like the Zika virus) and foodborne pathogens such as salmonella, listeria, and certain strands of *E. coli*. Finally, Category C focused on pathogens that "could be engineered for mass dissemination in the future." This highly heterogenous category included the bacteria causing tuberculosis, the viruses causing the flu, rabies, and tick-borne encephalitis, as well as drug-resistant pathogens – an expanding category that was listed in 2019 by the WHO as one of the top ten threats to global health, alongside the priority emerging pathogens identified in the WHO's 2016 report, flu viruses, HIV/AIDS, and other factors ranging from climate change to vaccine hesitancy.[18]

In addition to a broader range of emerging pathogens, outbreaks of infectious diseases have been occurring with increasing frequency in recent decades. In a 2014 study, Katherine F. Smith and colleagues mapped outbreaks of infectious diseases over thirty-three years (1980–2013) and found that both the number of outbreaks and the number of pathogens at their root had increased significantly over time.[19] During this period, there were 12,102 known outbreaks of 215 diseases. Collectively, these outbreaks resulted in over forty-four million cases of disease affecting people in 219 countries. Infection caused by salmonella bacteria was the most common type of disease, while viral gastroenteritis (often caused by norovirus) caused the most disease, with fifteen million recorded cases. Smith and colleagues concluded that recent outbreaks of infectious diseases pointed toward increased novelty in the infectious disease ecosystem, as pathogens "have undergone recent evolutionary change, entered the human population for the first time, or have been newly discovered."

[16] World Health Organization, "WHO Publishes List of Top Emerging Diseases Likely to Cause Major Epidemics" (December 10, 2015), www.who.int/medicines/ebola-treatment/WHO-list-of-top-emerging-diseases/en/, at 22.
[17] NIAID, note 10.
[18] World Health Organization, "Antimicrobial Resistance" (October 13, 2020), www.who.int/news-room/fact-sheets/detail/antimicrobial-resistance.
[19] Katherine F. Smith et al., "Global Rise in Human Infectious Disease Outbreaks" (December 6, 2014) 11 *Journal Royal Society Interface* 101, 1–6.

The increase in number and diversity of outbreaks is partly attributable to increased global mobility.[20] As humans travel or utilize transportation networks in the increasingly globalizing culture and economy of today, pathogens and their carriers also find new ways of circulating among increasingly larger networks. Additionally, the continued growth of urban centers, insufficiencies in public infrastructures, poverty, and climate change are all contributing factors.[21]

In spite of the quantitative and qualitative changes in the spread of infectious diseases in the late twentieth and early twenty-first centuries, the study conducted by Smith and colleagues also pointed out that, when measured against the growth in global population, the relative number of people infected during an outbreak has actually decreased.[22] The researchers attributed this improvement to the development and implementation of better prediction, detection, and response techniques.

Alongside interventions designed to monitor and curb the spread of infectious diseases, another key component of public health policy is the development of strategies to prevent the onset of disease in the first place, or to mitigate disease transmission, should an outbreak occur. Within the spectrum of preventative interventions, the administration of vaccines remains a touchstone of modern public health.

1.1.2 *The Road to Vaccines*

Attempts to prevent or curb the spread of disease in ways that anticipate the modern concept of vaccination have now existed for well over a millennium. Researchers credit eastern Asia as the birthplace of the earliest known process for deliberately triggering some form of immunity or resistance to disease: records show that, by 1000 CE, doctors were harvesting human smallpox scabs, which they then turned into a powder to be inhaled by young children.[23] This process, which became known as "nasal insufflation," was shown to reduce the severity of symptoms caused by smallpox infection, which in the most extreme cases included disfiguring scarring and could lead to death. Through the years, this technique became known across the Ottoman Empire and, later on, Europe. However, as noted by Michael Kinch in his history of vaccines, *Between Hope and Fear*, knowledge of techniques to trigger a protective reaction against smallpox arrived too late in western Europe, from where

[20]   A. J. Tatem et al., "Global Transport Networks and Infectious Disease Spread" (2006) 62 *Advances in Parasitology* 293–343.

[21]   Julia Belluz, "4 Reasons Disease Outbreaks are Erupting Around the World" (May 31, 2016) *Vox*, www .vox.com/2016/5/31/11638796/why-there-are-more-infectious-disease-outbreaks; J. A. Patz et al., "Global Climate Change and Infectious Diseases" (January 17, 1996) 275(3) *JAMA* 217–23; Asim Anwar et al., "Climate Change and Infectious Diseases: Evidence from Highly Vulnerable Countries" (December 2019) 48 *Iranian Journal of Public Health* 2187–95.

[22]   Smith et al., "Global Rise," note 19.

[23]   Michael Kinch, *Between Hope and Fear* (Simon and Schuster, 2018), 19.

participants in the Columbian voyages carried the disease across the Atlantic with catastrophic consequences for native populations.[24]

Physicians in the Ottoman Empire also practiced a technique that did not require insufflation, instead putting the infected matter directly into contact with the punctured skin of a healthy subject.[25] This practice, then known as inoculation and today also called variolation, was observed by Europeans visiting Constantinople, popularized in England in the 1720s, and subsequently adopted across the European continent.

As explored in Chapter 3 in connection with the idea of vaccine races, the first vaccine proper is usually credited to an English physician active in the late eighteenth and early nineteenth centuries.[26] Edward Jenner built on existing knowledge about the effects of cowpox, a disease caused by a virus closely related to the *vaccinia* virus, producing localized skin lesions in humans. People who had contracted cowpox appeared to develop some degree of immunity to smallpox, a much more severe, and often lethal, disease that was once described as "the scourge of mankind."[27] Jenner harvested matter from a sore on a cowpox patient and used it to inoculate a healthy boy, James Phipps. Several days later the doctor repeated the process, this time with matter harvested from smallpox sore. Exposed in later months to the virus that causes smallpox, Phipps never developed the disease. Borrowing from the name *vaccinia*, the process tested and later reported by Jenner is now regarded as marking the beginning of vaccination in the modern sense of the concept. Subsequent experimentation and improvements on smallpox vaccines would result in vaccination campaigns around the world, leading to the eradication of the disease by 1980.

Vaccines targeting many other pathogens were successfully developed building on the Jennerian method, as well as on processes and technological platforms developed throughout the nineteenth and twentieth centuries – and some even more recently, with events like the COVID-19 pandemic shedding new light on emerging types of vaccines.[28] Other quests in vaccinology have proven more elusive: to this day, even though enormous progress has been made in the fields of HIV/AIDS prevention and treatment, an effective vaccine has yet to emerge from the decades-long R&D efforts to produce one.

Unlike the Jennerian and immediately subsequent eras of vaccine development, today, there are different types of approaches to creating a new vaccine, relying on differentiated methods, components, and technological approaches, summarized in Section 1.3.1. Yet, the concept of "vaccine" as popularized from Jenner's experiments

---

[24]   Kinch, *Between Hope and Fear*, note 23.
[25]   Arthur Boylston, "The Origins of Inoculation" (2012) 105 *Journal of the Royal Society of Medicine* 309–13.
[26]   Stefan Riedel, "Edward Jenner and the History of Smallpox and Vaccination" (January 2005) 18(1) *Proceedings (Baylor University. Medical Center)* 21–25.
[27]   Riedel, "Edward Jenner," note 26.
[28]   See e.g. Rino Rappuoli et al., "Vaccinology in the Post–COVID-19 Era" (January 19, 2021) 118(3) *PNAS* e2020368118.

onward remains a unifiable one. While the book will often distinguish between forms of vaccine technology – older versus newer, patent-protected versus freely replicable – vaccines are treated as a cohesive group for specific purposes. Scientifically, vaccines are understood as particular types of biopharmaceutical products. The US National Academies of Science currently provides the following definition of vaccine:

> A biological preparation that improves immunity to a particular disease. A vaccine typically contains an agent that resembles a disease-causing microorganism and is often made from weakened or killed forms of the microbe or its toxins. The agent stimulates the body's immune system to recognize it as foreign, destroy it, and "remember" it, so that the immune system can more easily identify and destroy any of these microorganisms that it encounters later. The body's immune system responds to vaccines as if they contain an actual pathogen, even though the vaccine itself is not capable of causing disease.[29]

Drug regulators across the world match this scientific understanding by grouping vaccines with other biologic products for purposes of regulatory review and approval, a process described in Chapter 2. Similarly, most debates about vaccine hesitancy and vaccine misinformation focus predominantly on vaccines as a category, probing one's feelings or knowledge about vaccines as human-made products designed to coax a particular reaction from the human body.

From this unified perspective – one that regards vaccines as technological constructions devised with the purpose of priming the human body to better respond to potential attacks from pathogens – vaccines are widely considered as one of the greatest developments in the history of public health. As is the case with other pharmaceutical products, they also present inherent risks, which vaccine development and regulation have progressively sought to address and, wherever possible, minimize. Chapter 2 integrates the discussion of these risks into its surveys of the regulatory framework for vaccine approval. Section 1.2 now underscores the benefits that have long been recognized in connection with the use of vaccines – which, as the COVID-19 pandemic has highlighted, exceed the domain of public health and intersect with socioeconomic concerns at the community, national, and international levels.

1.2 BENEFITS OF VACCINATION

1.2.1 *Public Health Value of Vaccination*

Vaccines have long been recognized as one of the most cost-effective tools in public health to prevent, manage, and mitigate the spread of infectious diseases.[30] The

---

[29] Madeline Drexler, "Prevention and Treatment: Vaccines," in *What You Need to Know About Infectious Disease* (US National Academies of Science, 2011), 1–44.
[30] See e.g. Walter A. Orenstein & Rafi Ahmed, "Simply Put: Vaccination Saves Lives" (2017) 114 *PNAS* 4031–33.

development and administration of numerous new vaccines throughout the twentieth century have drastically reduced infection and disease rates, and in some cases contributed decisively to the eradication or quasi-eradication of disease.

Consider the following examples. A tetanus vaccine was introduced in the United States in 1938 and combined in the 1940s with vaccines against diphtheria and pertussis (whooping cough).[31] Broad administration of these vaccines has helped bring infection rates to extremely low levels. Since 1947, cases of tetanus have decreased by 95 percent and deaths by 99 percent.[32] Cases of diphtheria, which a century ago averaged 200,000 cases per year in the United States, have been reduced by 99.9 percent.[33]

Chapter 3 describes the polio vaccine race, which helped inform vaccine and drug testing procedures still in place. The first vaccines resulting from this race entered the market in the 1950s and early 1960s. In the United States, polio infection led to an average of 15,000 cases of paralysis each year.[34] After the vaccines were introduced, the overall polio case count dropped to less than a hundred during the 1960s, and less than ten during the 1970s. Since 1979, the United States has been polio-free. In 2002, the fifty-three countries that integrate the WHO's European Region were certified as being free of the disease.[35]

As explored in Chapter 4, public health gains achieved through vaccination can erode quickly. Cases of measles dropped by 99 percent since the first measles vaccine was introduced in the United States in 1963.[36] In the late 2010s, however, there were multiple outbreaks of measles across the United States, which have been connected to decreasing rates of measles vaccination within certain geographical communities with growing levels of hesitancy toward vaccination. The story of vaccines as scientific and technological advancements to improve public health is thus one that is closely intertwined with the ways in which vaccine technology is perceived by different communities and, ultimately, the public at large.

Finally, from a public health perspective, the narrative of vaccine development and broadly available vaccination is only reflective of certain regions of the world, largely corresponding to higher-income countries. Lower-income countries, by

---

[31] Jennifer L. Liang et al., "Prevention of Pertussis, Tetanus, and Diphtheria with Vaccines in the United States: Recommendations of the Advisory Committee on Immunization Practices (ACIP)" (April 27, 2018) 67(2) *Recommendations and Reports* 1–44.

[32] US Centers for Disease Control and Prevention, "Tetanus (Lockjaw)," (2021), www.hhs.gov/immun ization/diseases/tetanus/index.html; T. Tiwari et al., "Tetanus Surveillance – United States, 2001–2008" (April 1, 2011) 60(12) *Morbidity and Mortality Weekly Report (MMWR)* 365–69.

[33] US Centers for Disease Control and Prevention, "Diphtheria," (2021), www.hhs.gov/immunization/ diseases/diphtheria/index.html.

[34] US Centers for Disease Control and Prevention, "Polio Elimination in the United States," (2021), www.cdc.gov/polio/what-is-polio/polio-us.html.

[35] World Health Organization, "Poliomyelitis," www.euro.who.int/en/health-topics/communicable-diseases/poliomyelitis.

[36] US Centers for Disease Control and Prevention, "Measles," (2021), www.vaccines.gov/diseases/ measles.

contrast, continue to face significant limitations in access to vaccines – especially newly developed ones, as recent pandemics have amply illustrated, through a phenomenon now popularly known as "vaccine nationalism," which the book describes and critiques in Chapter 3. But even outside the context of highly disruptive events such as a pandemic, lower-income countries still often lack adequate and equitable access to vaccines, including those necessary to prevent routine childhood diseases. Consider again the case of measles. Before vaccination against measles became available globally, the disease was estimated to cause 2.6 million deaths each year.[37] By 2015, that number had dropped to just over 134,000 (although it surged to over 140,000 in the year that preceded the COVID-19 pandemic). Between 2000 and 2015 alone, global measles deaths dropped by 79 percent. In spite of these considerable public health achievements, the public health toll of measles continues to fall on populations in less affluent parts of the world. The disease, which remains one of the leading causes of vaccine-preventable deaths, continues to disproportionally affect populations in sub-Saharan countries, such as those located in Somalia and the Democratic Republic of the Congo.[38]

1.2.2 *Economic and Other Societal Benefits*

In addition to having a direct positive impact on health outcomes, widespread vaccination contributes toward several other societally desirable outcomes.[39] The COVID-19 pandemic shed renewed light on the potentially severe economic effects associated with curbing the spread of infectious disease pathogens.

Calculations focusing on the economic impact of routine childhood vaccination have consistently concluded that widespread vaccination practices in the United States have resulted in substantial economic savings. For example, a study published in *Pediatrics* in 2014 by Fangjun Zhou and colleagues calculated that administering routine vaccines to a birth cohort of just over four million infants would prevent approximately twenty million cases of disease and 42,000 early deaths.[40] The avoidance of these events would, in turn, result in US $13.5 billion in net savings in direct

---

[37] World Health Organization Regional Office for Africa, "Measles," www.afro.who.int/health-topics /measles.

[38] World Health Organization, "More Than 140,000 Die from Measles As Cases Surge Worldwide" (December 5, 2019), www.who.int/news/item/05-12-2019-more-than-140-000-die-from-measles-as-cases-surge-worldwide.

[39] R. F. Breiman, "Vaccines as Tools for Advancing More than Public Health: Perspectives of a Former Director of the National Vaccine Program Office" (2001) 32 *Clinical Infectious Diseases* 283.

[40] Fangjun Zhou et al., "Economic Evaluation of the Routine Childhood Immunization Program in the United States, 2009" (2014) 133 *Pediatrics* 577–85, https://pediatrics.aappublications.org/content/ 133/4/577. The study was based on recommended childhood vaccines with reference to the year 2009, which included the following vaccines: diphtheria and tetanus toxoids and acellular pertussis (DTaP), Haemophilus influenzae type b conjugate (Hib), inactivated poliovirus (IPV), measles/ mumps/rubella (MMR), hepatitis B (HepB), varicella (VAR), 7-valent pneumococcal conjugate (PCV7), hepatitis A (HepA), and rotavirus (Rota) vaccines.

costs and US $68.8 billion in net savings in total societal costs. Direct costs include medical costs, such as the treatment of a vaccine-preventable disease, and non-medical costs, such as the cost associated with providing special education to children disabled by a vaccine-preventable disease. Non-medical costs encompass productivity losses due to permanent disability or premature death, and opportunity costs for individuals who contract a vaccine-preventable disease (such as missed wages) or for parents who have to forego work in order to care for a child.

Several other studies point toward significant savings to health systems linked to vaccination. Vanessa Rémy and colleagues have calculated that robust administration of the diphtheria, tetanus, and pertussis (DTP) vaccine has helped the United States health system save an overall US $23.6 billion.[41]

Conversely, responding to an outbreak of a vaccine-preventable disease increases costs to health systems and society in general. Two recent cases may be instructive here. A measles outbreak affecting the Somali-American community in Minnesota in 2017 has been largely linked to the spread of misinformation about the measles, mumps, and rubella (MMR) vaccine.[42] Anti-vaccine activists specifically targeted this immigrant community, attending local events and spreading word that the administration of the MMR vaccine was linked to autism. As a result, measles vaccination rates within this community plunged over the course of a decade (2004–2014) from 92 percent to 42 percent.[43] Research by Dorit Rubinstein Reiss and John Diamond suggests that responding to this outbreak cost the local public health authorities in excess of one million dollars.[44]

Even more granular data are available about the economic impact of the response to a measles outbreak that took place between late December 2018 and late April 2019 in Clark County, in southwestern Washington State, and part of the larger Portland metropolitan area, a region known for high rates of vaccine hesitancy.[45] A study published in the journal *Pediatrics* calculated that the "overall societal cost" of the outbreaks was around US $3.4 million, which averaged to $47,479 per case or $814 per contact.[46] The majority of costs were those incurred by public health authorities in response to the

---

[41] Vanessa Rémy et al., "Vaccination: The Cornerstone of an Efficient Healthcare System" (2015) 3 *Journal of Market Access & Health Policy* 27041, 27044–46.

[42] Victoria Hall et al., "Measles Outbreak – Minnesota April–May 2017" (July 14, 2017) 66 *Morbidity & Mortality Weekly Report* 713–17; Helen Braswell, "Measles Sweeps an Immigrant Community Targeted by Anti-Vaccine Activists" (May 8, 2017) *Stat*, www.statnews.com/2017/05/08/measles-vaccines-somali/.

[43] Owen Dyer, "Measles Outbreak in Somali American Community Follows Anti-Vaccine Talks" (May 16, 2017) 357 *British Medical Journal* j2378.

[44] Dorit R. Reiss & John Diamond, "Measles and Misrepresentation in Minnesota: Can There Be Liability for Anti-Vaccine Misinformation That Causes Bodily Harm?" (2019) 56 *San Diego Law Review* 531, 531–80.

[45] Isaac Stanley-Becker, "Anti-Vaccination 'Hot Spot' in SW Washington Declares Emergency Over Measles Outbreak" (January 23, 2019) *Seattle Times*, www.seattletimes.com/seattle-news/an-anti-vaccination-hotspot-near-portland-declares-an-emergency-over-measles-outbreak/.

[46] Jamison Pike et al., "Societal Costs of a Measles Outbreak" (March 2021) 147(4) *Pediatrics*, https://doi.org/10.1542/peds.2020-027037.

outbreak, consisting of "labor, material, and contractor costs," which totaled around $2.3 million. Productivity losses resulting from "illness, home isolation, quarantine, or informal caregiving" were estimated to have cost around $1 million. And, finally, there were medical costs arising from "third party or patient out-of-pocket treatment costs," which rose to around $76,000.

1.3 VACCINES AS A FORM OF TECHNOLOGY

Even though the development of vaccines is geared toward the pursuit of the same overall goal – the prevention or mitigation of disease by triggering a protective reaction of the human immune system – modern vaccines rely on different technological approaches to exact that protective reaction. For example, some types of vaccines might incorporate a weakened form of a pathogen, while others rely on synthetic matter engineered to coax the human immune system to respond. While Chapter 2 will focus on commonalities between vaccines – namely, from a regulatory perspective, which treats vaccines as a group within the universe of biologics – this section emphasizes the differences between technological approaches to creating a vaccine. The implications of these differences are manifold. Varying degrees of technological complexity often affect the ease with which a given vaccine can be replicated by others, and even distributed or administered. In situations of vaccine scarcity, it is often the case that only a limited number of companies or institutions may be able to produce, or help produce, complex vaccines; existing manufacturing facilities may not be able to scale up the production of vaccines as quickly as it is often possible to increase the production of technologically simpler health goods; and some vaccines require storage and transportation at ultra-cold temperatures, as was the case with certain COVID-19 vaccines, a process that further complicates vaccine rollout and makes this type of vaccine poorly suited for distribution across regions with infrastructure gaps, as is the case of many areas in lower-income countries and even remote areas of higher-income ones. Moreover, under contemporary legal regimes applicable to innovative goods, several components of a vaccine – and especially newer components of complex vaccines – are often covered by patent rights which, as discussed in Chapter 3, may prevent the transfer of vaccine technology, or render it costlier, procedurally more complicated, or even politically fraught.

In this section, the book hones in on different types of vaccines currently available on domestic and global markets with reference to the scientific processes employed. While multiple, overlapping categorizations have been proposed by science-driven institutions, the book uses the definitional approach provided by the US Department of Health and Human Services, which as of 2021 categorizes commercially available vaccines into six groups.[47]

---

[47]   US Department of Health and Human Services, "Vaccine Types," (April 29, 2021), www.hhs.gov /immunization/basics/types/index.html.

1.3.1 *Different Types of Vaccine Technology*

The first group comprises vaccine products in which the pathogen has been killed, and the resulting vaccines are known as inactivated vaccines.[48] The seasonal flu shot, vaccines against rabies and hepatitis A, and the polio vaccine delivered through an injection – whose development in the mid-twentieth century the book chronicles in Chapter 3 – are all made according to this method. Many types of inactivated vaccines tend to confer protection for shorter periods of time than other types of vaccines, which is why booster doses may need to be administered after the initial shot.

The second group covers vaccine products in which the pathogen has been weakened but not killed, and resulting vaccines are known as live-attenuated vaccines.[49] The goal of this method is to diminish the virulence of the pathogen so that, when administered, the virus or bacterium will in principle be incapable of causing disease, but nonetheless prompt the human body to trigger a protective immune reaction. The most common way to weaken wild pathogens for vaccine-making purposes is through repeated culturing in a lab. These viruses and bacteria grow progressively weaker as they reproduce in controlled cell cultures, a process that may take close to a decade to complete.[50] For instance, the first measles vaccine was developed by scientists who collected blood from a child suffering from measles, David Edmonston, and managed to isolate the virus and then cultivate it in kidney cells for nearly ten years. The Edmonston strain became the basis of measles vaccines used in the United States to this day.[51] The measles vaccine is now most commonly administered together with two other vaccines in a combination vaccine often called MMR (measles, mumps, rubella). Other examples of live-attenuated vaccines include the oral vaccine against rotavirus (a pathogen causing diarrhea and potential dehydration in babies and young children) and the injectable vaccines against chickenpox (a virus causing rashes and, in serious cases, lung disease) and yellow fever (a potentially fatal disease caused by the bite of a mosquito endemic to parts of Africa and South America).

Instead of the pathogen itself, other types of vaccine technology use a variety of techniques that require only a fragment of a pathogen, such as a sugar or protein. The US Department of Health and Human Services groups these types of technology under a third group that serves as an umbrella and is called "subunit, recombinant, polysaccharide, and conjugate vaccines."[52] This type of technology leverages the part of a pathogen that is best at stimulating a protective response from the human immune system. Examples of these vaccines include the PPSV23 vaccine,

---

[48] US DHHS, "Vaccine Types," note 47.
[49] US DHHS, "Vaccine Types," note 47.
[50] US Centers for Disease Control and Prevention, "Principles of Vaccination," (2021), www.cdc.gov /vaccines/pubs/pinkbook/downloads/prinvac.pdf.
[51] Jeffrey P. Baker, "The First Measles Vaccine" (September 2011) 128(3) *Pediatrics* 435–37.
[52] US DHHS, "Vaccine Types," note 47.

a polysaccharide vaccine against twenty-three types of bacteria causing pneumococ-cal diseases like pneumonia and certain bloodstream infections, and the hepatitis B vaccine, a recombinant vaccine developed by inserting part of the DNA of the hepatitis B virus into yeast cells, which are then able to produce one of the proteins found in the surface of the hepatitis B virus.[53] In addition to generally triggering a strong immune response, one advantage of vaccines that are not made by using the whole pathogen is that they can be given to people with weakened immune systems who may not be able to receive some inactivated or live-attenuated vaccines.[54]

The fourth group is comprised of toxoid vaccines, which are made by using harmful substances (toxins) produced by bacteria causing certain diseases.[55] Unlike other types of vaccines, toxoid vaccines are designed to confer protection against the toxins and not the pathogens themselves. The most common examples of toxoid vaccines include those against tetanus (a disease causing symptoms ranging from stiff muscles to seizures) and diphtheria (a disease causing symptoms ranging from sore throat to organ damage).

These four groups used to cover the spectrum of commercially available vaccines in the United States and Europe, even though several other types of vaccine technology have long been in development across the world. In late 2020, the authorization of COVID-19 vaccine by regulators in multiple countries marked the introduction of a new type of vaccines: mRNA vaccines, as was the case with the COVID-19 vaccines manufactured by the American company Moderna and by the American company Pfizer in partnership with the German company BioNTech. These vaccines use a lab-engineered form of messenger RNA – genetic material that directs the human body to produce specific proteins; in the case of COVID-19, the mRNA vaccines caused the body to produce some of the proteins produced by the SARS-CoV-2 coronavirus, which in turn prompted the immune system to respond. For purposes of categorization, the US Department of Health and Human Services has placed mRNA vaccines in their own group.

The sixth and final group encompasses yet another emerging type of vaccine technology: viral vector vaccines, which use a modified version of a virus that is different from the one the vaccine is designed to protect the body from; for example, an influenza virus or the virus causing the common cold (adenovirus) may be used to trigger protection against a virus that causes neither flu nor the common cold. The Johnson & Johnson COVID-19 vaccine was based on viral vector technology – also successfully applied to the development of Ebola vaccines, which the book recounts in Chapter 3.

Several other technological approaches to vaccine development are currently being studied and tested, likely resulting in continued heterogeneity in the types

---

[53] Mirella Bucci, "First Recombinant DNA Vaccine for HBV" (September 28, 2020) *Nature Portfolio*, www.nature.com/articles/d42859-020-00016-5.

[54] US DHHS, "Vaccine Types," note 47.

[55] US DHHS, "Vaccine Types," note 47.

of vaccines coming to the market in coming decades. Moreover, many of the more recent techniques used to develop new vaccines are now being used in R&D aimed at developing non-vaccine products. For instance, in an initial overview of the state of vaccine technology as the world emerges from the COVID-19 pandemic, Rino Rappuoli and colleagues noted in a *Proceedings of the National Academies of Science* report published in early 2021 that "some of the vaccine technologies that are fast-tracked by the urgency of COVID-19 may also be the answer for other health priorities, such as antimicrobial resistance, chronic infections, and cancer, that the post-COVID-19 world will urgently need to face."[56] An example of this potential for use outside the traditional context of vaccinology is the case of the mRNA technology utilized to produce some of the first COVID-19 vaccines, and which is currently being studied in multiple other areas, including cancer R&D, Parkinson's, and several autoimmune diseases.

From a technological perspective, vaccine R&D has thus diversified significantly since the dawn of Jennerian vaccinology and continues to evolve in response to both persistent and newer challenges posed by infectious disease pathogens. At the same time, we may in the near future be facing a progressive blurring of frontiers between what counts as vaccine technology and what may be best regarded as platform technology – that is, technology that can be used or adapted for the development of both vaccine and non-vaccine products. As seen in Chapters 3 and 5, this blurring will likely have important consequences for the ways in which vaccine R&D is funded, the relevance of intellectual property rights, and ultimately the allocation of newly developed vaccines.

Against this backdrop of burgeoning scientific and technological change, there are longstanding structures in place to vet new vaccines before they come to market, as well as to monitor vaccines once they are authorized or approved for commercialization. The book now explores the vaccine R&D ecosystem from this perspective, which applies common regulatory principles to all types of products falling under the umbrella of "vaccine."

---

[56] Rappuoli et al., "Vaccinology," note 28.

2

The Vaccine Development Ecosystem

2.1 THE REGULATORY FRAMEWORK SURROUNDING VACCINE DEVELOPMENT

As vaccines are complex technologies that interact with the human body, their development is overseen by regulators in the administrative state. Countries structure the review of pharmaceutical products according to domestic rules and institutional design. As such, vaccines are reviewed as biologic products by regulatory authorities at the domestic level, such as the Therapeutic Goods Administration in Australia or the Pharmaceutical and Medical Devices Agency in Japan. The national basis of vaccine regulation inevitably leads to country-specific processes and timelines and may in some cases lead to different decisions.[1] However, in spite of these geographical and jurisdictional limitations, drug and vaccine regulatory processes across the world share most defining features. In part, this is due to the fact that the regulation of pharmaceutical products incorporates scientific and ethical principles now regarded as universal: the law imposes conditions on the development and testing of these products, offers protections to volunteers participating in clinical trials, and prompts regulators to examine data generated during the R&D process when performing a risk–benefit assessment and deciding whether to allow the commercialization of new pharmaceuticals. Additionally, national regulators communicate and collaborate with one another. Moreover, international institutions – chief among which the WHO – promote and coordinate knowledge-sharing and communication among country-level pharmaceutical regulators.[2]

This chapter provides an overview of the standard model of regulatory review and approval of new vaccines with reference to the United States, where the Center for Biologics Evaluation and Research (CBER) at the Food & Drug Administration (FDA) is responsible for the review of applications to bring new vaccines to market.

---

[1] See e.g. "COVID Vaccines: The World's Medical Regulators Need Access to Open Data" (2020) 588 *Nature* 195 (arguing that, during a public health crisis such as COVID-19, vaccine regulators should employ a "more harmonized" vaccine approval process).

[2] World Health Organization, "Vaccine Regulation," note 14.

2.1.1 *The Dawn of Vaccine Regulation: The Case of the United States*

Vaccine regulation as we know it today is largely a product of the twentieth century, even though vaccines have been produced in the United States in quasi-industrial conditions since the nineteenth century. The seeds for the modern vaccine industry were planted in the form of vaccine farms that emerged in response to the introduction of an animal-based smallpox vaccine in the United States in the 1870s.[3] Although initially focused solely on the production of smallpox vaccines, these farms quickly began expanding into the development and manufacturing of other types of vaccine products, such as diphtheria vaccines.[4]

These farms, the antecedent of modern vaccine manufacturers, operated in a largely unregulated environment.[5] There were some early attempts to regulate the vaccine ecosystem, although primarily from the perspective of preventing the circulation of infectious disease pathogens, promoting vaccination, or facilitating the distribution of vaccines. For instance, as early as 1792, Virginia passed an act consolidating previous attempts to regulate inoculation against smallpox; the law included monetary penalties and the possibility of imprisonment for anyone who willfully spread smallpox outside the contexts allowed by the act.[6] In 1813, Congress passed the first federal piece of legislation focused exclusively on the topic, titled An Act to Encourage Vaccination.[7] The Act, which was in force until 1822, allowed for the appointment of a federal agent to "preserve the genuine vaccine matter," gave the agent the authority to distribute or have vaccines distributed, and established that vaccines could be distributed through use of the postal service free of charge. Massachusetts was the first state to enact both a general vaccination mandate (through an 1809 law requiring vaccination against smallpox) and a school vaccination mandate (through an 1855 law, which also focused on vaccination against smallpox, then the only disease for which a vaccine was available).[8]

This lightly regulated environment contributed to multiple malfunctions within the vaccine production system. Two large incidents in 1901 called attention to the

---

[3] José Esparza et al., "Early Smallpox Vaccine Manufacturing in the United States: Introduction of the 'Animal Vaccine' in 1870, Establishment of 'Vaccine Farms', and the Beginnings of the Vaccine Industry" (June 19, 2020) 38(30) *Vaccine* 4773–79.

[4] Esparza et al., "Early Smallpox Vaccine Manufacturing," note 3.

[5] Walter Reed, "What Credence Should Be Given to the Statements of Those Who Claim to Furnish Vaccine Lymph Free of Bacteria?" (1895) 5 *Journal of Practical Medicine* 532–34, at 532.

[6] History of Vaccines, "Commonwealth of Virginia Consolidation Act for Smallpox Regulation" (1792), www.historyofvaccines.org/content/stricter-regulations-passed-inoculation.

[7] An Act to Encourage Vaccination, ch. 37, 2 Stat. 806 (1813) repealed by An Act to Repeal the Act to Encourage Vaccination, ch. 50, 3 Stat. 677 (1822).

[8] Philip J. Smith et al., "Highlights of Historical Events Leading to National Surveillance of Vaccination Coverage in the United States" (2011) 126(Suppl 2) *Public Health Reports* 3–12. See also Kevin M. Malone & Alan R. Hinman, "Vaccination Mandates: The Public Health Imperative and Individual Rights," in *Law in Public Health Practice*, Richard A. Goodman et al., eds. (Oxford University Press, 2007); History of Vaccines, "Vaccination Exemptions" (2018), www.historyofvaccines.org/index.php/content/articles/vaccination-exemptions.

problems posed by poor vaccine manufacturing practices, which were fairly common then. The first took place in Saint Louis, Missouri, and has been called the "first modern medical disaster."[9] Employees of the Saint Louis Health Department failed to discard serum extracted from an animal that developed tetanus a few days after the extraction. The serum was used to produce diphtheria antitoxin, which was mislabeled and administered, without being tested, to children suffering from diphtheria, as well as prophylactically to healthy children. As a result, thirteen children died. That same year, there was an outbreak of tetanus in Camden, New Jersey, involving approximately eighty people and resulting in eleven deaths. The outbreak affected individuals who had recently been administered a vaccine against smallpox manufactured by Mulford, a company based in Philadelphia. Although the ensuing investigation did not produce definitive evidence of vaccine contamination, it raised several concerns about the conditions under which the Mulford vaccines were being produced as well as their safety.[10]

The Saint Louis and Camden incidents were merely the most visible face of systemic, substandard practices in the budding vaccine industry. Around the same period, tetanus outbreaks associated with the administration of smallpox vaccines occurred elsewhere in the East Coast and Midwest. The growing concerns surrounding vaccine safety strengthened the case for a model of stringent and centralized vaccine regulation. This model was introduced the year after the Saint Louis and Camden outbreaks and refined through continued legislative interventions thereafter.

2.1.2 *Vaccine Regulators: The Case of the FDA*

In 1902, Congress passed the Biologics Control Act, which gave the Hygienic Laboratory of the Public Health and Marine Hospital Service the authority to regulate the manufacturing process and the sale of vaccine products.[11] Vaccine manufacturers were required to undergo an annual licensure process and have their facilities periodically inspected, as well as comply with labeling requirements. Although expanded through subsequent legislation, similar obligations remain at the core of the modern regulation of vaccines and other biologic products.[12]

In 1906, Congress passed the Pure Food and Drugs Act, which did not directly regulate vaccines and other biologics, but established a comprehensive regulatory regime for food and drugs. Although the law that superseded it – the 1938 Federal

9   Ross E. DeHovitz, "The 1901 St Louis Incident: The First Modern Medical Disaster" (June 2014) 133 (6) *Pediatrics* 964–65.
10   Linda Bren, "The Road to the Biotech Revolution – Highlights of 100 Years of Biologics Regulation" (January–February 2006) *FDA Consumer Magazine*, Centennial edition.
11   Pub. L. No. 57–244, 32 Stat. 728 (1902) (repealed in 1944); Bren, "The Road to the Biotech Revolution," note 10.
12   Terry S. Coleman, "Early Developments in the Regulation of Biologics" (2016) 71 *Food and Drug Law Journal* 544–607, at 551.

Food, Drug, and Cosmetic Act – deemed biologics as drugs,[13] it did not unify the regulation of drugs and biologics. As seen in Section 2.1.3, to this day the regulation of biologics – including vaccines – is governed by segments of the Food, Drug, and Cosmetic Act in articulation with another law, the 1944 Public Health Service Act.[14] In the meantime, the Hygienic Laboratory became the National Institute of Health in 1930, the precursor to the National Institutes of Health (NIH) in 1948, and it continued to regulate vaccines until 1972, at which point the authority to regulate biologics shifted from the NIH to the FDA.

Today, the FDA remains the primary regulator of drugs and biologics, including vaccines, even though the agency was not initially designed as a drug regulation-oriented institution. The agency traces its origins to a chemical office created within the Patent Office in the mid-nineteenth century focusing on issues related to the analysis and monitoring of agricultural products.[15] The Agricultural Division of the Patent Office later integrated with the structure of the Department of Agriculture, from which it eventually evolved into an institutional figure with an increasingly large footprint (from the Division of Chemistry in 1890 to the Bureau of Chemistry in 1901) and with subject-matter jurisdiction that greatly exceeded the food-related and agricultural domains. In 1927, it became the Food, Drug and Insecticide Administration and, in 1930, the FDA. Presently, the FDA has jurisdiction over a broad range of products – food, drugs, medical devices, cosmetics, and tobacco – with 2018 estimates indicating that approximately 20 percent of products purchased by consumers in the United States are regulated by the FDA.[16]

In the case of pharmaceutical products, there are currently more than 19,000 prescription drugs approved by the FDA. According to calculations released by the agency in 2018, biologics – the scientific and regulatory category to which vaccines belong – represent a relatively smaller area, with around 340 products approved.[17]

2.1.3 *Vaccines as Biologics: The Applicable Legal Framework*

The basic structure of the regulatory review process for vaccines is set forth in the Food, Drug, and Cosmetic Act and the Public Health Service Act, which are supplemented by FDA-issued guidance.[18] Collectively, these legal frameworks

---

[13]   Bren, "The Road to the Biotech Revolution," note 10.
[14]   Public Health Service Act § 351, 42 US Code § 262; Federal Food, Drug, and Cosmetic Act § 505, 21 US Code § 355.
[15]   Peter Barton Hutt, "A Historical Introduction" (1990) 45 *Food, Drug, Cosmetic Law Journal* 17–19.
[16]   US Food & Drug Administration, "Fact Sheet: FDA at a Glance" (2018), www.fda.gov/about-fda/fda-basics/fact-sheet-fda-glance.
[17]   US Food & Drug Administration, "FDA at a Glance," note 16.
[18]   FDA guidance consists of documents reflecting the agency's thinking on a specific topic or series of topics. Although nonbinding, guidance informs interested parties of FDA's interpretation of the law or regulatory policy in a given area. See US Food & Drug Administration, "Guidances" (February 10, 2021), www.fda.gov/industry/fda-basics-industry/guidances. For an overview of FDA guidance on vaccines and related products, see US Food & Drug Administration, "Vaccine and Related

treat vaccines from complementary perspectives. First and more broadly, vaccines are considered pharmaceutical products – they fit under the general category of "drugs" as opposed to other types of FDA-regulated products such as food or medical devices. For regulatory purposes, the Food, Drug, and Cosmetic Act considers drugs to include "articles intended for use in the diagnosis, cure, mitigation, treatment, or prevention of disease in man or other animals."[19] Before a new drug can be distributed in interstate commerce, the FDA is required to perform a risk–benefit analysis based on available data generated through clinical trials and determine if the product is "safe" and "effective." This idea permeates the regulation of all types of drugs or what most people might think of as pharmaceuticals. Therefore, even when laws and regulations distinguish between different types of pharmaceutical products, a demonstration of safety and effectiveness remains the touchstone of any process designed to bring these products to market.

Even though the concept of vaccines – and especially their preventative function – fits under the umbrella definition of drugs found in the Food, Drug, and Cosmetic Act, they are further regulated under the legal framework applicable to biologics. This framework includes the basic principles undergirding drug regulation in the Act, as well as the regulatory process specific to biologics set forth in the Public Health Service Act.

Biologics form a large and highly heterogenous subset of drugs. The Public Health Service Act defines "biological product" as "a virus, therapeutic serum, toxin, antitoxin, vaccine, blood, blood component or derivative, allergenic product, protein, or analogous product, or arsphenamine or derivative of arsphenamine (or any other trivalent organic arsenic compound), applicable to the prevention, treatment, or cure of a disease or condition of human beings."[20] The common trait among these seemingly different products is that they are structurally large and complex drugs made from, or including parts of, living things. This sets them apart from other types of pharmaceutical products – the ones regulated under the umbrella of "drugs" by the Food, Drug, and Cosmetic Act – which are structurally smaller and less complex.

Recall the case of the different types of vaccine technology surveyed in Chapter 1: although there are markedly different processes for producing a vaccine, they all rely on the use of a biological component, such as a weakened virus or part of a protein. By contrast, nonbiological drugs, which are often called conventional drugs or small-molecule drugs, are chemically synthesized instead of being made out of living organisms or components thereof. The vast majority of pharmaceutical products available to patients fall under the umbrella of small-molecule drugs. Examples include aspirin, corticosteroids, and many of the existing drugs in the

Biological Product Guidances" (2020), www.fda.gov/vaccines-blood-biologics/biologics-guidances/vaccine-and-related-biological-product-guidances.
[19]   21 US Code § 321(g).
[20]   42 US Code § 262(i)(1).

treatment of high cholesterol. To put things in perspective, consider how legal scholars Nicholson Price and Arti Rai have described the relative differences between small-molecule drugs and biologics and then within the realm of biologics itself: "In terms of size and rough complexity, if an aspirin [a small-molecule drug] were a bicycle, a small biologic would be a Toyota Prius, and a large biologic would be an F-16 fighter jet."[21]

These differences in size and structure between biologics and small-molecule drugs have important implications. While it is relatively easy to reverse-engineer and replicate an existing small-molecule drug, it is not only difficult to reverse-engineer a biologic but also impossible to create a perfect replica thereof. From a regulatory perspective, one of the major implications of the differences between vaccines and other biologics on the one hand, and small-molecule drugs on the other, is that there has been a regulatory pathway in place for the FDA to approve generic versions of small-molecule drugs since the 1980s.[22] Because it is scientifically impossible to produce a generic version of a biologic, a separate regulatory framework is in place for the counterparts to generics in the field of biologics – biosimilars. The legal framework for biosimilars to undergo FDA review and enter the market was not created until 2010, however, as part of the Affordable Care Act.[23] The different timeline is also a reflection of the fact that the biologics industry is much more recent than the pharmaceutical industry, which produced the small-molecule drugs that constituted the backbone of drug products for most of our history. The first biosimilar to enter the US market was approved by the FDA in 2015. As of early 2021, there is a total of twenty-nine approved biosimilars and none is a vaccine.[24]

Vaccines are thus grouped together with other biologics from both a scientific and a regulatory perspective. Nonetheless, the properties of vaccines as products of biotechnology render most vaccines a poorer fit for market-driven R&D models than most emerging biologics. Collectively, biologics are currently considered "the most promising" type of pharmaceutical products available to patients in a variety of areas,[25] ranging from oncology to autoimmune diseases, and several biologics rank among the most profitable drugs in the world. Even though they fall within the larger category of biologics, most vaccines are produced under much more resource-constrained R&D conditions and, once approved, face considerably smaller markets than best-selling biologics, as discussed at length in Chapter 3.

---

[21] W. Nicholson Price II & Arti K. Rai, "Manufacturing Barriers to Biologics Competition and Innovation" (2016) 101 *Iowa Law Review* 1023, at 1026–63.

[22] Drug Price Competition and Patent Term Restoration Act of 1984, Pub. L. No. 98–417, 98 Stat. 1585 (codified as amended in scattered sections of 15, 21, 35 and 42 US Code).

[23] Patient Protection and Affordable Care Act of 2010, Pub. L. No. 111–48, 124 Stat. 119, 804 (codified as amended in scattered sections of US Code). See also 42 US Code § 262(k) (regulating the approval of biosimilars).

[24] US Food & Drug Administration, "Biosimilar Product Information," (2021), www.fda.gov/drugs/biosimilars/biosimilar-product-information.

[25] See Price & Rai, "Manufacturing Barriers," note 21, at 1026.

2.1.4 *From the Lab to the Market: An Overview of the Standard Vaccine Regulatory Process*

Absent certain types of emergencies, the pathway to bring new vaccines to market is subject to the parameters applicable to drugs in general, and biologics in particular, as seen in the previous section. A vaccine sponsor must ultimately present the FDA with data that enable the agency to determine that there is substantial evidence that the vaccine is safe and effective. If such a determination is made, the FDA issues a biologics license, the legal instrument that allows a company or any other vaccine sponsor to start marketing their product.[26] Until there is a permissive gesture from the agency, the Public Health Service Act prohibits the introduction of unapproved vaccines into interstate commerce.[27]

The data submitted to the FDA in support of a biologics license application (BLA) are typically gathered throughout an R&D process that spans several years, sometimes even more than a decade. As discussed in the subsequent sections, the R&D timeline may be shorter for the development of vaccines during a large public health crisis, such as the COVID-19 pandemic, particularly in cases in which it is possible to adapt preexisting vaccine technology to create a vaccine targeting a new pathogen.

Irrespective of the length of the R&D process, vaccine candidates generally traverse the same phases of development. First, the vaccine undergoes an initial period of preclinical studies, which, if successful, is followed by testing on human volunteers. The preclinical stage encompasses different types of tests, both in vitro (outside a living organism) and in vivo (in or on a living organism), during which scientists experiment with different formulations, gathering multiple data, including information on toxicity levels and the ability of the vaccine to trigger an immune response when administered to animals.[28]

A promising vaccine candidate may then be allowed to move to the clinical stages, in which it is tested on humans. The vaccine sponsor is required to submit an investigational new drug (IND) application to the FDA before initiating this stage. The IND prompts a vaccine sponsor to disclose detailed information about the vaccine, how it works, and how it is made. This information includes a description of the vaccine, its safety and immunogenicity (its ability to trigger a protective immune response), manufacturing method, quality control testing, and the proposed protocols for clinical trials.[29]

---

[26]   See 42 US Code § 262(a).
[27]   42 US Code § 262(a).
[28]   World Health Organization, "Nonclinical Evaluation of Vaccines" (2014), www.who.int/biologicals/vaccines/nonclinial_evaluation_of_vaccines/en/.
[29]   US Food & Drug Administration, "Investigational New Drug Applications (INDs) for CBER-Regulated Products" (2021), www.fda.gov/vaccines-blood-biologics/development-approval-process-cber/investigational-new-drug-applications-inds-cber-regulated-products.

If the IND is authorized, the vaccine may then be tested on human subjects through clinical trials, which typically unfold in three phases. Phase 1 clinical trials enroll a limited number of volunteers – typically between twenty and one hundred participants – and are designed to test the safety and immunogenicity of the vaccine. Phase 2 involves a larger number of volunteers, up to several hundred, representing different demographics. This phase allows researchers to start forming early assessments of the effectiveness of the vaccine while continuing to gather information on the safety of the vaccine. Finally, if trials progress that far, phase 3 enrolls thousands or tens of thousands of volunteers, generating substantial data on the effectiveness of the vaccine, as well as additional information on its safety. In addition to data about the clinical properties of the vaccine as a product, vaccine sponsors are also required to submit detailed information to the FDA about the manufacturing process and manufacturing facilities that have been used to produce doses of the experimental vaccine and that will continue to be used to produce the vaccine if and when the FDA approves or otherwise authorizes it for commercialization.

If clinical testing of a vaccine candidate yields positive results from a scientific standpoint, the vaccine sponsor then seeks review of the data and approval from the FDA to bring the vaccine to market. This is done through the submission of a BLA.[30] A multidisciplinary team at the CBER at the FDA evaluates the application. The agency currently defines a "typical FDA team" as comprising "physicians, chemists, statisticians, pharmacologists/toxicologists, microbiologists, experts in postmarketing safety, clinical study site inspectors, manufacturing and facility inspectors, and labeling and communications experts."[31] The FDA team assigned to the review of any given vaccine BLA may also consult with the Vaccines and Related Biological Products Advisory Committee, a group formed by independent scientific and public health experts.[32]

Ultimately, the FDA is the sole decisor of whether a new vaccine should be deemed "safe" and "effective." In order to make this decision, the agency performs a risk–benefit analysis based on the data submitted as part of the BLA. When reviewing the effectiveness of a vaccine candidate, the FDA is bound by the statutory standard of "substantial evidence."[33] The Food, Drug, and Cosmetic Act defines the standard as being satisfied by

> evidence consisting of adequate and well-controlled investigations, including clinical investigations, by experts qualified by scientific training and experience to

[30] US Food & Drug Administration, "Biologics License Applications (BLA) Process (CBER)" (2021), www.fda.gov/vaccines-blood-biologics/development-approval-process-cber/biologics-license-applications-bla-process-cber.

[31] US Food & Drug Administration, "Vaccine Development – 101" (2020), www.fda.gov/vaccines-blood-biologics/development-approval-process-cber/vaccine-development-101.

[32] US Food & Drug Administration, "Vaccines and Related Biological Products Advisory Committee" (2019), www.fda.gov/advisory-committees/blood-vaccines-and-other-biologics/vaccines-and-related-biological-products-advisory-committee.

[33] 21 US Code § 355(d).

evaluate the effectiveness of the drug involved, on the basis of which it could fairly and responsibly be concluded by such experts that the drug will have the effect it purports or is represented to have under the conditions of use prescribed, recommended, or suggested in the labeling or proposed labeling thereof.[34]

Under the separate regulatory regime codified in the Public Health Service Act, vaccines and other biologics have to be deemed "safe, pure, and potent" in order to be approved by the FDA.[35] Potency is defined in regulations as "the specific ability or capacity of the product, as indicated by appropriate laboratory tests or by adequately controlled clinical data obtained through the administration of the product in the manner intended, to effect a given result."[36] This definition thus incorporates the notion of effectiveness into the concept of potency, and the FDA has long relied on this textual construction to require a demonstration of effectiveness before approving vaccines and other biologics.[37] The agency has further interpreted the Public Health Service Act as imposing the same evidentiary standard with regard to effectiveness as the one established in the Food, Drug, and Cosmetic Act – substantial evidence.[38]

If the FDA finds a vaccine to be safe and effective according to the scientifically informed parameters set forth in the law, the agency will approve it for the US market, and the vaccine is said to be licensed. It can thus be commercialized with the caveat that its use is restricted to the populations covered in the license. A vaccine manufacturer wishing to market the vaccine outside the United States will have to submit data about the vaccine candidate to drug regulators in the relevant jurisdictions, where the vaccine will be subject to regulatory review according to the specifications established in the laws and regulations of those countries.

The national basis of this process increases the complexity and cost of the regulatory review of vaccines and may prolong the timeframe according to which vaccines are made available to populations in need. However, there are two factors that mitigate these disadvantages. First, from a systemic perspective, the existence of multiple regulators means that there are multiple decisors performing the function of market gatekeepers and examining scientific data from viewpoints that are similar and tend to converge, but nonetheless independent from one another. And second, because national regulatory processes are designed around scientific paradigms, the

---

[34]   21 US Code § 355(d). See also Russell Katz, "FDA: Evidentiary Standards for Drug Development and Approval" (2004) 1 *NeuroRx* 307–16.

[35]   42 US Code § 262(C)(i)(I).

[36]   21 CFR 600.3(s).

[37]   US Food & Drug Administration, "Demonstrating Substantial Evidence of Effectiveness for Human Drug and Biological Products: Guidance for Industry" (2019) (hereinafter "FDA Guidance on Substantial Evidence"), www.fda.gov/media/133660/download, at 3.

[38]   "FDA Guidance on Substantial Evidence," note 37, at 3–4. See also US Food & Drug Administration Modernization Act of 1997, Pub. L. 105–15, § 123(f) (which directs the FDA to "minimize differences in the review and approval" of biologics and conventional drugs), cited in "FDA Guidance on Substantial Evidence," note 37, at 4.

structure of vaccine regulatory review as outlined earlier is very similar across the world. As the head of Biological Health Threats and Vaccines Strategy at the European Medicines Agency noted during the multi-country race to develop COVID-19 vaccines, "[o]verall, there are no major differences and we [regulatory agencies overseeing vaccine development and licensure] are all following the same powerful requirements with, of course, some variation also on a case by case basis."[39]

Under extraordinary circumstances, such as a large-scale public health crisis, drug regulators across the world have the ability to greenlight the use of products that are not fully approved. The FDA, for instance, has the authority to authorize the use of unapproved drugs or other medical products, as well as unapproved uses of approved products, by issuing an emergency use authorization (EUA) instead of a full license.[40] The agency has exercised this authority on multiple occasions and resorted to it during the COVID-19 pandemic to authorize the expedited commercialization of COVID-19 vaccines. In the context of an EUA application, the sponsor of a vaccine must submit data that may enable the FDA to determine that "it is reasonable to believe" that a vaccine "may be effective."[41] The amount of data that a sponsor is required to submit to meet the EUA standard is less than when seeking full approval. While set lower than the threshold for full approval under the BLA pathway, the EUA framework still binds the agency to a risk–benefit analysis driven by scientific principles. The COVID-19 vaccines authorized by the FDA in December 2020 marked the first time that newly developed vaccines entered the US market through the EUA model.

Other countries have used similar pathways to bring products to market when extraordinary circumstances arise. The European Medicines Agency, for example, started granting "conditional marketing authorizations" to qualifying COVID-19 vaccines at roughly the same time the FDA used the EUA pathway to authorize the commercialization of COVID-19 vaccines in the United States.[42]

2.1.5 *The Post-market: Continued Regulatory Oversight*

Although vaccine candidates are tested and evaluated for safety and effectiveness before being licensed by the FDA or its counterparts in other countries, it is understood that the continued production of information about approved vaccines – and pharmaceuticals in general – after they become commercially available is desirable both from a scientific and a regulatory perspective. The licensure of pharmaceutical products is based on extensive yet limited datasets. Having cleared the "substantial evidence" standard required by the law for licensure, these products

---

[39]   Natalia Oelsner, "How Does a Vaccine Get Approved in Europe? The Process, Explained" (July 6, 2020) *EuroNews*, www.euronews.com/2020/07/03/how-does-a-vaccine-get-approved-in-europe-the-process-explained.

[40]   21 US Code § 360bbb-3.

[41]   21 US Code § 360bbb-3.

[42]   European Medicines Agency, "Conditional Marketing Authorization," www.ema.europa.eu/en/human-regulatory/marketing-authorisation/conditional-marketing-authorisation.

continue to be studied, now in "real world" and at a larger scale. They are also monitored for potential problems that might have gone undetected during the pre-licensure stages of development and regulatory review. In addition to adhering to scientific precepts of continued knowledge acquisition and interventive adjustments to reflect these knowledge gains, continued study and monitoring of licensed pharmaceuticals also help build overall trust in these products. As discussed in Chapter 4, issues of trust surrounding vaccines are especially fraught, with recent drops in vaccination rates for diseases like measles being linked to declining public trust in vaccines.

Continued regulatory oversight of vaccines after licensure thus contributes to scientific, regulatory and public trust goals. The period during which licensed vaccines and other pharmaceutical products are commercialized is often called the "post-market"– a hint to the idea that drug regulators have exercised their market gatekeeping functions and that they will now act predominantly in a monitoring or surveillance capacity.

One of the main mechanisms of regulatory oversight of vaccines in the post-market is through phase 4 clinical trials, which generate additional data about the safety and efficacy of licensed vaccines. Unlike pre-licensure clinical trials, post-market trials do not always take place, and depend on the regulator's evaluation of the data on, and characteristics of, a given pharmaceutical product. However, phase 4 clinical trials remain common in the case of vaccines.[43] The results of post-market studies inform evolving scientific understandings about a specific vaccine, providing both researchers and regulators with more granular data as the vaccine is administered to an increasingly larger number of people over a longer time span than the one during which pre-market clinical trials are conducted.

In addition to the possibility of phase 4 trials, there are several mandatory requirements in place during the post-market designed to coax the production of information about approved vaccines, as well as to monitor their manufacturing and distribution. Regulators across the world inspect samples of vaccines, as well as the manufacturing facilities where vaccine doses are produced, and require vaccine manufacturers to submit detailed information about their product. For example, in the United States, the law has codified a mechanism known as a "lot release" that prevents manufacturers of licensed vaccines from distributing a batch of vaccine before the agency analyzes samples and data about each specific batch.[44] In addition to samples of the vaccine, manufacturers must submit the protocols and test results for each new batch of vaccine they intend to distribute.

Alongside these monitoring requirements, there are different types of surveillance programs that engage other participants in the vaccine ecosystem – including laypeople who have received a vaccine.[45] Some of these programs are designed

---

[43] See e.g. European Union, "E.U. Clinical Trials Register: Clinical Trials for Cervarix," (January, 2021), www.clinicaltrialsregister.eu/ctr-search/search?query=Cervari (listing ongoing clinical trials around the world for Cervarix, an HPV vaccine further described in Chapter 3).

[44] 21 US Code of Federal Regulations §610.1–2.

[45] US Food & Drug Administration, "Vaccine Development – 101," note 31.

specifically for vaccines, as is the case of the Vaccine Adverse Event Reporting System (VAERS) in the United States, a reporting system available to any individuals wishing to report side effects after the administration of a vaccine.[46] Reports are entered into a database made publicly available online. The FDA co-manages VAERS with another agency within the Department of Health and Human Services, the Centers for Disease Control and Prevention (CDC).

Another vaccine-specific surveillance program is the Vaccine Safety Datalink, managed by the CDC.[47] The program, which performs studies on vaccine safety, is conducted in partnership with nine health-care organizations, such as Kaiser Permanente and HealthPartners. Data collected by the Vaccine Safety Datalink comes from a broader array of sources than VAERS, and it includes information obtained during hospital stays, as well as during visits to doctors' offices, emergency rooms, and urgent care. The program also conducts studies prompted by ongoing discussions in the scientific literature and arising out of data collected by VAERS.[48]

As biologics – and, more broadly, as pharmaceutical products – licensed vaccines are also subject to surveillance programs that are not specifically designed for vaccines. In the United States, these programs include the Sentinel Program, FDA's growing "national electronic system" for evaluating the safety of prescription drugs, and the FDA-administered Biologics Effectiveness and Safety System (FDA BEST), which is part of Sentinel and focuses on the gathering of data on the safety and effectiveness of biologics.[49]

Finally, as seen later in the text, drug regulators and other public health-oriented agencies often play an important complementary function in the vaccine and drug ecosystem as funders of, or the locus for, vaccine and drug R&D. The involvement of the public sector in scientific research has been especially salient in the case of vaccine R&D.

2.2 THE CENTRALITY OF CLINICAL TRIALS TO VACCINE DEVELOPMENT AND APPROVAL

The development of new vaccines hinges, as seen earlier, on the production of data that will allow regulators to make a cost–benefit analysis about each vaccine candidate. The production of these data is anchored on the clinical trial model – a model whose evolution is intertwined with the history of vaccine research and testing. This

---

46   Vaccine Adverse Event Reporting System, "About VAERS," https://vaers.hhs.gov/about.html.
47   US Centers for Disease Control and Prevention, "Vaccine Safety Datalink (VSD)," (2020), www
     .cdc.gov/vaccinesafety/ensuringsafety/monitoring/vsd/index.html.
48   US Centers for Disease Control and Prevention, "Vaccine Safety Datalink," note 47.
49   US Food & Drug Administration, "CBER Biologics Effectiveness and Safety (BEST) System" (2020),
     www.fda.gov/vaccines-blood-biologics/safety-availability-biologics/cber-biologics-effectiveness-and
     -safety-best-system; US Food & Drug Administration, "FDA's Sentinel Initiative" (2019), www
     .fda.gov/safety/fdas-sentinel-initiative.

book takes a closer look at how data supporting vaccine licensure is generated and shared with both the research community and society at large.

2.2.1 *Vaccine Clinical Trials in Historical Context*

The polio vaccine clinical trials that took place across the United States in the 1950s were instrumental in establishing the clinical trial model in use today for both drugs and vaccines. These trials were then described as the largest experiment in public health on record.[50] They followed a period of intense research on the poliovirus and the highly infectious disease it causes, poliomyelitis, which until the mid-twentieth century caused cyclical outbreaks with devastating consequences, particularly among young children.[51] While the overwhelming majority (90 percent) of people who contract polio feel no symptoms or relatively mild ones, such as fever or fatigue, the disease leads to some form of paralysis in the remaining 10 percent of cases.[52] In most cases, polio-induced paralysis is irreversible, and the disease can be lethal to patients experiencing paralysis symptoms (at rates varying around 5–10 percent).[53] Children younger than five were particularly susceptible to the disease until polio vaccines were developed.

Several research teams based in the United States worked concurrently on different R&D approaches to developing a polio vaccine. Building on scientific advances in polio research that took place in the late 1940s and early 1950s, the research team of Jonas Salk was the first to produce a polio vaccine candidate.[54] Sponsored by the National Foundation for Infantile Paralysis, now renamed March of Dimes, the vaccine entered human trials in April 1954. The trials had a dual design. Over 600,000 children participated in a placebo-controlled trial, in which some received the vaccine and others received a substance with no therapeutic effect.[55] Additionally, more than one million children received the vaccine with no placebo controls. The results of these trials indicated that the vaccine developed by the Salk team was effective in protecting against polio at rates between 80 percent and 90 percent.[56] Upon evaluation of those data, the FDA licensed the vaccine in 1955. Continued administration of this and, later on, other polio vaccines led to the elimination of the disease in the United States in 1979.[57]

---

[50] Paul Meier, "The Biggest Public Health Experiment Ever: The 1954 Field Trial of the Salk Poliomyelitis Vaccine," in *Statistics: A Guide to the Unknown*, Judith M. Tanur et al., eds. (Holden Day, 1972).

[51] See generally David M. Oshinsky, *Polio: An American Story* (Oxford University Press, 2006).

[52] See World Health Organization, "Poliomyelitis (Polio): Symptoms," www.who.int/health-topics /poliomyelitis#tab=tab_1.

[53] See World Health Organization, "Poliomyelitis (Polio): Symptoms," note 52.

[54] Oshinsky, *Polio*, note 51.

[55] Marcia Meldrum, "'A Calculated Risk': The Salk Polio Vaccine Field Trials of 1954" (1998) 317 *British Medical Journal* 1233–36.

[56] Meldrum, "A Calculated Risk," note 55, at 1233.

[57] US Centers Disease Control & Prevention, "Polio Elimination in the United States" (2019), www .cdc.gov/polio/what-is-polio/polio-us.html.

In addition to its direct impact on disease prevention and management, the polio trials were instrumental in making the case for the formalization of the placebo-controlled randomized model for clinical trials, not just for vaccines but for drugs and biopharmaceutical products in general. At that point, the law did not require pharmaceutical companies to submit data supporting the efficacy of the products they were seeking to bring to market. The 1938 Federal Food, Drug, and Cosmetic Act (FDCA) was the first statute in the United States to mandate that drug and vaccine sponsors present the FDA with data showing that their product is safe. It was not until 1962, with the Kefauver-Harris Amendments to the FDCA, that a similar requirement was introduced with regard to efficacy.[58] By then, clinical trials had become understood within the scientific community as the best available mechanism to test new medical products and generate data about their effectiveness. Accordingly, the 1962 Amendments established that drug and vaccine sponsors had to submit data to the FDA garnered through "adequate and well-controlled studies" demonstrating "substantial evidence" of the effectiveness of their product.[59] This shift in the legal paradigm reflected the underlying evolution in scientific consensus, with the role of clinical trials becoming pivotal to the development of new drugs and vaccines.

The polio vaccine trials were not the immediate catalyst for the 1962 statutory changes. That role was largely played by the thalidomide crisis of 1961, the year in which a drug approved by several foreign counterparts to the FDA was linked to significant birth defects in children. A similar crisis was averted in the United States almost singlehandedly by the work of a medical officer at the FDA, Dr. Frances Kelsey, who rejected the application for thalidomide after finding the data submitted by the drug sponsor lacking.[60] While from a regulatory perspective the ultimate problem with thalidomide was that the information available about the drug was not enough to establish its safety and efficacy, the root of the problem harked back to the absence of properly conducted clinical trials capable of generating scientifically sound data. For example, in the case of thalidomide, many patients who formally participated in "trials" were never tracked after receiving the drug.[61]

Regulators across the world reacted to the thalidomide crisis by bolstering their drug review frameworks. Virtually every regulatory agency in the world started requiring the submission of data on both the safety and efficacy of new drugs and vaccines. This obligation to produce adequate data elevated clinical trials to a core

---

[58] Suzanne White Junod, "FDA and Clinical Drug Trials: A Short History" (2008), www.fda.gov/media/110437/download, at 5.

[59] See Junod, "FDA and Clinical Drug Trials," note 58, at 11–12.

[60] US Food & Drug Administration, "Frances Oldham Kelsey: Medical Reviewer Famous for Averting a Public Health Tragedy" (2018), www.fda.gov/about-fda/fda-history-exhibits/frances-oldham-kelsey-medical-reviewer-famous-averting-public-health-tragedy.

[61] Bara Fintel, Athena T. Samaras, & Edson Carias, "The Thalidomide Tragedy: Lessons for Drug Safety and Regulation" (2009) *Helix*. www.helix.northwestern.edu/article/thalidomide-tragedy-lessons-drug-safety-and-regulation.

component of drug and vaccine R&D. And the model after which clinical trials now had to be structured in order to meet the threshold of "adequate and well-controlled studies" had roots in the large-scale placebo trial conducted in 1954 during the polio vaccine race.

The trials were thus instrumental in the short term by generating the data that supported the licensure of a health good critical in tackling the public health crisis posed by cyclical polio outbreaks. They were also instrumental in the long term by providing a blueprint that aligned vaccine- and drug-testing processes and regulatory review with scientific parameters. While paving the way for the introduction of a highly beneficial health good, the polio vaccine trials were not exempt from severe flaws, with researchers relying on several practices that violate core principles of biomedical ethics, including the administration of the vaccine to institutionalized children with physical and intellectual disabilities.[62]

These problems were not unique to the polio vaccine trials. Even against the backdrop of a progressively more regulated clinical trial environment, ethical violations continued to occur in the decades that followed, both in vaccine and drug R&D. The Tuskegee Study, which spanned over forty years, remains perhaps the most well-known embodiment of these manifold violations, and an enduring illustration of how porous safeguards for participants in biomedical research tend to detrimentally affect the most vulnerable and disadvantaged populations.[63] Funded by the federal government, the study ran from 1932 to 1972, and was billed as a medical research program designed to observe the evolution of untreated syphilis – a disease whose course was fairly well understood even at the outset of the study, thus rendering the study unnecessary. The target population were Black male volunteers, who were enrolled from a pool of individuals in disadvantaged socioeconomic conditions, and who were largely kept unaware of the real purpose of the study and the fact that researchers withheld effective treatment for the disease even after it became widely available. In addition to these informational gaps, the Tuskegee Study resulted in poor health outcomes for individual participants, who went on to endure a plethora of symptoms known to develop when syphilis remains untreated, and which range from fever and hair loss to paralysis, blindness and dementia. Eventually, the disease leads to death.[64] Research published in 2018, almost five decades after the study ended, confirmed that the Tuskegee Study "correlated with increases in (. . .) mortality and decreases in both outpatient and inpatient physician interactions for older black men."[65]

[62] History of Vaccines, "Polio Brochure 1" (1953), www.historyofvaccines.org/content/salk-begins-early-polio-vaccine-tests-0; Allan M. Brandt, "Polio, Politics, Publicity, and Duplicity: Ethical Aspects in the Development of the Salk Vaccine" (1979) 8 *International Journal of Health Services* 257.

[63] See Ruqaiijah Yearby, "Exploitation in Medical Research: The Enduring Legacy of the Tuskegee Syphilis Study" (2017) 67 *Case Western Reserve Law Review* 1171–226.

[64] Thomas A. Peterman & Sarah E. Kidd, "Trends in Deaths Due to Syphilis, United States, 1968–2015" (January 2019) 46(1) *Sexually Transmitted Diseases* 37–40.

[65] Marcella Alsan & Marianne Wanamaker, "Tuskegee and the Health of Black Men" (2018) 133 *Quarterly Journal of Economics* 407–55, https://pubmed.ncbi.nlm.nih.gov/30505005/.

The families of the participants in the Tuskegee Study, as well as their communities, also suffered mental health and socioeconomic strains directly attributable to the study, as they coped personally and financially with the challenges posed by prolonged disease and death. At an even broader level, the egregiousness of the bioethical violations committed throughout the Tuskegee Study had a compounding effect on levels of trust in biomedical research, which have been consistently lower among minority populations in light of the historically disparate and detrimental treatment afforded to ethnically and racially diverse minorities in biomedical research.[66]

While the Tuskegee Study was not directly related to the field of vaccine research, it helps situate problems with vaccine-related research within a broader context, one that reflects systemic unethical practices in the history of biomedical R&D – and which also affected vaccine R&D. Between 1955–56 and 1971, for example, researchers studying the hepatitis C virus with the long-term goal of developing a vaccine conducted what became known as the Willowbrook State School "experiment."[67] Their research involved children with developmental disabilities at this Staten Island-based institution, which were deliberately infected with the virus. In addition to purposefully worsening the health of participants and having no therapeutic goals, the research was performed on especially vulnerable individuals. Consent given by parents and legal representatives was often heavily conditioned. Journalist Leah Rosenbaum interviewed the mother of a child who was part of the Willowbrook study and noted how her description of agreeing to let her daughter participate was akin to a "Faustian bargain":

> In order to get [her severely autistic daughter] a spot at the overcrowded facility, however, she had to make a Faustian bargain – consenting to allow her daughter to be part of a quest to find a vaccine for hepatitis. "I had no choice," McCourt says, "I had tried so many different places and so many arrangements, and they didn't work out, so I went along with it."[68]

The public outcry that followed the publicization of the findings about the bioethical violations committed throughout the Tuskegee Study, allied to the

---

[66] Harriet A. Washington, *Medical Apartheid: The Dark History of Medical Experimentation on Black Americans from Colonial Times to the Present* (Doubleday, 2006); V. L. Shavers et al., "Knowledge of the Tuskegee Study and Its Impact on the Willingness to Participate in Medical Research Studies" (2000) 92 *Journal of the National Medical Association* 563–72.

[67] See Stephen Goldby, "Experiments at the Willowbrook State School" (1971) 297 *Lancet* 749. Sources report disparate starting dates for the study. See e.g. "Willowbrook Hepatitis Experiments" in National Institutes of Health, *Exploring Bioethics* (NIH, 2009) (listing a 1955 starting date); James M. DuBois, "Hepatitis Studies at the Willowbrook State School for Children with Mental Retardation," *Ethics in Mental Health Research*, (2007), https://sites.google.com/a/narrativebioethics.com/emhr/contact/hepatitis-studies-at-the-willowbrook-state-school-for-children-with-mental-retardation (listing a 1956 starting date).

[68] Leah Rosenbaum, "The Hideous Truths of Testing Vaccines on Humans" (June 12, 2020) *Forbes*, www.forbes.com/sites/leahrosenbaum/2020/06/12/willowbrook-scandal-hepatitis-experiments-hideous-truths-of-testing-vaccines-on-humans/. See also Carl H. Coleman et al., *The Ethics and Regulation of Research with Human Subjects* (LexisNexis, 2005).

knowledge of pervasive problems elsewhere in the R&D ecosystem, such as the ones that occurred during the Willowbrook study, prompted the codification of norms of conduct governing scientific research involving human subjects. In the United States, this codification took the form of the Belmont Report, which was published in 1979. The Belmont Report laid out a set of core ethical principles that should guide all types of clinical research: respect for persons, beneficence, and justice.[69]

The bioethical framework introduced by the Belmont Report became the touchstone of the systemic regulation of informed consent in the United States. In 1981, the Department of Health and Human Services issued regulations governing federally funded research involving human subjects.[70] In 1991, these regulations were adopted as a Common Rule by sixteen federal agencies.[71] The Common Rule, which still governs federally funded research and has become the paradigm for most university-based research, was last revised in 2018.[72] Other regulatory interventions have targeted aspects of biomedical R&D beyond the protection of human subjects involved in clinical research. As seen in the following section, data collected in clinical trials has often failed to properly represent certain populations – usually racial and ethnic minorities, as well as women – which have remained historically under-enrolled in clinical trials. Seeking to correct this problem, in 1993 the United States passed the NIH Revitalization Act, which mandates appropriate inclusion of minority volunteers in R&D receiving funding from the NIH.[73] However, as seen later, this particular legal intervention seems to have had limited effect. In a 2018 study, researcher Stacie Geller found that "NIH policies have not resulted in significant increases in reporting results by sex, race, or ethnicity."[74]

2.2.2 *Persistent Shortcomings of Vaccine Clinical Trials: Racial and Ethnic Disparities*

As seen earlier, the approval of a new vaccine hinges on the examination of data by experts tasked with assessing the safety and efficacy of new medical products. Even though the production of data on a vaccine candidate begins during the preclinical

---

[69] "Belmont Report: Ethical Principles and Guidelines for the Protection of Human Subjects of Research" (April 18, 1979) Report of the National Commission for the Protection of Human Subjects of Biomedical and Behavioral Research, 44 *Federal Register* 23,192, 23,194.

[70] General Requirements for Informed Consent, 45 C.F.R. § 46.116 (2005).

[71] See 45 C.F.R. § 46 and 21 C.F.R. § 50 (collectively laying out the regulatory regime for the protection of human subjects in clinical trials, the former in the context of federally funded research, and the latter in the context of clinical trials overseen by the FDA).

[72] Department of Health & Human Services, "Revised Common Rule," (2018), www.hhs.gov/ohrp/regula tions-and-policy/regulations/finalized-revisions-common-rule/index.html. See also Jerry Menikoff et al., "The Common Rule, Updated" (2017) 376 *New England Journal of Medicine* 613–15.

[73] NIH Revitalization Act of 1993, Pub. L. No. 103–43.

[74] Stacie E. Geller et al., "The More Things Change, the More They Stay the Same: A Study to Evaluate Compliance with Inclusion and Assessment of Women and Minorities in Randomized Controlled Trials" (2018) 93 *Academic Medicine* 630–35.

stages – and is a precondition of moving a vaccine candidate to tests involving human subjects – information gathered through clinical trials is key to the scientific and regulatory processes that control which products will eventually be made available to patients.

A robust system for generating and evaluating clinical trial data is critical not only to the soundness of regulatory processes, but also to promote trust in newly approved vaccines. Notwithstanding the centrality of clinical trial data to vaccine development and approval, the ways in which it is collected and shared remain far from ideal. Even though the laws governing clinical trials have been regularly bolstered to tighten data collection reporting requirements, there are still several holes in the data infrastructure – and not all requirements are observed or enforced, as described later.

Data about a vaccine candidate can be seen as building blocks of scientific knowledge. These building blocks are useful to different players for a variety of purposes: researchers fine-tuning the development of that particular vaccine candidate; regulators trying to determine its safety and efficacy; scientists working on ongoing or future R&D projects involving similar or related vaccine technology; and the public at large, who needs to be able to trust the reliability of the information on which scientific and regulatory decisions that result in the commercialization of a vaccine are made. If the building blocks produced during vaccine clinical trials are somehow imperfectly generated, these players will operate in an environment characterized by intrinsically limited data, in which trust deficits are likely to occur.

The most significant example in this area is data that, albeit collected in formal compliance with existing laws and regulations, fail to reflect the diversity of the patient population indicated for a particular vaccine – and for whom sponsors of a vaccine undergoing clinical trials are seeking regulatory approval. This has long been the case of racial and ethnic minorities, which have been historically underrepresented in clinical trials – including vaccine trials – and remain so to this day.

The COVID-19 vaccine race provides a recent illustration of this problem. As the leading vaccine candidates moved from the preclinical to the clinical R&D stages, the National Institute of Allergy and Infectious Diseases (NIAID) in the United States created a clinical trials network to coordinate and facilitate the enrollment of volunteers.[75] The COVID-19 Prevention Trials Network (COVPN) resulted from the merger of NIAID-funded networks that had been operating predominantly in the HIV/AIDS clinical trial space.[76] COVPN created an online registry for volunteers to express interest in participating in COVID-19 vaccine trials.[77] By late August 2020, the registry had around 350,000 registered participants, of which only 10–11 percent

---

[75] National Institute of Allergy and Infectious Diseases, "NIH Launches Clinical Trials Network to Test COVID-19 Vaccines and Other Prevention Tools" (July 8, 2020), www.nih.gov/news-events/news-releases/nih-launches-clinical-trials-network-test-covid-19-vaccines-other-prevention-tools.

[76] These networks are located in Seattle, Durham NC, Atlanta, and Los Angeles, and added COVID-19 vaccine clinical trials to their ongoing work on HIV vaccine clinical trials, as well as clinical trials on vaccines targeting other infectious diseases. See note 75.

[77] CoVPN Volunteer Screening Registry, https://covpn.oracle.com/register/f?p=610000:1:5870322253512.

identified as Black or Hispanic.[78] According to estimates from the US Census Bureau, individuals identifying as "Black or African American" accounted for 13.4 percent of the United States population, while individuals identifying as "Hispanic or Latino" accounted for 18.5 percent.[79] The registry thus contained a pool of potential clinical trial volunteers that underrepresented the two largest minority groups in terms of racial and ethnic diversity in the United States.

Underrepresentation of racial and ethnic minorities was confirmed by actual enrollment levels in COVID-19 vaccine clinical trials, albeit at less disproportionate rates. Preliminary phase 3 data reported by Pfizer in December showed that trials for this vaccine candidate had enrolled 44,863 participants in six countries, including the United States.[80] While the overall diversity rate was 42 percent, the rate for the US-based trial population was 30 percent.[81] Demographic data on the US trials for Pfizer's vaccine candidate indicated that 13% of the participants identified as Latinx, 10% as Black, 6% as Asian, and 1.3% as Native American.[82] The December 2020 report did not specify the rate of enrollment of participants identifying as White, but adding up the diversity rates disclosed by Pfizer indicates that 69.7 percent of the US participants did not belong to racial or ethnic minorities. The 30 percent diversity rate registered in the US trial is below 2020 census projections of an overall 40 percent diversity rate in the US population makeup.[83]

This was not the only case in which a representation in trial populations lagged behind national diversity rates. According to preliminary data, phase 3 trials for the Moderna vaccine candidate met the target enrollment of 30,000 volunteers across dozens of sites in more than half of the states in the United States.[84] Interim demographic data released by Moderna in October 2020 showed that 63% of the participants identified as White, 20% as Latinx, 10% as Black or African American, 4% as Asian, with all other races and ethnicities accounting for 3% of the trial population.[85] At 37 percent, the diversity rate for the Moderna vaccine rate was thus higher than Pfizer's, but slightly below the overall US populational diversity rate. The clinical trials for Moderna's vaccine were closer to the national diversity

---

[78] Carolyn Y. Johnson, "Large US Covid-19 Vaccine Trials Are Halfway Enrolled, But Lag on Participant Diversity" (August 27, 2020) *Washington Post*, www.washingtonpost.com/health/2020/08/27/large-us-covid-19-vaccine-trials-are-halfway-enrolled-lag-participant-diversity/.

[79] US Census, "Quick Facts," (2020), www.census.gov/quickfacts/fact/table/US/PST045219. These data were originally released in 2019 and then updated in mid-2020.

[80] Pfizer, "Our Progress in Developing an Investigational Covid-19 Vaccine" (December 14, 2020), www.pfizer.com/science/coronavirus/vaccine.

[81] Pfizer, "Our Progress in Developing an Investigational Covid-19 Vaccine," note 80.

[82] Pfizer, "Our Progress in Developing an Investigational Covid-19 Vaccine," note 80.

[83] See e.g. William H. Frey, "The Nation is Diversifying Even Faster than Predicted, According to New Census Data" (July 1, 2020) *Brookings*, www.brookings.edu/research/new-census-data-shows-the-nation-is-diversifying-even-faster-than-predicted/.

[84] Moderna, "Moderna Cove Study" (2020), www.modernatx.com/sites/default/files/content_documents/2020-COVE-Study-Enrollment-Completion-10.22.20.pdf, at 2.

[85] Moderna, "Moderna Cove Study," note 84.

rates than Pfizer's – even slightly surpassing the 18.5 percent mark in representativity of Latinx populations.[86] However, certain segments of the US population were underrepresented in trials for both vaccines, as was the case with populations identifying as Black or African American, for which representativity in both trials fell below the national mark of 13.4 percent.[87]

Contrasting vaccine trial diversity rates with the racial and ethnic makeup of the US population is a rather blunt tool, and using it alone does not convey the granularity of the scientific processes supporting each specific clinical trial, and which are outside the scope of this book.[88] It may also lead to the oversimplification and under-acknowledgment of centuries-long asymmetries in racial and societal dynamics in the United States, including its checkered history of medical research, particularly involving minority or vulnerable populations.[89] Yet this contrast is commonly alluded to in public health – and the book introduces it here – because it is indicative of systemic problems in the medical research ecosystem that have long resulted in the underproduction of scientific knowledge about minority populations. If anything, in the case of COVID-19 vaccines, the way in which diversity rates for enrollment lagged behind populational diversity rates provides just a glimpse into the magnitude of underrepresentation problems. Noting the disproportionately higher burden that COVID-19 placed on minority populations throughout the United States, NIAID Director Dr. Anthony Fauci noted that trials for COVID-19 vaccines should aim for diversity enrollment at significantly higher rates than the ones in trials for other medical products.[90] Dr. Fauci acknowledged that, given both current clinical trial recruitment practices and the urgency posed by the pandemic, it would be virtually impossible to meaningfully improve representativity paradigms in vaccine clinical trials. Yet, he argued that enrollment for COVID-19 vaccine trials in the United States should aim for diversity rates twice as high as diversity rates in the US population.[91]

Dr. Fauci's oversampling approach is shared by other members of the scientific community concerned with the heightened burden of several infectious diseases on

---

[86]   Both Moderna and the Pfizer study referred to Latinx populations.
[87]   The Moderna study referred to both Black and African American populations, while Pfizer's only referred to Black populations.
[88]   For more information, see the protocols for Pfizer and Moderna's phase 3 vaccine clinical trials. "Study to Describe the Safety, Tolerability, Immunogenicity, and Efficacy of RNA Vaccine Candidates against COVID-19 in Healthy Individuals" (2021), https://clinicaltrials.gov/ct2/show/ NCT04368728; "A Study to Evaluate Efficacy, Safety, and Immunogenicity of mRNA-1273 Vaccine in Adults Aged 18 Years and Older to Prevent COVID-19" (2021), https://clinicaltrials.gov/ct2/show/ NCT04470427.
[89]   For a discussion of the history of medical research involving African American populations in the United States, see Harriet A. Washington's comprehensive treatment of the subject in Washington, *Medical Apartheid* (2006).
[90]   Elizabeth Cohen, "Despite Effort, Enrollment of Minorities for Coronavirus Vaccine Trial is Lagging" (August 22, 2020) CNN, www.cnn.com/2020/08/22/health/coronavirus-moderna-minorities-lag/index.html.
[91]   Cohen, "Despite Effort," note 90.

socioeconomically disadvantaged populations, coupled with the fact that clinical trials for most types of medical products have long been disproportionately focused on White populations.[92]

The optimal diversity rate prescribed by Dr. Fauci for COVID-19 vaccine trials reflects ongoing concerns shared by at least some strands of the scientific community, but does not constitute a legally or scientifically required standard for data produced through clinical trials to be validated and used as part of an application to bring a vaccine to market. In this sense, current practices of vaccine testing and evaluation coexist with the collective knowledge that the data building blocks used to make both scientific and regulatory decisions have been imperfectly generated and need improving upon. This contributes to trust problems that have long been especially heightened in connection with vaccines as opposed to many other types of medical technologies.

There have been multiple legal interventions designed to address these problems. At the international level, the Declaration of Helsinki, adopted by the World Medical Association in 1964 and last revised in 2013, provides a "statement of ethical principles for medical research involving human subjects" and mandates the registration of clinical trials in publicly accessible databases.[93] Countries have progressively incorporated these requirements into domestic legislation. In the United States, for example, the Food and Drug Administration Modernization Act of 1997 imposed registration requirements for clinical trials involving medical products for serious or life-threatening conditions.[94] These requirements were later expanded by the Food and Drug Administration Amendments Act of 2007.[95] Since 2000, the NIH has maintained an online database through the National Library of Medicine (Clinicaltrials.gov) that records information about clinical trials conducted both in the United States and elsewhere in the world. As of mid-2021, there were over 372,000 registered studies, taking place across the fifty US states and in 219 countries.[96]

Even though the Declaration of Helsinki and several national laws mandate the disclosure of the results of clinical trials involving human subjects, studies have long documented significant delays in the reporting of results from vaccine clinical trials.[97] In several cases, those data were not even published or otherwise

[92]   See e.g. Johnson, "Large US Covid-19 Vaccine Trials," note 78.

[93]   World Medical Association, "Declaration of Helsinki: Ethical Principles for Medical Research Involving Human Subjects" (2018), www.wma.net/policies-post/wma-declaration-of-helsinki-ethical-principles-for-medical-research-involving-human-subjects/.

[94]   Food and Drug Administration Modernization Act of 1997, Pub. L. No. 105–15, 111 Stat. 2296. See also US Food & Drug Administration, "Regulations: Good Clinical Practice and Clinical Trials" (2021), www.fda.gov/science-research/clinical-trials-and-human-subject-protection/regulations-good-clinical-practice-and-clinical-trials.

[95]   Food and Drug Administration Amendments Act of 2007, Pub. L. No. 110–85, 121 Stat. 823.

[96]   Clinicaltrials.gov, https://clinicaltrials.gov.

[97]   See e.g Christopher W. Jones & Timothy F. Platts-Mills, "Delayed Publication of Vaccine Trials" (2014) 348 *British Medical Journal* 3259.

disclosed.[98] For example, Lamberto Manzoli and colleagues have surveyed the publication of vaccine clinical trial data related to different types of vaccines tested in 384 clinical trials, which had collectively enrolled over 400,000 participants.[99] The survey looked at vaccine clinical trial data generated through standard R&D processes (such as clinical trials for pneumococcal and meningococcal vaccines), as well as data generated through R&D taking place during a large-scale public health crisis (as was the case of the H1N1 vaccines developed during the 2009 pandemic). The researchers found that "delays to publication of several years are common." On average, only half of the clinical trials included in the study were published within twenty-six months of the end of the trial, with publication being characterized as "one or more of the main outcomes appeared in a peer reviewed journal, either online or in print."

The same study also found several instances of non-publication, which the researchers measured as vaccine clinical trial data that had not been published six or more years after the conclusion of a given trial. In addition to clashing with reporting principles and requirements applicable to contemporary biomedical research, lack of publication of clinical trial data may pose further systemic problems. As Manzoli and colleagues noted, "when non-publication is considerable, published articles, as well as early reviews or meta-analyses that incorporate them, may be unreliable and overestimate the benefits of an intervention."

The problems described in this section – underrepresentation of certain populations and underreporting of clinical trial data – combine to affect the trust that both specific populations and society in general place in the R&D and regulatory processes that enable new vaccines to come to market.[100] The book raises these issues here not in support of ongoing movements encouraging individuals to skip vaccinations for which they (or their children) are indicated, but to highlight systemic flaws that need remedying. While reflective of the scientific process and producing products that have consistently been assessed by independent scientists as safe and effective, the vaccine ecosystem can and should be improved upon. This chapter has surveyed problems connected to the structure in place for the review and approval of vaccines. As seen throughout the rest of the book, the vaccine ecosystem is marked by several other failures. While underrepresentation and underreporting problems are unfortunately not exclusive to clinical research on vaccines, some of the other failures play out in highly idiosyncratic ways where vaccines are concerned – starting with the longstanding scarcity of funding for vaccine R&D addressed in the next section and Chapter 3, and stretching to the way in which we collectively communicate about vaccines in the post-market.

[98] Jones & Platts-Mills, "Delayed Publication of Vaccine Trials," note 97.
[99] Lamberto Manzoli et al., "Non-Publication and Delayed Publication of Randomized Trials on Vaccines: Survey" (2014) 348 *British Medical Journal* 3058.
[100] See e.g. Kay Dickersin & Drummond Rennie, "Registering Clinical Trials" (2003) 290 JAMA 516–23.

2.3 OTHER PLAYERS IN VACCINE R&D

The chapter thus far has focused on the pathway designed to bring new vaccines to market. In so doing, it has highlighted the role of regulators as market gatekeepers, as well as the role of vaccine sponsors – predominantly, pharmaceutical companies – as the regulated industry. This section briefly surveys other players in the vaccine R&D ecosystem, whose role often precedes or otherwise conditions the very existence of vaccine candidates going through the R&D pipeline and being brought to drug regulators for review. As discussed at length in the following chapter, one longstanding problem in vaccine R&D – often more pronounced in the case of vaccines against emerging pathogens – is that there is scarce funding for both foundational and late-stage R&D work on new vaccine candidates. This section provides an overview of players in the vaccine development ecosystem who have no regulatory functions but whose role is vital to vaccine R&D.

2.3.1 *The Public Sector*

Public-sector funding has always played a prominent role in R&D connected to vaccine-preventable infectious diseases, domestically and internationally. A study published in 2016 found that the United States provided almost two-thirds of all public-sector funding for R&D on neglected diseases.[101] However, in recent years, public-sector funding in general has decreased in these and other areas of scientific and technological research. Data collected by the National Science Foundation shows that the federal funding for basic research, which in the 1970s accounted for more than 70 percent of all funding available for basic research in the United States, dropped below 50 percent in 2013.[102] By 2015, it had further dipped to 44 percent. This was the first time since World War II that the public sector did not fund the majority of basic research being performed in the United States.[103] Global funding for R&D on neglected diseases similarly declined throughout the 2010s.[104]

Funding available for work on vaccines targeting emerging diseases should therefore be understood against a backdrop of significant limitations that generally affect R&D on "neglected diseases." These diseases are estimated to affect over one billion people around the world.[105] In spite of this tremendous toll on

---

[101]   Policy Cures Research, "Neglected Disease Research and Development: A Pivotal Moment for Global Health" (2016), https://s3-ap-southeast-2.amazonaws.com/policy-cures-website-assets/app/uploads/2020/01/09162330/2016-G-FINDER-report.pdf, at 5.

[102]   Jeffrey Mervis, "Data Check: Federal Share of Basic Research Hits New Low" (2017) 355 *Science* 1005.

[103]   Mervis, "Data Check," note 102.

[104]   Policy Cures Research, "Neglected Disease Research," note 101.

[105]   National Institutes of Health, "Neglected Diseases," https://rarediseases.info.nih.gov/files/neglected_diseases_faqs.pdf.

individual, community and public health, funding for R&D on neglected diseases has been historically low – in relative terms (when compared to funding available for R&D on other diseases) and in terms of what is projected to be necessary to improve R&D structures and innovation in the area of neglected diseases (Figure 2.1.).[106]

Consider the following comparison between funding for neglected diseases versus non-neglected diseases, measured in millions of USD:

Even within the realm of underfunded diseases, the funding landscape is highly heterogenous. Some diseases are able to attract suboptimal yet continued levels of investment. For instance, R&D on malaria – including malaria vaccines – has consistently been supported by several major funders, including the United States and European public sectors, and philanthropic actors such as the Gates Foundation.[107] Between the early 1990s and the mid-2010s, funding for malaria R&D alone increased four-fold, reaching US $565 million in 2015.[108] This field has also benefited from work performed by dedicated organizations, such as the Medicines for Malaria Venture and the Roll Back Malaria Partnership.[109]

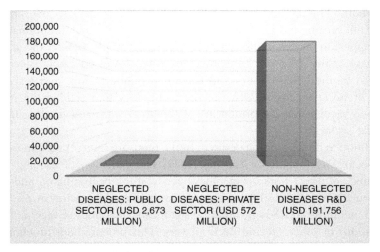

FIGURE 2.1 Funding for R&D on neglected versus non-neglected diseases[110]

---

[106] World Health Organization, "R&D Blueprint," note 8, at 6.
[107] "Higher Research Funding Leads to 4x Rise in New Anti-Malaria Product Pipeline" (June 29, 2011) *Malaria.com*, https://perma.cc/5LSF-Z37D.
[108] PATH, "Staying the Course? Malaria Research and Development in a Time of Economic Uncertainty" (2011), at 13, www.path.org/resources/staying-the-course-malaria-research-and-development-in-a-time-of-economic-uncertainty/; Policy Cures Research, "Neglected Disease Research," note 101, at 28.
[109] See Chapter 5 for a description of emerging vaccine-dedicated international public–private partnerships.
[110] Adapted from World Health Organization, "R&D Blueprint," note 8, at 6.

Even within the realm of neglected diseases, most funding is absorbed by a limited number of research areas, with over two-thirds of global funding being allocated to three diseases: HIV/AIDS, malaria, and tuberculosis.[111] This means that there are many emerging diseases known to be vaccine-preventable for which little to no vaccine R&D is occurring.[112] Moreover, vaccine research tends to slow down, and in some cases come close to a halt, after outbreaks of infectious diseases start winding down. An example further explored in Chapter 3 is that of one of the leading Zika vaccine candidates, which was quickly developed during the 2015–2016 Zika outbreak through public funding and direct US public-sector R&D. Even though existing vaccine technology was used to develop this Zika vaccine candidate in a matter of months – much like what happened with the COVID-19 vaccine candidates – once the severity of the outbreak began diminishing, so did public funding available for Zika vaccine R&D. As of mid-2021, and in spite of promising results gleaned from initial data, late-stage R&D has yet to be finalized.[113]

Even though, from a funding perspective, vaccine R&D faces significant limitations, the role of the public sector in this area is critical – as is funding provided by the private sector, public–private collaborations, and international organizations. The public sector, nonetheless, plays an especially relevant role at the start of vaccine R&D, often by taking on projects that traditionally have limited appeal to players in the private sector. For example, besides the aforementioned case of the Zika vaccine candidate, initial R&D on Ebola vaccines was performed by the United States and Canadian public sectors, and a significant amount of R&D on the mRNA vaccine technology that yielded the Moderna COVID-19 vaccine was performed in collaboration with, and funding from, the US public sector.

In addition to direct funding or direct R&D, there are indirect ways in which the public sector can incentivize vaccine R&D. The provision of funding and the performance of direct work on vaccines operate at the beginning of, and possibly throughout, the vaccine R&D time line. However, the public sector can also provide financial incentives to R&D by ordering significant quantities of vaccine from the private sector or other vaccine R&D players. This procurement function of the public sector was evidenced during the COVID-19 pandemic: For instance, the US government placed an initial order for 100 million doses of vaccine from Pfizer and 200 million from Moderna, which combinedly would be enough to vaccinate 150 million Americans.[114] This procurement mechanism has also been used by

[111] Policy Cures Research, "Neglected Disease Research," note 101.
[112] Plotkin et al., "Establishing a Global Vaccine-Development Fund," note 12 (listing vaccine-preventable diseases with no available vaccine).
[113] Aryamav Pattnaik et al., "Current Status of Zika Virus Vaccines: Successes and Challenges" (2020) 8 (2) *Vaccine* 266.
[114] Sarah Kliff, "The Vaccines Are Supposed to Be Free. Surprise Bills Could Happen Anyway" (December 17, 2020) *New York Times*, www.nytimes.com/2020/12/17/upshot/vaccines-surprise-bills.html.

international organizations operating in the vaccine field, chief among which Gavi (the Vaccine Alliance) and more recently COVAX (COVID-19 Vaccines Global Access), both public–private partnerships that the book describes in Chapter 5 as one of the emerging mechanisms to counter the dearth of financial incentives for vaccine R&D.

2.3.2 *The Case of Military R&D*

The military, particularly in the United States, has historically played an important role in pharmaceutical R&D, including the development of new vaccines.[115] Infectious diseases can spread quickly among military personnel operating in close contact and shared facilities, conditioning or even driving the outcomes of military campaigns. During the American Revolutionary War, the Continental Army was exposed to smallpox while fighting British troops in Quebec. Most soldiers in the British Army came from areas where smallpox was endemic, while most soldiers in the Continental Army had never been exposed to it. As a result, the virus disproportionately infected the Continental Army, prompting George Washington to quip that soldiers should be more afraid of smallpox than the enemy.[116]

Research-oriented arms of the military also have heightened incentives to conduct R&D on vaccines targeting emerging infectious diseases. Many of the pathogens causing these diseases have historically been endemic to areas in the Global South where vaccine R&D is lacking and where the military might have, or anticipate having, personnel. As the mission statement for the US Military Infectious Diseases Research Program notes, "(i)nfectious diseases historically cause more casualties than enemy fire in deployment to tropical regions. The impact on soldiers ranges from loss of man-days to death and can severely hamper combat effectiveness while increasing the logistical burden for diagnosis, treatment and evacuation."[117] Accordingly, the Army has continued to a play a significant role in modern vaccine R&D processes, particularly in terms of catalyzing early-stage research.

In the United States, the Army Medical Research and Development Command (USAMRDC) plays a salient role in R&D focused on infectious diseases. Through its eight subordinate commands, which include the Walter Reed Army Institute of Research and the US Army Medical Research Institute of Infectious Diseases, USAMRDC is routinely involved in vaccine R&D. USAMRDC maintains research laboratories in the United States (the Maryland-based Walter Reed Army Institute of Research, Naval Medical Research Center and Army Medical

---

[115] See Kendall Hoyt, "Vaccine Innovation: Lessons from World War II" (2006) 27(1) *Journal of Public Health Policy* 38–57.

[116] Joseph B. Cantey, "Smallpox Variation during the Revolutionary War" (2011) 30 *Pediatric Infectious Disease Journal* 821–918.

[117] US Army Medical Research & Material Command, "Military Infectious Diseases Research Program (MIDRP)," (2019), https://mrdc.amedd.army.mil/index.cfm/program_areas/medical_research_and_development/midrp_overview.

Research Institute of Infectious Diseases) as well as in five other countries (Egypt, Indonesia, Kenya, Peru, and Thailand).[118]

The footprint of vaccine R&D performed or otherwise supported by the military is considerable. The Army was involved in the development of a quarter of the new vaccines that entered the market in the United States between the early 1960s and the first decade of the twenty-first century.[119] It is also regularly one of the first institutional players to support vaccine R&D on emerging pathogens. For instance, it started, and continues to maintain, a research program on HIV/AIDS vaccine R&D since 1985.[120] More recently, the Army was involved in response to major public health crises linked to emerging pathogens, performing R&D on a COVID-19 vaccine[121] and, as seen in Chapter 3, through the development of Ebola and Zika vaccine candidates.

As with public-sector funding in general, military funding for vaccine R&D has decreased considerably over time.[122] Budgetary cuts and the resetting of strategic priorities in the 1990s prompted the Army to start prioritizing vaccine R&D targeting bioterrorism agents over vaccine R&D on naturally acquired infectious diseases.[123] In a 2011 report, Colonel Kenneth Hall vehemently criticized both the decline in vaccine R&D funding and the narrowing of the types of vaccine R&D supported by the military, and called on the Department of Defense to "revitalize its infectious-disease vaccine program."

A complementary institutional player in this area worth mentioning here is the Defense Advanced Research Projects Agency (DARPA), which operates under the umbrella of the Department of Defense. DARPA was created in direct response to the launch of the Soviet satellite *Sputnik 1* in 1957, as a way to position the United States in the forefront of strategic technological research.[124] DARPA presently defines its mission as driven by making "pivotal investments in breakthrough technologies for national security."[125] While the pursuit of goals related to national security vastly exceeds both the realm of military activity and that of R&D on infectious diseases, the agency has long been a major funder of vaccine R&D.

[118] US Army Medical Research & Material Command, "Military Infectious Diseases Research Program," note 117.
[119] US Department of Defense, "The US Commitment to Global Health R&D," *Research America*, www.researchamerica.org/sites/default/files/uploads/DoDFactsheet.pdf.
[120] US Army Medical Research & Material Command, "Military Infectious Diseases Research Program," note 117.
[121] Kyle Rempfer, "Army's Own Vaccine That Could Fight COVID Variants Begins Clinical Trials" (April 7, 2021) *Army Times*, www.armytimes.com/news/your-army/2021/04/07/armys-own-vaccine-that-could-fight-covid-variants-begins-clinical-trials/.
[122] Col. Kenneth E. Hall, "The Dangerous Decline in the US Military's Infectious-Disease Vaccine Program" (2011) *Air & Space Power Journal* 101–15.
[123] Hall, "The Dangerous Decline," note 122.
[124] US Defense Advanced Research Projects Agency, "About DARPA," www.darpa.mil/about-us/about-darpa.
[125] DARPA, note 124.

There is also an important link between infectious diseases, vaccine R&D, and bioterrorism. Albeit in limited settings, biological agents have successfully been deployed with the purpose of causing injury or death among humans. The development of vaccines targeting pathogens that can be used as bioterrorism agents – such as anthrax, Ebola viruses, or smallpox – is a key component of bioterrorism preparedness.[126]

2.3.3 *The Interplay between the Public and Private Sectors*

As a catalyst for basic research, the public sector has long played a critical role in vaccine R&D, both through scientific work performed by its own scientists and indirectly, as the funder of work on vaccines carried out by nongovernmental R&D players. Yet, the public sector alone does not have the capacity to bring vaccines to market on its own. As epidemiologist Michael Osterholm has observed, because "the only real expertise in the world to make these vaccines in a quantity and a safety environment is in the private sector (. . .), (i)f the private sector isn't fully engaged and involved, it's a show stopper."[127]

As seen in the following chapter, vaccines represent a relatively small sliver of pharmaceutical products entering the market each year, and are often considered as peripheral R&D priorities for most private-sector R&D players. Pharmaceutical companies, however, have played an important role in bridging the gap between the early and late stages of vaccine development and production. Throughout this chapter, the word "sponsor" has been used to refer to the person or institution seeking regulatory review and approval of a vaccine, reflecting the regulatory parlance long used in this area. The US Code of Federal Regulations explains that, in the general context of drug regulation, "sponsor means a person who takes responsibility for and initiates a clinical investigation. The sponsor may be an individual or pharmaceutical company, governmental agency, academic institution, private organization, or other organization."[128] Typically, the sponsor of a vaccine in the United States, Europe, and many other jurisdictions is a private-sector pharmaceutical company. This is why during the COVID-19 pandemic the reader may have heard of, or even talked about, *the Moderna* vaccine, *the Pfizer* vaccine, *the Johnson & Johnson* vaccine, *the AstraZeneca* vaccine, and so on. None of these vaccines were developed and produced exclusively by the companies whose names now attach to them, and work on all of these vaccines benefited from

---

[126] See e.g. Philip K. Russell, "Vaccines in Civilian Defense against Bioterrorism" (1999) 5 *Emerging Infectious Diseases* 531–53; Philip M. Polgreen & C. Helms, "Vaccines, Biological Warfare, and Bioterrorism" (2001) 28(4) *Primary Care* 807–21.

[127] See Helen Branswell, "Who Will Answer the Call in the Next Outbreak? Drug Makers Feel Burned by String of Vaccine Pleas" (January 11, 2018) *Stat*, www.statnews.com/2018/01/11/vaccines-drug-makers//. See also Kendall Hoyt, *Long Shot* (Harvard University Press, 2012), 32 (noting that, apart from a few cases, "vaccines are manufactured in United States by the private sector").

[128] 21 US Code of Federal Regulation 312.3(b).

multiple sources of funding ranging from the public to the private and philanthropic sectors. But these companies were the sponsors of these vaccines, precisely because from an R&D perspective, they are the players with the adequate infrastructure, know-how, and personnel to perform late-stage vaccine R&D and seek regulatory approval. In spite of its critical contributions to vaccine R&D, the public sector alone lacks these types of capabilities.

At the end of the day, as the remaining chapters will continue to show, vaccine R&D, production, and distribution is not an isolated endeavor ascribable only – and often not even predominantly – to a single entity or sector. Rather, it consists of a highly collaborative process, often spanning national borders and co-involving heterogenous players, which in the case of nonpublic-sector actors often also includes institutions outside the pharmaceutical industry, such as international organizations and nonprofits. Chapter 5 describes the increased role that international organizations – particularly those structured as public–private partnerships – took on from the beginning of the twenty-first century onward in financing the purchase of vaccines and, more recently, in creating incentives for vaccine R&D.

To illustrate the interplay between these different sectors in modern-day vaccine development, consider the following snapshot of the breadth of collaborations taking place during the 2014–2016 Ebola outbreak. The graph groups the most relevant participants by their predominant role in the development of one of the leading vaccine candidates during 2014–2016, which was known at the time as the rVSV-ZEBOV vaccine (Figure 2.2); it ultimately came to market in late 2019 under the brand name *Ervebo*, becoming the first approved Ebola vaccine in history.[129]

Recent public health crises – from Ebola and Zika to COVID-19 – have shown that the vaccine ecosystem can be quite supple in bringing heterogenous parties together when there is sudden demand for a vaccine. However, many impediments remain to the development of new vaccines against emerging pathogens, as well as to the timely and equitable distribution of vaccines that succeed in navigating the R&D and regulatory pathways.

As the next chapter demonstrates, many of these cross-sector collaborations have traditionally occurred as reactions to already unfolding public health crises, as opposed to focusing on the production of vaccine-related knowledge and vaccine development ahead of severe outbreaks of infectious diseases. Moreover, even when multiple players combine resources and expertise to develop a vaccine in response to especially severe outbreaks, the existing infrastructure is insufficient to produce the doses needed to respond to global outbreaks of infectious diseases, as abundantly illustrated by the COVID-19 pandemic, during which the public health need for

[129]   US Food & Drug Administration, "First FDA-Approved Vaccine for the Prevention of Ebola Virus Disease, Marking a Critical Milestone in Public Health Preparedness and Response" (December 19, 2019), www.fda.gov/news-events/press-announcements/first-fda-approved-vaccine-prevention-ebola-virus-disease-marking-critical-milestone-public-health.

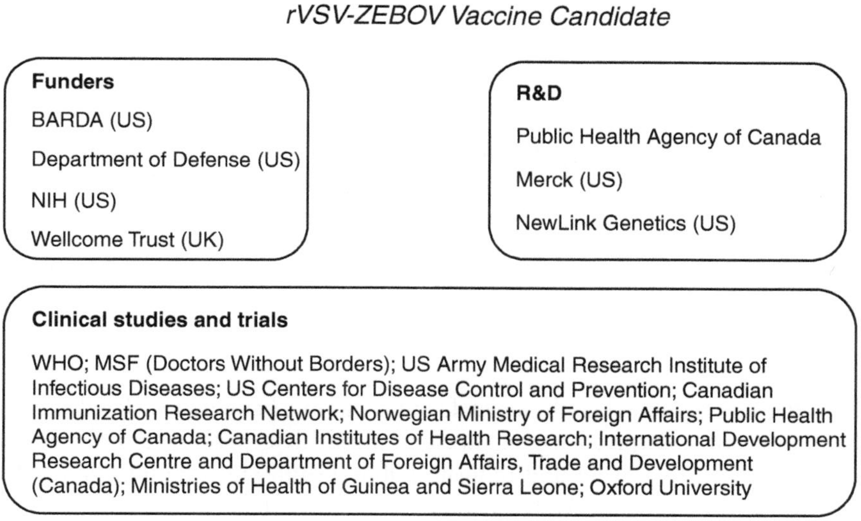

rVSV-ZEBOV Vaccine Candidate

Funders

BARDA (US)

Department of Defense (US)

NIH (US)

Wellcome Trust (UK)

R&D

Public Health Agency of Canada

Merck (US)

NewLink Genetics (US)

Clinical studies and trials

WHO; MSF (Doctors Without Borders); US Army Medical Research Institute of Infectious Diseases; US Centers for Disease Control and Prevention; Canadian Immunization Research Network; Norwegian Ministry of Foreign Affairs; Public Health Agency of Canada; Canadian Institutes of Health Research; International Development Research Centre and Department of Foreign Affairs, Trade and Development (Canada); Ministries of Health of Guinea and Sierra Leone; Oxford University

FIGURE 2.2 Main players involved in the development of the rVSV-ZEBOV vaccine during the 2014–2016 Ebola outbreak[130]

vaccines was only fractionally met for months on end, and to the detriment of populations in countries where the toll of COVID-19 was often the highest.

Having laid out the basic architecture of the system currently in place to bring new vaccines to market, the book now turns to structural and dynamic problems in the way players in the vaccine ecosystem – interacting within legal frameworks and policies seemingly capable of supporting the public health desideratum of robust vaccine development and distribution – invest in, produce, and allocate vaccines against emerging pathogens.

---

[130]   Adapted from Ana Santos Rutschman, "IP Preparedness for Outbreak Diseases" (2018) 65 *UCLA Law Review* 1200–66.

3

Vaccine Development under Proprietary Paradigms

Given the strong public health, societal, and economic benefits associated with the availability and widespread use of vaccines, an ideal scenario would dictate that vaccines needed to prevent and mitigate public health crises be treated as R&D priorities. Both domestic and international innovation policies would prioritize their development, and there would be mechanisms in place to ensure an equitable distribution of these vaccines. In practice, that is not the case.

Vaccine R&D pipelines have long remained underfunded and underpopulated, with spikes occurring when a public health crisis of considerable proportions is already underway, at which point a vaccine race typically begins and ends within an extremely compressed time line. When new vaccines emerge during one of these races – which is not always the case, as epidemic- and pandemic-spiked funding for vaccine R&D quickly dwindles – they may be captured by a limited number of countries, as happened most recently with COVID-19.

This chapter explores the reasons for this dissociation between public health goals and modes of production and distribution of new vaccines. It does so through the lens of proprietary paradigms: first, those applicable to vaccine R&D and technology transfer through intellectual property regimes; and second, those governing the allocation of newly developed vaccines, embodied primarily through bilateral contracts between countries or quasi-sovereign entities and vaccine manufacturers.

3.1 THE PROBLEM OF THE COMMODIFICATION OF VACCINES

Vaccines are perhaps most commonly regarded as tools for the promotion of public health goals, and this is the dimension that the book has highlighted so far. At the same time, they can be conceptualized from several other perspectives. Some of these perspectives are compatible with public health-informed views, while others negate the public health value of vaccines and vaccination. For example, as seen in Chapter 4, vaccines are portrayed across the spectrum of vaccine-questioning discourses as instruments of oppression and deceit, tools for the advancement of government or individual agendas, and even as causes of disease.

The main argument throughout the book is that, in many practical situations, vaccines are treated in ways that are often virtually indistinguishable from the ways in which the development and distribution of other goods occur. From a legal perspective, two branches of the law – intellectual property and contracts – treat vaccines as privatizable technologies produced primarily through market-driven models. Barring a few exceptions, emphasized in Chapter 5, the intellectual property and contractual principles applicable to vaccines are the same that are routinely applied to most transactable commodities. Over time, this approach has often resulted in scenarios that are at odds with public health goals.

An alignment between public health and innovation policy in the area of vaccines would lead to substantial investment in the development of new vaccines against emerging pathogens, improvement of existing ones, as well as to collaborative approaches to vaccine distribution. By contrast, many players in the vaccine ecosystem treat vaccines as commodities and transact them according to the dynamics of supply and demand. This chapter thus shifts the viewpoint to a more technology-centric angle – one through which the legal and policy regimes usually tasked with promoting innovation in socially valuable goods cabin vaccine production and distribution into proprietary paradigms. While these paradigms may work relatively well for a wide array of goods, they constitute a poor fit for the precise characteristics of vaccine technologies and fail to adequately reflect the public health, societal, and economic value of vaccines and vaccination.

3.1.1 *Characteristics of Vaccines That Render Them Unappealing for Market-Based R&D Approaches*

In some cases, scientific complexity and intractability have posed insurmountable challenges to the development of new vaccines against emerging pathogens. For example, in 1984 the US Health and Human Services Secretary expressed hope that an HIV vaccine would be ready for testing within two years.[1] Nearly four decades later, that hope has yet to materialize – not because of lack of support for vaccine R&D, but rather due to the complex scientific and technical challenges undergirding this area of vaccinology.

There are however many vaccine-preventable diseases for which vaccine development does not progress for reasons that are not solely (or even predominantly) attributable to scientific or technical complexity. Writing alongside several colleagues, physician Stanley Plotkin – one of the developers of the modern vaccine against rubella, a disease also known as German measles – has noted that the

---

[1] History of Vaccines, "The Development of HIV Vaccines," (2018), www.historyofvaccines.org/content/articles/development-hiv-vaccines.

prospective size of the market influences the allocation of funding and other resources to a given vaccine R&D project:

> Vaccine development is facing a crisis for three reasons: the complexity of the most challenging targets, which necessitates substantial investment of capital and human expertise; the diminishing numbers of vaccine manufacturers able to devote the necessary resources to research, development, and production; and the prevailing business model, which prioritizes the development of vaccines with a large market potential.[2]

This has led to a paradoxical situation. Vaccine manufacturers flocked to the market in the early twentieth century, contributing decisively to the development of products that greatly reduced the burden of many diseases – and, in some cases, led to their eradication. Once, however, many of these vaccine-preventable diseases were controlled or eradicated, private-sector interest in vaccine R&D shrunk considerably, both in terms of the number of R&D players and in terms of funding available for work on vaccines. At the same time, as seen earlier, public-sector funding for basic science has shrunk considerably in countries including the United States, one of the major centers for vaccine R&D.

Within a universe of finite funding and other resources, vaccines compete with other biomedical technologies for R&D attention. Regarding vaccines strictly from a public health perspective would suggest that vaccines would have the upper hand against other types of drugs because they prevent disease – which is largely preferable to having to treat disease. In some cases, vaccines also mitigate the effects of disease – which is also preferable to treating more severe effects of disease, enduring long-term disability or having patients die from a vaccine-preventable disease. Yet, under a market-based approach to R&D, it is precisely the specific characteristics of vaccines as products of biotechnology that render them less attractive to potential R&D funders than many other technologies competing for R&D interest.

In particular, R&D on vaccines targeting emerging pathogens is regarded as carrying a heightened degree of *risk*. First, there are issues of predictability. Even though early-detection and predictive technologies are becoming increasingly sophisticated, it is difficult to calculate which pathogens are likely to cause an outbreak in the short-, medium-, and long-terms.[3] That being said, current predictive frameworks do yield valuable insights and have enabled actors in the public health arena to accurately flag out areas of R&D in need of greater attention. For instance, recall that the emerging pathogen list published by the WHO in the wake of the 2014–2016 Ebola outbreak included both filoviruses (the viral family Ebola

---

[2]   Plotkin et al., "Establishing a Global Vaccine-Development Fund," (2015) 373 *New England Journal of Medicine* 297–300, note 12.

[3]   Eirini Christaki, "New Technologies in Predicting, Preventing and Controlling Emerging Infectious Diseases" (2015) 6 *Virulence* 558–65.

viruses belong to) and coronaviruses.[4] Since then, there have been multiple Ebola outbreaks, as well as the emergence of the novel coronavirus causing COVID-19.

Another aspect of risk often alluded to in debates about the development of new vaccines is the risk of failure of the research project itself. Most vaccine candidates never reach phase 3 clinical trials, and even within those that advance into phase 3 clinical trials, the majority fail on scientific grounds.[5] Recent calculations indicate only around 7 percent of vaccine candidates move beyond preclinical development.[6] Of those entering clinical trials, only 15–20 percent eventually receive approval to be marketed.[7] For context, it is important to understand that, in this regard, vaccines are not fundamentally different from other pharmaceutical products. These are extremely complex technologies and R&D in this area has long been recognized as carrying a higher risk of failure when compared to other areas of science and technology. As seen in Section 3.1.2, the inherent complexity of R&D on pharmaceutical products has long been invoked as one of the reasons intellectual property rights are necessary as incentives to investment in R&D.

Yet another aspect of risk is linked to pathogen mutation and the emergence of new variants. This phenomenon was vividly illustrated during the COVID-19 pandemic, when multiple variants of the SARS-CoV-2 virus emerged across the world and quickly spread to populations in other countries. In some cases, vaccines already under development or production may still be effective against newer variants, while in other cases R&D on vaccines responding to these variants may be necessary. This problem is not restricted to pandemic R&D. For example, the development of seasonal flu vaccines for the northern hemisphere is based on a prediction of which influenza viruses are likely to emerge based on flu patterns observed earlier in the southern hemisphere. By the time these newly developed vaccines come to market, some of these viruses have mutated, rendering the vaccines much less effective than hoped.[8] While risk of failure is something that most pharmaceutical R&D has to contend with, not all areas of R&D face problems posed by pathogen mutation.

In addition to risk, the development of many vaccines is also constrained by the prospect of *limited markets,* often with limited opportunities for repeat consumption.[9] As seen in the previous chapters, many of the diseases for which new vaccines are needed are often endemic to poorer regions of the world, where

---

[4] World Health Organization, "R&D Blueprint," note 8.
[5] World Health Organization, "R&D Blueprint," note 8.
[6] See Helen Branswell, "WHO, Partners Unveil Ambitious Plan to Deliver 2 Billion Doses of Covid-19 Vaccine to High-Risk Populations" (June 26, 2020) *Stat,* www.statnews.com/2020/06/26/who-partners-unveil-ambitious-plan-to-deliver-2-billion-doses-of-covid-19-vaccine-to-high-risk-populations/.
[7] Branswell, "WHO, Partners Unveil Ambitious Plan," note 6.
[8] Leigh Krietsch Boerner, "The Flu Shot and the Egg" (February 26, 2020) 6(2) *ACS Central Science* 89–92.
[9] Patricia M. Danzon et al., "Vaccine Supply: A Cross-National Perspective" (2005) 24 *Health Affairs* 706–17, 707.

demand may be high, but where vaccine manufacturers struggle to monetize their product. There are also diseases that emerge during a pandemic or epidemic, creating a sudden uptick in vaccine demand, but these markets are temporally limited and hard to predict. Moreover, vaccines may confer long-term immunity after the administration of a single dose, in some cases followed by a limited number of booster shots. By contrast, other health goods, including many types of drugs and biologics, are prescribed for continued or periodic consumption over long periods of time. Longer courses of treatment and the associated possibility for repeated consumption mean that these goods will be deemed as offering better prospects of monetization when compared to vaccines.

While furthering public health goals through the administration of a preventative, vaccination also tends to erode the underlying vaccine market. A lot of demand for COVID-19 vaccines is a sign of a public health problem. The reduction in the burden of COVID-19 partially brought about by the use of vaccines is a good sign from a public health perspective, but it also signals that the market for COVID-19 vaccines is shrinking.

Against this backdrop, how is an actor driven predominantly by market forces likely to behave? By allocating resources to areas of pharmaceutical R&D that, albeit risky, face fewer constraints likely to result in diminished chances of generating revenue.

This is, admittedly, a reductionist perspective on vaccine development. It leaves out players motivated to engage in vaccine R&D for reasons related to public health and other non-market factors that many players in the vaccine ecosystem take into account. While Chapter 5 explores these beyond-market forces behind contemporary vaccine R&D, the book here pauses to consider the pervasiveness of predominantly market-driven approaches. This pervasiveness, intimately connected to the legal and policy treatment of vaccines as privatizable commodities, has shaped the vaccine R&D ecosystem in considerable ways.

A 2017 report from the Department of Health and Human Services noted that "the prevailing business model prioritizes vaccine candidates with large markets; yet market sizes are likely smaller for many remaining targets."[10] The private sector itself recognizes that vaccine R&D as a whole is often seen as "not a priority for industry" because there are many fewer prospects of return on investment than in other areas of pharmaceutical R&D.[11] An article published in *The Economist* in 2010 put it more bluntly, describing vaccine R&D as a "neglected corner of the drugs business, with old technology, little investment and abysmal profit margins."[12]

---

[10]　US Department of Health and Human Services, "Encouraging Vaccine Innovation: Promoting the Development of Vaccines That Minimize the Burden of Infectious Diseases in the 21st Century," (December 2017) Report to Congress, www.hhs.gov/sites/default/files/2018-06-25_nvac_curesreport_ presentation.pdf, at 3,

[11]　Rino Rappuoli et al., "The Intangible Value of Vaccination" (2002) 297 *Science* 937–39.

[12]　"A Smarter Jab" (October 14, 2010) *Economist*.

Although there have been important achievements in the development of new vaccine technology – including those that allowed for the first mRNA vaccines to come to market in late 2020 – the diagnosis of vaccine R&D as not being afforded mainstream status remains valid.

A further comparison between vaccines and other pharmaceutical products may help situate vaccines as relatively peripheral technologies in market contexts. The following graph (Figure 3.1) illustrates the relative frequency of vaccine licensure in the United States. It maps the number of product approvals by the FDA between 2000 and 2017, contrasting vaccines (shown on top of each bar) with other types of biologics and drugs.

Over a span of eighteen years, thirty-two new vaccines entered the market in the United States. During that period of time, the greatest number of vaccine licenses issued in a single year was five (2005). In three different years, no new vaccines were licensed (2004, 2015, and 2017). Overall, the average number of new vaccines entering the market between 2000 and 2017 was just shy of 1.8 per year. As seen in the graph, these numbers stand in sharp contrast with those representing the licensure of other types of new pharmaceutical products – some of which routinely registered yearly market entrance numbers in the double digits.

Even a shift to less market-centric vaccine R&D models would be unlikely to alter these disparities in the rate of market entrance – which is not a problem, as relative market entrance tells us nothing about how robust or lacking vaccine R&D might be at a point in time. It is nonetheless important to keep in mind the relative status of vaccines vis-à-vis other pharmaceutical products in a market-driven economy. As the

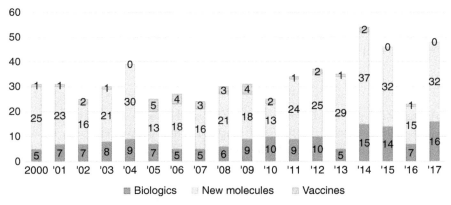

FIGURE 3.1 FDA drug approvals 2000–2017[13]

[13] Adapted from Laura DeFrancesco, "Drug Pipeline: 1Q18" (May 9, 2018) 5 *Nature Biotechnology* 386 and from US Food & Drug Administration, "Vaccines Licensed for Use in the United States" (2021), www.fda.gov/vaccines-blood-biologics/vaccines/vaccines-licensed-use-united-states.

book delves further into the proprietary frameworks that feed into the current dynamics of vaccine R&D, this relative status – allied to the particular characteristics of vaccines as biotechnologies – will help elucidate why vaccine R&D remains underfunded, and why some vaccine candidates linger in the R&D pipeline for years instead of being brought to market in a timely fashion.

3.1.2 *The Paradoxically Corrective Function of Public Health Crises*

From a public health perspective, one reason vaccines are valued so highly is their preventative function. Markets, by contrast, might undervalue vaccines in the absence of a pandemic or epidemic precisely because prevention of disease is a nonevent that is difficult to monetize. This misalignment between public health and the commodification of vaccines is nonetheless periodically bridged. A significant outbreak of an infectious disease causes a sudden surge in demand for vaccines. A pandemic or epidemic can thus have a catalytic effect, eliminating or lessening problems in attracting funders and R&D players to vaccine R&D – and triggering a phenomenon now commonly described as a vaccine race.[14]

As seen later, this corrective function of large-scale public health crises is temporary, and – unlike the COVID-19 pandemic – often insufficient to propel new vaccines through the R&D pipeline and into the market. These bursts of vaccine development also fit poorly into the preparedness paradigms that guide public health, which place a premium on proactive interventions, rather than focusing most activity on reacting to crises as they unfold.

R&D performed during pandemics and epidemics remains nonetheless a critical component of vaccine development. The following subsections illustrate how the market dynamics created by a public health crisis functions as a corrective to the otherwise widespread problem of underfunding of vaccine R&D.

3.1.2.1 The Zika Vaccine Race

Although Zika did not become widely discussed outside scientific circles until a quasi-global outbreak occurred in 2015–2016, the disease has been known to scientists for longer than several other infectious diseases – including, for instance, Ebola. Transmitted primarily by daytime mosquitoes, Zika was first identified in 1947 in Uganda and since then it had been primarily associated with a range of symptoms considered relatively mild.[15] These symptoms included fever, muscle or

---

[14]   See, e.g. Meredith Wadman, *The Vaccine Race: Science, Politics, and the Human Costs of Defeating Disease* (Penguin, 2017).

[15]   Oumar Faye et al., "Molecular Evolution of Zika Virus during Its Emergence in the 20th Century" (2014) 8(1) *Plos Neglected Tropical Diseases*.

joint pain, and rash.[16] As such, as virologist Alan D. Barrett, puts it, for most of its known history, Zika "was not considered to be a major pathogen."[17]

Until 2007, there had only been fourteen documented cases of Zika virus disease in humans.[18] That year, an outbreak in the small Island of Yap, in the Federated States of Micronesia, led to forty-nine confirmed cases, coupled with calculations suggesting that 74 percent of the island population might have been infected with the virus.[19] This prompted further research on Zika, and a 2012 study found that, in addition to the African lineage of the virus, there was now a distinct lineage of the virus circulating in the Eastern regions of the globe.[20] An outbreak of the Asian lineage of the virus in French Polynesia in 2013 led some scientists to suggest that Zika virus disease in humans might produce more serious consequences than previously known.[21] These included a rare neurological disorder known as Guillain–Barré syndrome, which can produce symptoms ranging from numbness and weakness to paralysis. An outbreak caused by the same lineage of the virus took place in 2015–2016 and quickly reached much larger dimensions. It also renewed concerns about possible neurological effects associated with Zika virus disease.[22] These concerns, allied to the magnitude of the outbreak, prompted a spike in Zika R&D and triggered a vaccine race.

Studies performed early in the outbreak reinforced the link between Zika virus disease and Guillain–Barré syndrome, and further suggested that the virus could lead to congenital defects.[23] In February 2016, the WHO declared a Public Health Emergency of International Concern.[24] The declaration lasted until November 2016, at which point there were nineteen groups conducting late-stage Zika vaccine R&D – some of them working on multiple types of vaccine technology – as well as several groups doing early stage or otherwise exploratory Zika vaccine R&D.[25]

The mobilization of resources around the development of Zika vaccine candidates illustrates not only a profound change to the market-based landscape of

[16] World Health Organization, "Zika Virus," (2021), www.who.int/en/news-room/fact-sheets/detail/zika-virus.

[17] Alan D. T. Barrett, "Zika Vaccine Candidates Progress through Nonclinical Development and Enter Clinical Trials" (November 10, 2016) 1 *NPJ Vaccines*.

[18] Mark R. Duffy et al., "Zika Virus Outbreak on Yap Island, Federated States of Micronesia" (June 11, 2009) 360 *New England Journal of Medicine* 2536–43, at 2536.

[19] Duffy, "Zika Virus Outbreak," note 18; Jon Cohen, "Zika's Long, Strange Trip into the Limelight" (February 8, 2016) *Science*, www.science.org/content/article/zika-s-long-strange-trip-limelight.

[20] Cohen, "Zika's Long, Strange Trip," note 19.

[21] Van-Mai Cao-Lormeau et al., "Guillain-Barré Syndrome Outbreak Associated with Zika Virus Infection in French Polynesia: A Case-Control Study" (2016) 387 *Lancet* 1531.

[22] Michael A. Johansson et al., "Zika and the Risk of Microcephaly" (2016) 375 *New England Journal of Medicine* 1; Thais dos Santos et al., "Zika Virus and the Guillain-Barré Syndrome Case Series from Seven Countries" (2016) 375 *New England Journal of Medicine* 1598.

[23] Fernanda R. Cugola et al., "The Brazilian Zika Virus Strain Causes Birth Defects in Experimental Models" (2016) 534 *Nature* 267.

[24] World Health Organization, "Zika Virus and Complications: 2016 Public Health Emergency of International Concern," (2016), www.who.int/emergencies/zika-virus-tmp/en/.

[25] World Health Organization, "Current Zika Product Pipeline 5" (2016), https://perma.cc/8X7D-AGKB.

incentives to R&D, but also how R&D on some types of vaccine technology can occur on extremely compressed timelines: US Army scientists made the decision to develop a Zika vaccine candidate in January 2016; testing began the following April; results were submitted for peer-review in May and published in the journal *Nature* in June; patent applications were filed in May and August; clinical trials began in November 2016.[26] By contrast, it takes on average between ten to fifteen years to develop and bring a vaccine to market.[27]

3.1.2.2 The Coronavirus Vaccine Races

Unlike Zika, the pathogen at the root of the COVID-19 pandemic, the SARS-CoV-2 virus, was not previously known. In a strict sense, there was no underfunding problem prior to the outbreak, as R&D on a vaccine against this particular pathogen was not a possibility. SARS-CoV-2 emerged in late 2019. The WHO declared a pandemic in mid-March 2020.[28] By July 2020, there were around 150 vaccine candidates in development, with twenty-three undergoing different phases of clinical trials. By April 2021, that number had swollen to over 200 vaccine development projects, with ninety-two in clinical trials.[29] The COVID-19 vaccine race thus illustrates the specific, yet not isolated, case of a crisis during which public health needs and market-driven demand aligned early on – although, as seen in Section 3.2 of the chapter, this alignment was not as immediate and seamless as it appeared.

Not all vaccine races triggered by severe public health crises result in the development and commercialization of new vaccines. Such was the case of the first coronavirus vaccine race that took place in the twenty-first century. SARS coronavirus (SARS-CoV), a pathogen causing severe acute respiratory syndrome (SARS), was first identified in 2003 and connected to cases of atypical pneumonia that started being reported in November 2002.[30] The outbreak caused by the virus would result in over 8,000 probable cases in almost thirty countries, and 774 reported deaths.[31] The identification

[26] Annette M. Boyle, "Army Research Produces Zika Vaccine Candidate in Record Time" (August 2016) *US Medicine*, www.federalregister.gov/documents/2016/12/09/2016-29514/intent-to-grant-an-exclusive-license-of-us-government-owned-patents; Rafael A. Larocca et al., "Vaccine Protection against Zika Virus from Brazil" (2016) 536 *Nature* 474; " Intent to Grant an Exclusive License of US Government-Owned Patents Notice" (December 9, 2016) 81(237) *Federal Registry* 89087–88.

[27] History of Vaccines, "Vaccine Development, Testing, and Regulation," (2018), www.historyofvaccines.org/content/articles/vaccine-development-testing-and-regulation .

[28] World Health Organization, "Timeline of WHO's Response to COVID-19" (June 29, 2020), www.who.int/news-room/detail/29-06-2020-covidtimeline.

[29] World Health Organization, "Timeline of WHO's Response to COVID-19," note 28. See also Jonathan Gardner et al., "The Coronavirus Vaccine Frontrunners Have Emerged. Here's Where They Stand" (June 9, 2020) *Biopharma Drive*, www.biopharmadive.com/news/coronavirus-vaccine-pipeline-types/579122/.

[30] National Institute of Allergy and Infectious Diseases, "Coronaviruses," (2021), www.niaid.nih.gov/diseases-conditions/coronaviruses.

[31] James D. Cherry, "The Chronology of the 2002–2003 SARS Mini Pandemic" (2004) 5 *Paediatric Respiratory Review* 262–69.

of the novel pathogen in early 2003, associated with the increase in case numbers, quickly prompted a vaccine race.[32] Different types of SARS vaccine candidates were developed throughout the outbreak, as well as in the years that followed it.[33] None, however, made it to market. The virus all but disappeared from circulation within less than a year,[34] and the vaccine R&D gradually petered out.

Although there have been no new reported cases of SARS since 2004, the virus is still considered a threat to public health. In 2012, the US National Select Agent Registry Program designated SARS-CoV a "select agent."[35] This program, jointly run by divisions within the Centers for Disease Control and Prevention and the Plant Health Inspection Service, regulates the possession, use and transfer of biologic materials with the "potential to pose a severe threat to public, animal or plant health or to animal or plant products."[36] The 2016 list published by the WHO on emerging diseases in critical need of increased funding for R&D included the diseases triggered by SARS and other coronaviruses.[37] SARS was deemed a "priority" disease for which there were insufficient levels of vaccine and drug R&D – the highest category in the WHO's hierarchization of R&D shortcomings, followed by "serious" diseases like Zika, where insufficient levels of R&D were deemed problematic but relatively not as acute as for top-tier diseases.

This is not to say that R&D on SARS vaccines was inexistent. Between 2011 and 2016, for example, a group of public–private R&D players worked on vaccines targeting both SARS and Middle East respiratory syndrome (MERS).[38] The latter disease, caused by the MERS coronavirus (MERS-CoV), was first identified in 2011 and cases have been reported ever since.[39] The R&D group that came together in 2011 to develop vaccines for both types of coronaviruses then known to cause disease in humans included participants from Baylor and Texas universities, the Texas Children's Hospital's Center for Vaccine Development, the New York Blood Center, UTMB Galveston, and the Walter Reed Army Institute of Research.[40]

---

[32] See e.g. Shibo Jiang et al., "SARS Vaccine Development" (2005) 11 *Emerging Infections Diseases* 1016, www.ncbi.nlm.nih.gov/pmc/articles/PMC3371787/.

[33] See generally Deborah R. Taylor, "Obstacles and Advances in SARS Vaccine Development" (2006) 24 *Vaccine* 863, www.ncbi.nlm.nih.gov/pmc/articles/PMC7115537/; Rachel L. Roper & Kristina E. Rehm, "SARS Vaccines: Where Are We?" (2009) 8 *Expert Review of Vaccines* 887, www.medscape.com/viewarticle/706717_1; See e.g. Jiang et al., "SARS Vaccine Development," note 32.

[34] See e.g. Wei-Jie Guan et al., "Severe Acute Respiratory Syndrome: A Vanished Evil?" (2013) 5 *Journal of Thoracic Disease* S87, www.ncbi.nlm.nih.gov/pmc/articles/PMC3747533/.

[35] US Centers for Disease Control and Prevention, "Severe Acute Respiratory Syndrome (SARS)," (2017), www.cdc.gov/sars/index.html.

[36] US Centers for Disease Control and Prevention, "Federal Select Agent Program," (2021), www.selectagents.gov.

[37] World Health Organization, "WHO Publishes List," note 16, at 22.

[38] See PATH, "Could a Vaccine Candidate for SARS Also Prevent COVID-19?" (May 7, 2020), www.path.org/articles/could-vaccine-candidate-sars-also-prevent-covid-19/.

[39] World Health Organization, "Middle East Respiratory Syndrome Coronavirus (MERS-CoV)," (2019), www.who.int/health-topics/middle-east-respiratory-syndrome-coronavirus-mers#tab=tab_1.

[40] PATH, "Could a Vaccine Candidate," note 38.

Given the genetic similarities between viruses in the coronavirus family, interest in this R&D project – and, more broadly, on preexisting work on coronavirus vaccines – resurfaced during the COVID-19 pandemic, which marked the third time in the twenty-first century in which a novel pathogen in the coronavirus family (SARS-CoV-2) capable of causing serious disease in humans emerged.

3.1.3 *The Exceptionalism of Outbreak-Spiked Funding for Vaccine R&D*

The evolution of the SARS vaccine race narrated in the previous section provides a glimpse into the ephemeral nature of funding for vaccine R&D triggered by a severe outbreak of an infectious disease. Hopefully, crises of the magnitude of COVID-19 will remain the exception rather than becoming the norm – and while this is good from a public health perspective, it also means that most outbreak-spiked funding is usually short-lived.

In early 2017 – a few months after the 2014–2016 Ebola outbreak ended – epidemiologist Michael Osterholm offered an illuminating comment on the status of Ebola vaccine R&D: "I can't say that all the momentum has been lost. But it's pretty hard to run a semi-truck on a lawnmower motor. There's not enough push and pull right now. Things are happening in more of what I'd call a routine matter of trying to follow through on this."[41] As seen throughout Section 3.2, most vaccine races prompted by a pandemic or epidemic resemble the SARS and Ebola races from a funding perspective: Resources committed to vaccine R&D increase exponentially during the course of a short period of time and begin waning toward the later stages of an outbreak. R&D might come close to a halt and only resume if and when another public health crisis rekindles interest in a particular disease.

One of the primary ways through which policymakers and legislators have long sought to solve problems like this – as well as the broader problem of chronically underfunded R&D on socially valuable goods – is through the use of intellectual property rights as incentives to innovation. The book now surveys how intellectual property has helped shape the vaccine R&D ecosystem, and how, in so doing, it has accentuated the market-driven nature of current models of vaccine development.

3.2 THE INTELLECTUAL PROPERTY OF VACCINES

Most new vaccines that come to market are "protected" by one or more layers of intellectual property rights in the form of patents.[42] This protection consists in the ability of rightsholders to prevent others from competing with their products for a certain period

---

[41]   Helen Branswell, "We're Not Prepared for Future Ebola Outbreaks, Experts Warn" (January 17, 2017) *Stat*, www.statnews.com/2017/01/17/ebola-vaccine-warning/.

[42]   A vaccine may be covered by additional intellectual property rights, such as trademarks. Unlike patents, these rights do not play a significant role in the R&D process leading up to the production and distribution of a vaccine, although they can help with brand recognition once the vaccine enters the market.

of time. By indirectly – yet deliberately – restricting competition, intellectual property does something that other branches of the law seek to prevent altogether. Consider antitrust and competition laws, which heavily scrutinize any business practices that may unduly restrict competition. Intellectual property, by contrast, enables producers of qualifying goods to effectively operate in monopoly-like conditions.

By and large, intellectual property precepts apply to all fields of technology – across the spectrum of most pharmaceutical technologies and beyond, from electronics to agriculture, transportation, sports gear, household items, and clothing, just to give a few examples. This section begins by providing a brief overview of how intellectual property works and how its application to the field of vaccines has influenced vaccine research, development, and allocation.

3.2.1 *Intellectual Property*

Intellectual property is a relatively recent branch of the law. Throughout history, there were occasional instances of legally established monopolies, grants of rights, or normative practices that would today loosely fit the concept of intellectual property. For instance, precursors to what we now understand to be copyrights were documented in ancient Greece and Rome, as well as across pre-Islamic societies. The Venetian Republic in the Renaissance is usually credited with having passed the first law creating a system of patent protection for several technologies, including its burgeoning glass-blowing industry. But the generalized and systemic adoption of intellectual property laws – and in particular of patents – is a product of the late nineteenth and twentieth centuries, ushered in by international conventions through which a large number of countries agreed to implement relatively similar patent, trademark, and copyright protection.[43]

The expression "intellectual property" is used to designate a set of laws and doctrines governing intangible goods and processes.[44] The existence of, and need for, rights governing these types of goods have been justified in different ways.[45] The dominant narrative has regarded these rights from a utilitarian perspective. Absent some form of property-like rights over their emerging creations, innovators might not spend time and resources developing new goods in the first place, especially if these goods can be replicated by others with relative ease. According to this worldview of intellectual property, these rights are justified instrumentally as functioning as a system of incentives

---

[43]   Paris Convention for the Protection of Industrial Property (1883); Berne Convention for the Protection of Literary and Artistic Works (1886).

[44]   See generally Wendy J. Gordon, "Intellectual Property," in *Oxford Handbook of Legal Studies*, Peter Cane & Mark Tushnet, eds. (Oxford University Press, 2003).

[45]   William Fisher, "Theories of Intellectual Property," in *New Essays in the Legal and Political Theory of Property*, Stephen R. Munzer, ed. (Cambridge University Press, 2001), 168; Gordon, "Intellectual Property," (2005); Richard Posner & William Landes, *The Economic Structure of Intellectual Property Law* (Harvard University Press, 2005); Robert P. Merges, *Justifying Intellectual Property* (Harvard University Press, 2011).

to innovation. They give innovators exclusive rights for certain periods of time, during which they are able to occupy a market position similar to that of a monopolist. This lead time on the market allows them to potentially recover the costs they have incurred and make a profit – should there be enough demand for their goods.

To be sure, there have been other historically influential justifications for intellectual property emphasizing nonutilitarian principles, such as theories drawing from Locke's philosophical writings on property arguing that innovators should acquire property-like rights over the fruits of their labor. The contemporary intellectual property regime, however, was developed according to predominantly utilitarian principles. Within the umbrella of intellectual property, the patent system in particular is regarded as a way to solve underinvestment problems, and is often described as most needed for those areas of science and technology marked by especially costly and risky R&D processes – as is the case with pharmaceutical technologies.[46]

Today, the patent system is largely understood as a bargain between innovator and society at large: In exchange for conveying information about an invention – through the formal and substantive requirements set forth in the patent application process – the innovator is granted a set of exclusionary rights. These rights are valid for a period of time, currently set at twenty years – which in the case of pharmaceutical products, including vaccines, is in practice somewhat shorter, as drug and vaccine sponsors may not start commercializing their products before receiving authorization from national drug regulators, as seen in Chapter 2.

The rights conferred by a patent prevent second-comers from competing with the originator of a new drug or vaccine having incurred substantially fewer R&D costs and risk. Some commentators have compared the position of a patent holder to that of a monopolist.[47] In general, legal systems around the world – and especially those associated with Western economies – look disfavorably on monopoly-like market positions. As British historian and politician Thomas Babington Macaulay famously remarked, the "effect of monopoly generally is to make articles scarce, to make them dear, and to make them bad."[48] Yet patent law adopts a lesser-of-two-evils approach: policymakers in this area operate under the assumption that it is better to deal with monopoly-like effects for a period of time than risk not having sufficient investment in costly and risky R&D.

This theoretical framework to justify patents as tools to promote innovative R&D does not always hold. As seen before, many areas in pharmaceutical R&D – including many vaccine-preventable diseases – have long been significantly underfunded,

---

[46] See e.g. Michael A. Heller & Rebecca S. Eisenberg, "Can Patents Deter Innovation? The Anticommons in Biomedical Research" (1998) 280 *Science* 698–701.

[47] Benjamin N. Roin, "Intellectual Property versus Prizes: Reframing the Debate" (2014) 81 *University of Chicago Law Review* 999–1078, at 1001.

[48] Thomas Babington Macaulay, *Speeches of Lord Macaulay: Corrected by Himself* (Longman, Green, and Company, 1877), 112.

and are likely to remain so under predominantly market-driven funding models, which is essentially the ethos of the patent system. In this sense, if understood as a catalyst for investment in R&D, the patent system often fails in critical areas of public health.

Moreover, in cases in which there is investment conducive to the production of new drugs and vaccines, the system may fail in a different way. By allowing for periods of monopoly-like market positions, patents enable drug and vaccine manufacturers to charge supracompetitive prices for their products, as well as to allocate them as desired – which may not result in the provision of these goods to the patient populations who need them the most. This translates into deadweight losses, the economic term for the number of would-be consumers of a good that is excessively priced.[49] From a public and individual health perspective, however, deadweight loss translates into increased disease burdens.

Called to analyze the patent system in the mid-twentieth century, economist Fritz Machlup offered the following insight:

> If we did not have a patent system, it would be irresponsible, on the basis of our present knowledge of its economic consequences, to recommend instituting one. But since we have had a patent system for a long time, it would be irresponsible, on the basis of our present knowledge, to recommend abolishing it.[50]

Even though Machlup's recommendation that the current patent structure remain in place was made in reference to the United States patent system, he noted that his findings were likely applicable to countries with a "large industrial economy." For lower-income countries, Machlup posited, "a different weight of argument might well suggest another conclusion."[51] Nevertheless, the evolution of patent systems since Machlup's 1958 study converged into widespread adoption of intellectual property protections, and today virtually all countries grant patents on products and processes deemed innovative by their domestic patent offices.

3.2.2 *The TRIPS Agreement and the Global Reach of Intellectual Property*

The evolution of intellectual property has resulted in the implementation of patent systems at the national level that are relatively similar to one another. Although domestic patent offices and courts create different procedural, administrative, and substantive rules about patents, most countries in the world are bound by the same

---

49 Steven Shavell & Tanguy van Ypersele, "Rewards versus Intellectual Property Rights" (2001) 44 *Journal of Law and Economics* 525–47, at 529.

50 Fritz Machlup, "An Economic Review of the Patent System" (1958) Study commission by the Subcommitttee on Patents, Trademarks, and Copyrights of the Committee on the Judiciary, US Senate, 85th Congress, second session, Washington, DC, at 80. https://cdn.mises.org/An%20Economic%20Review%20of%20the%20Patent%20System_Vol_3_3.pdf.

51 Machlup, "An Economic Review," note 50.

international intellectual property standards. These standards were comprehensively negotiated in the 1990s and codified in the World Trade Organization Agreement on Trade-Related Aspects of Intellectual Property Rights (TRIPS), which entered into force on January 1, 1995.[52] The TRIPS Agreement directs countries to enact laws implementing a set of minimum standards in different areas of intellectual property. Among these mandatory standards, TRIPS establishes that "patents shall be available for any inventions, whether products or processes, in all fields of technology."[53] The Agreement limits the grant of a patent to inventions that "are new, involve an inventive step and are capable of industrial application."[54] While it allows for limited cases in which countries may elect to exclude a product or process from patentability – the most notable examples in the field of biomedical innovation are the cases of diagnostic, therapeutic and surgical methods[55] – the overarching principle of TRIPS is that countries must award patents to inventions meeting the cumulative criteria of novelty, inventiveness and susceptibility of industrial application.

As a result, TRIPS signatories are bound by international law to set up national patent systems that reflect these requirements, and to make patents available for a period that lasts twenty years from the date a patent application is filed.[56] All 164 member-countries of the World Trade Organization are parties to the TRIPS Agreement. This has resulted in the quasi-global adoption of highly harmonized patent regimes. Moreover, many of the sovereign states that are not parties to TRIPS – including several micro-states like San Marino and Polynesian island-countries, or recently formed countries like South Sudan – tend to recognize some form of patent protection at the domestic level.

A second implication of this largely harmonized legal architecture is that the current international intellectual property laws bind countries to offer patent protection to inventions meeting the substantive requirements of novelty, inventiveness, and usefulness. For the majority of countries in the world, the TRIPS Agreement reinforces this point by establishing that "patents shall be available and patent rights enjoyable without discrimination as to (...) the field of technology."[57] Even if, in light of the particular characteristics of certain goods, a country wants to create

---

[52] For a comprehensive view of the TRIPS Agreement, including its gestation, negotiation and legal analysis, see Daniel Gervais, *The TRIPS Agreement: Drafting History and Analysis*, 5th ed. (Sweet & Maxwell, 2021).

[53] TRIPS Agreement, article 27.1.

[54] TRIPS Agreement, article 27.1.

[55] TRIPS Agreement, article 27.3(a). Other cases include exclusions from patentability based on *ordre public* or morality concerns (article 27.2) and "plants and animals other than micro-organisms, and essentially biological processes for the production of plants or animals other than non-biological and microbiological processes" (article 27.3(b)). The Agreement mandates, nonetheless, that countries resort to patent protection, sui generis rights or a combination thereof to protect plant varieties (article 27.3(b)).

[56] TRIPS Agreement, article 30.

[57] TRIPS Agreement, article 27.1.

a differentiated legal regime for those goods alone, it is legally impermissible to eliminate the possibility of patenting a subset of technologies – such as vaccines against emerging pathogens.

TRIPS recognizes the instrumental nature of intellectual property rights as utilitarian tools to incentivize innovation in ways that promote economic *and* social welfare. Article 7 establishes that "(t)he protection and enforcement of intellectual property rights should contribute to the promotion of technological innovation and to the transfer and dissemination of technology, to the mutual advantage of producers and users of technological knowledge and in a manner conducive to social and economic welfare, and to a balance of rights and obligations." Moreover, it expressly carves out room for the adoption of measures specifically designed to protect the public health: Article 8 gives countries the possibility of "formulating or amending their laws and regulations, adopt measures necessary to protect public health and nutrition and to promote the public interest in sectors of vital importance to their socio-economic and technological development." Additionally, the Doha Declaration on the TRIPS Agreement and Public Health, adopted in 2001, reiterated that the "TRIPS Agreement does not and should not prevent Members from taking measures to protect public health."[58]

Neither TRIPS nor the Doha Declaration, however, fundamentally displace the centrality of patents to vaccine R&D processes – and the consequent possibility of a restricted number of players largely controlling uses of vaccine technology. Attempts to privatize components of vaccines, in fact, predate intellectual property frameworks, and they were an early indicator that the development of new vaccines would come to unfold in a race-like format not only for public health reasons, but also as R&D players tried to position themselves as sole market suppliers ahead of their competitors.

3.2.3 *Proprietary Approaches to Vaccine R&D: Before Patents*

The first vaccines were developed in an environment in which proprietary conceptions of the scientific method played a marginal role when compared to the present day. As seen in Chapter 1, Edward Jenner is usually credited as the developer of the first vaccine in 1796, by successfully inoculating a healthy eight-year-old boy against smallpox. Several commentators have pointed out that Jenner's contributions are best framed less in terms of vaccine inventorship – he relied on knowledge and techniques already employed, albeit in scattered fashion, by other country doctors like himself[59] – and more in terms of having generated, collected, and reported evidence

---

[58] Doha Declaration, para. 4.
[59] Patrick J. Pead, "Benjamin Jesty: The First Vaccinator Revealed" (2006) 368 *Lancet* 2202; Susan Brink, "What's the Real Story about the Milkmaid and the Smallpox Vaccine?" (February 1, 2018) *NPR*, www.npr.org/sections/goatsandsoda/2018/02/01/582370199/whats-the-real-story-about-the-milkmaid-and-the-smallpox-vaccine.

about the process that would become known as vaccination.[60] In so doing, Jenner managed to drum up interest and confidence in vaccination among growing segments of the medical community. Importantly, he sent vaccine matter to colleagues who requested it, enabling them to use it for immediate medical purposes within their local communities, as well as launching the basis of scientific experimentation – and, to a certain extent, cooperation – that would result in the development of vaccines for other diseases and, more broadly, the establishment of the field of vaccinology and the industry that soon was born to support it.[61]

Even though intellectual property rights played no role at this point, proprietary approaches to vaccine development were quick to emerge. In the late eighteenth and early nineteenth centuries, access to vaccine matter was limited, with Jenner himself facing periodic shortages of product to share.[62] This scarcity would soon lead some vaccine developers to behave in ways that anticipated the exclusionary aspects of contemporary vaccine races. In the case of smallpox vaccines, product scarcity was especially acute in the United States, where there was no naturally occurring cowpox, the animal disease producing the raw material harvested by Jenner and others in order to inoculate patients against smallpox. This forced doctors to import the product from Europe, increasing both the costs and timeliness of preventing and responding to smallpox outbreaks, which were then frequent.[63] Benjamin Waterhouse, a leading figure in the United States medical community, tapped into his connections in England to obtain vaccine matter and became the first physician to provide inoculation against smallpox in America.[64] Although Waterhouse's efforts were instrumental in promoting vaccination in the United States,[65] he took a less freely collaborative approach than Jenner's by trying to monetize his quasi-exclusive access in the United States to a crucial raw material. As the author and journalist Arthur Allen has put it:

> Waterhouse's first blunder would perhaps seem natural in today's patent-crazy biomedical community: he tried to extract generous terms for himself from physicians in exchange for sharing the material. In a September 1800 proposal sent to Dr. Lyman Spalding of Portsmouth, NH, Waterhouse demanded exclusive rights to supply the vaccine – plus a quarter of Spalding's fees.[66]

While Waterhouse's behavior was against the norm in the then-incipient field of vaccinology, it anticipated the proprietary parameters according to which vaccine

---

[60]   Riedel, "Edward Jenner," note 26.

[61]   Riedel, "Edward Jenner," note 26.

[62]   Riedel, "Edward Jenner," note 26.

[63]   Arthur Allen, *Vaccine: The Controversial Story of Medicine's Greatest Lifesaver* (W. W. Norton, 2007), 50.

[64]   E. Ashworth Underwood, "Edward Jenner, Benjamin Waterhouse, and the Introduction of Vaccination into the United States" (1949) 163 *NATURE* 823–28.

[65]   Robert H. Halsey, "How the President, Thomas Jefferson, and Doctor Benjamin Waterhouse Established Vaccination as a Public Health Procedure" (1936) 27 *American Journal of Public Health* 1183–84.

[66]   Allen, *Vaccine*, note 63.

R&D processes would later unfold. The royalty-based licensing framework that he proposed to Spalding is today understood as a corollary of our patent-intensive R&D culture: Anyone wishing to use technology developed by others and protected by patents has the option of either licensing it or working around it. As detailed later, these new dynamics have a significant impact on the cost of vaccine R&D, as well as on frameworks for equitable access to vaccines. In some cases, they drive purchasers of vaccines with limited economic means to acquire older types of vaccine technology – for instance, by foregoing a vaccine with an improved formulation and buying instead an older, off-patent vaccine against the same disease. In other cases, impoverished populations may lack access altogether to certain on-patent vaccines, if prices are set prohibitively high.

It would be almost seven decades from the time Jenner's inoculation methods were introduced in the United States to the emergence of the first vaccine farms – the direct ancestors of the modern pharmaceutical industry.[67] These farms began establishing themselves from the 1870s onward, soon after animal-based smallpox vaccines were introduced in the United States. This type of vaccine – which no longer required arm-to-arm vaccination – was successfully tested in Naples in 1840 and attracted attention at a medical congress held in Paris in 1860, quickly gaining favor over Jennerian vaccination practices. In 1870, a Boston-based physician, Henry Austin Martin, imported lab-grown virus from France and introduced this type of vaccine technology to the United States. Researchers think that "the vaccine stock from Dr. Martin was the one exclusively used in the United States for the following six years."[68]

The business model pioneered by these farms would later evolve into the modern corporate structure we now tend to associate with private-sector R&D, with whole companies or branches of large pharmaceutical companies dedicated to vaccine discovery, testing, and manufacturing. As seen in Chapter 2, this evolution took place against a progressively more stringent regulatory background, to which intellectual property frameworks were later added.

The expansion of intellectual property throughout the twentieth century does not squarely match the rise of the pharmaceutical and biopharmaceutical industries, but it coincides with many of the important landmark achievements in these areas – and, in some cases, intellectual property laws and court decisions have had significant influence over the types of health goods that have received the most R&D attention, as well as how these goods are made available to those who need them.

3.2.4 *The Rise of the Vaccine Patent Culture*

Segments of the episode of *See it Now* that aired on CBS on April 12, 1955 can be easily located today through an online search by including the words "could you

---

[67] Esparza, "Early Smallpox Vaccine Manufacturing," note 3.
[68] Esparza, "Early Smallpox Vaccine Manufacturing," note 3.

patent the sun?"[69] Several clips show snippets of journalist Edward R. Murrow interviewing Jonas Salk, the most well-known member of the research team that produced the first polio vaccine. At this point, as seen in Chapter 2, the vaccine had been tested in large-scale trials and produced highly effective results. It would contribute, in just over two decades, to the elimination of polio in the United States.

In this particular episode, Murrow asked the famed scientist "Who owns the patent on this vaccine?" Immortalized in black-and-white footage, Salk can be seen pondering the issue for an infinitesimal moment, and answering: "Well, the people, I would say. There is no patent." After a brief pause, the scientist switches gears and adds "Could you patent the sun?" with a smile that evolves into a quick laughter.

Much as public health might owe to the research conducted by the Salk team and the preceding research they relied on, Salk's remarks about the intellectual property of the first polio vaccine were not entirely accurate. He was correct that it is legally impossible to patent the sun, as it is something that was not created by man – a long tradition in patent law observed by courts and legislators around the world tells us that it is only possible to patent man-made inventions. The United States Supreme Court famously articulated this principle in a 1980 case, *Diamond v. Chakrabarty*, defining patentable subject matter as "anything under the sun that is made by man."[70] Vaccine technology, as opposed to natural phenomena and similarly unpatentable categories, was patentable at the time the polio vaccine was developed, and remains so as long as it meets the criteria of novelty, nonobviousness and utility codified in domestic patent laws around the world.

We may of course take Jonas Salk's words in metaphorical stride, which seems closer to the spirit in which they appear to have been spoken – engaging perhaps with the more philosophical question of whether patent rights, which are by definition exclusionary mechanisms, *should* be granted over health goods like vaccines. It is worth noting, nonetheless, that research performed by Jane Smith has shown that the patentability of Salk's polio vaccine was actually evaluated by a legal team.[71] The team concluded that, even though it made an important contribution to public health, the vaccine would in all likelihood fail to meet some of the requirements for a patent, given the fact that the Salk team relied on several products and methods that had been previously invented by others. For instance, building on groundbreaking contributions from Yale scientist Dorothy Horstmann on the pathogenesis of the

---

[69] "Could You Patent the Sun?" (January 30, 2013) *YouTube*, www.youtube.com/watch?v=erHXKP386Nk.

[70] *Diamond v. Chakrabarty*, 447 US 303 (1980).

[71] Jane Smith, *Patenting the Sun: Polio and the Salk Vaccine* (W. Morrow, 1990). See also Robert Cook-Deegan, "Patent and Penicillin" (June 22, 2006) *Mises Wire*, https://mises.org/wire/patent-and-penicillin.

polio virus, a team led by John Enders at the Children's Medical Center in Boston succeeded in growing poliovirus in a lab in 1949.[72] Salk would rely on this step a few years later in the development of the first polio vaccine. Having examined preexisting inventions in the areas related to the polio vaccine – the universe that in patent law is known as the "prior art" – the legal team advised that "there was nothing to patent." As physician and researcher Robert Cook-Deegan has pointed out, "(w)e will never know whether the National Foundation on Infantile Paralysis or the University of Pittsburgh [who supported the development of the vaccine] would have patented the vaccine if they could."[73]

The process of seeking a patent has since become ingrained in contemporary vaccine R&D models. The year in which the Salk polio vaccine came to market there were only four applications for patents covering vaccine technology.[74] The patenting landscape changed quickly from that point onward. Today, a situation like the one surrounding the first polio vaccine – the development of a groundbreaking vaccine for which all components are deemed unpatentable – is now exceedingly rare.[75] As seen later in the text, the first vaccines developed to prevent certain types of cervical cancers that were brought to market in the late 2000s were covered by more than eighty patents.[76]

In 2012, the World Intellectual Property Organization conducted a survey of vaccine-related patent applications.[77] The survey mapped filing activity from before the polio vaccine race through the early twenty-first century (Figure 3.2), showing that the number of worldwide applications covering vaccine technology began increasing in the mid-twentieth century, with noticeable increases from the 1960s onward and sharp surges in the 1990s.

The study was based on filing activity reported by fifty-seven countries. Through the 1930s and 1940s – the period leading up to discoveries in vaccinology that ultimately resulted in the development of several of the basic vaccines now routinely administered to children – patent applications for components of a vaccine were sporadic. Applications started increasing in the mid-1950s, with seven in 1956, nine in 1958, and seventeen in 1959. Applications remained in the low two-digits throughout the 1960s and up to the 1970s. The 1980s marked an explosion in patent applications, with 87 in 1981, 186 five years later, and 218 in 1989. The numbers grew steadily in the

---

[72] Allen, *Vaccine*, note 63, at 196–97; Heather A. Carleton, "Putting Together the Pieces of Polio: How Dorothy Horstmann Helped Solve the Puzzle" (2011) 84 *Yale Journal of Biology and Medicine* 83–85.

[73] Cook-Deegan, "Patent and Penicillin," note 71.

[74] World Intellectual Property Organization, "Patent Landscape Report on Vaccines for Selected Infectious Diseases" (2012), at 25. www.wipo.int/edocs/pubdocs/en/patents/946/wipo_pub_946_3.pdf.

[75] World Intellectual Property Organization, "Patent Landscape Report," note 74, at 740–44. See also generally David M. Oshinsky, *Polio: An American Story* (2006).

[76] Swathi Padmanabhan et al., "Intellectual Property, Technology Transfer and Developing Country Manufacture of Low-cost HPV vaccines – A Case Study of India" (2010) 28(7) *Nature Biotechnology* 671–78, at 671.

[77] World Intellectual Property Organization, "Patent Landscape Report," note 74.

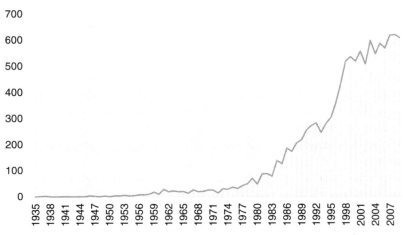

FIGURE 3.2 Number of worldwide first filings (1935–2009)[78]

1990s, breaking the 500 mark in 1998 and the 600 mark in 2007.[79] It should be noted that one limitation of this survey is that it uses incomplete data on applications taking place in the United States – historically the country issuing the largest number of vaccine-related patents per year – because the US Patent and Trademark Office did not adopt a policy of publishing patent applications until November 2000.[80]

While the number of patent applications does not tell us how many patents were actually granted, it illuminates the centrality of the race of modern vaccine R&D processes. But while this race-like format may be attractive to many well-funded private-sector companies that might not engage in vaccine R&D absent the possibility of patent protection, it also entails economic, social, and public health costs.

Patent applications might never mature into *granted* patents – in which case no exclusionary rights arise in connection with the underlying product or method. An application may be abandoned by the inventor, rejected by the patent examiner, or reexamined after it is granted and potentially found invalid. Additional empirical work is necessary to further explore the evolution of patent applications into actual patents across different types of vaccine technology. However, the survey performed by the World Intellectual Property Organization did provide valuable clues on at least one example – patents covering active ingredients in human influenza vaccines. The survey looked at patent

---

[78] Adapted from the data provided in World Intellectual Property Organization, "Patent Landscape Report," note 74.
[79] World Intellectual Property Organization, "Patent Landscape Report," note 74.
[80] US Patent & Trademark Office, "USPTO Will Begin Publishing Patent Applications" (November 27, 2020), www.legistorm.com/stormfeed/view_rss/219384/organization/32318.html.

families – clusters of patents covering similar vaccine technology – and found that there was a noticeable upward tick in the number of patents granted by patent offices around the world throughout the second half of the twentieth century and into the twenty-first (Figure 3.3).[81]

Shortly before the World Intellectual Property Organization's survey on vaccine patents was published, the WHO had conducted a study to assess how this patent landscape affected vaccines deemed "basic."[82] A wide array of vaccines makes up this group: the vaccines against diphtheria, tetanus, whooping cough, hepatitis B, haemophilus influenzae type B, polio, measles, mumps, rubella, and yellow fever. The survey found "no relevant intellectual property" covering these vaccines. This is because, from a technological perspective, these vaccines rely on components and manufacturing processes that have been in place for more than twenty years – the term of a patent, which means that any existing patents have expired.

However, the same study found that improved formulations and manufacturing processes for these vaccines were in some cases still covered by patents. For instance, this was the case with one vaccine against whooping cough, for which the British pharmaceutical companies GlaxoSmithKline and Medeva controlled the intellectual property over one of the components: pertactin, a type of protein that helps the bacterium causing whooping cough infect the tissue of a host. In this particular case,

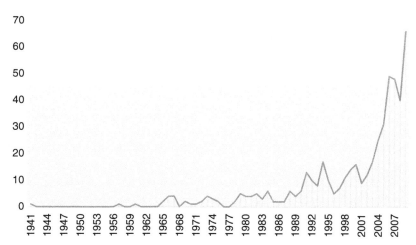

FIGURE 3.3 Granted patents covering active ingredients of human influenza vaccines[83]

---

[81] World Intellectual Property Organization, "Patent Landscape Report," note 74, at 112.

[82] Martin Friede, "Intellectual Property and License Management with Respect to Vaccines" (2010) *World Health Organization*, www.who.int/phi/news/Presentation15.pdf.

[83] Adapted from the data provided in World Intellectual Property Organization, "Patent Landscape Report," note 74, at 112.

the WHO noted that those seeking to make or buy vaccines against whooping cough but who could not afford licensing the relevant intellectual property or buying vaccine doses from GlaxoSmithKline and Medeva – such as countries or organizations with limited budgets – should look for "work-arounds" by buying whooping cough vaccines using older types of technology, or make vaccines without using the patented components. The WHO also recommended this approach at a broader level, advising that whenever a basic vaccine is protected by intellectual property rights R&D players had the option of "stick(ing) to 'old' formulation or develop(ing) work-arounds."[84]

While this work-around strategy has positive economic and practical effects by allowing for the development or acquisition of vaccines at lower costs, it poses trade-offs: on the one hand, it constrains the type of vaccine technology available to certain populations, likely those in more economically disadvantaged parts of the world; and on the other, as the WHO recognized in its study, the development of vaccines that work around patented technology nonetheless requires the commitment of R&D resources.[85] Relatedly, the WHO also noted that many lower-income countries lacked patent attorneys "with understanding of the science behind the technology" and "scientists with understanding of IP searching and interpreting."[86]

In higher-income countries, the average number of patents covering vaccine technology has also increased greatly since the polio vaccine race. For example, a study published in *Nature Biotechnology* by Swathi Padmanabhan and colleagues in 2010, shortly after the vaccines sold under the trade names *Gardasil* and *Cervarix* entered the United States market, found that there were eighty-one patents covering different components of these vaccines.[87] *Gardasil* and *Cervarix* are the first vaccines to target several strains of the human papillomavirus (HPV), which has been linked to numerous diseases, including several types of cancers. At US $300 at the time of the study, the full regimen for HPV vaccination was among the costliest for a vaccine product anywhere in the world.[88] This is not to say that the public health value of HPV prevention does not warrant incurring higher costs for the acquisition of the required health goods; rather, the point here is to underscore the market effects of patent protection, which is now the norm for most newly developed vaccines. Exclusionary rights enable market positions similar to those of a monopolistic price-setter, and as such health systems are likely to have to incur higher acquisition costs for vaccine technology that might be available at lower price points if vaccine development were not so dependent on patent-driven R&D models.

[84]   Friede, "Intellectual Property," note 83, at 5.
[85]   Friede, "Intellectual Property," note 83, at 5.
[86]   Friede, "Intellectual Property," note 83, at 16.
[87]   Padmanabhan et al., "Intellectual Property," note 76, at 671–78.
[88]   Padmanabhan et al., "Intellectual Property," note 76, at 671.

3.3 INTELLECTUAL PROPERTY AS INCENTIVES TO R&D: LIMITATIONS OF CURRENT MODELS

While the COVID-19 vaccine race will likely be remembered as one in which multiple companies and institutions rushed to develop a vaccine candidate – and while engagement of the private sector was critical to bringing the leading vaccine candidates to market – the reality is that there was a brief period early in the pandemic in which the R&D players with the resources needed to jumpstart vaccine development were initially less than enthusiastic to enter the field. In mid-February 2020, Dr. Anthony Fauci, the director of the US National Institute of Allergy and Infectious Diseases, publicly admitted to problems in attracting private-sector pharmaceutical companies to COVID-19 vaccine R&D, characterizing negotiations with these players as "very difficult and very frustrating."[89] Dr. Fauci added: "Companies that have the skill to be able to do it are not going to just sit around and have a warm facility, ready to go for when you need it."[90] However, as the magnitude of COVID-19 increased, dozens of pharmaceutical companies of varying sizes entered the vaccine race, alongside many other R&D players.

This moment of reluctance of the private sector to engage in vaccine R&D may register as infinitesimal in a public health crisis as prolonged as COVID-19. But it is a constant in vaccine R&D dynamics, with players capable of bringing vaccines through the R&D pipeline often choosing to allocate their resources elsewhere. Even though patent rights are available for qualifying vaccine technologies, and even though spikes in vaccine demand periodically occur, the vaccine R&D ecosystem as presently structured functions in a reactive mode – typically as a crisis is already underway – and not in a preparedness mode, which the patent system in theory would seem to support by providing incentives to innovation. The examples surveyed in this section showcase the distinct ways in which the logics of patent-based incentives have proved, time and again, a poor policy lever to nudge R&D players to bring vaccines to market.

3.3.1 *Insufficiencies of Market-Driven Incentives: R&D on Ebola Vaccines*

Consider the case of the Ebola vaccine candidate developed in the early 2000s in Canada. Ebola virus disease is highly infectious and potentially lethal. Scientists first identified Ebola viruses in 1976 during outbreaks in Zaire (now the Democratic Republic of the Congo) and Sudan.[91] The Zaire outbreak, near the river Ebola, after which the disease was then named, was caused by a species of the virus that became

---

[89] Nicholas Florko, "Major Drug Makers Haven't Stepped Up to Manufacture NIH Coronavirus Vaccine, Top US Health Official Says" (February 11, 2020) *Stat*, www.statnews.com/2020/02/11/major-drug-makers-havent-stepped-up-to-manufacture-coronavirus-vaccine-top-u-s-health-official-says/.

[90] Florko, "Major Drug Makers," note 89.

[91] Centers for Disease Control & Prevention, "History of Ebola Virus Disease (EVD) Outbreaks," (2021), www.cdc.gov/vhf/ebola/outbreaks/history/chronology.html.

known as *Zaire ebolavirus* and caused 318 reported cases and 280 reported deaths, for an overall 88 percent fatality rate. The outbreak in Sudan, triggered by a different species of the virus (*Sudan ebolavirus*), led to 284 reported cases and 151 reported deaths, for a fatality rate of 53 percent.[92] Since then, a total of six different species of Ebolavirus have been identified.[93] Four are known to cause disease in humans and, apart from a period of no known activity throughout most of the 1980s, they have caused recurring outbreaks with fatality rates ranging from 25 percent to 90 percent and an average fatality rate of 50 percent.

At the turn of the century, the most promising R&D on an Ebola vaccine was being performed by the Canadian public sector through scientists at the National Microbiology Laboratory, which integrates the Infectious Disease Prevention and Control Branch of the Public Health Agency of Canada.[94] In 2003, the Canadian government obtained a patent on this Ebola vaccine candidate.[95] R&D on the vaccine continued until 2005, both in Canada and in the United States, through animal tests conducted by the US Army's Medical Research Institute of Infectious Diseases. Preclinical data published in peer-reviewed journals suggested that the vaccine was "highly efficacious."[96] The results were also widely publicized through the popular press,[97] and scientists projected that the beginning of clinical trials would occur in 2008, with a tentative date for the licensure of the vaccine set for 2010–2011.[98]

Given the fact that there was no approved Ebola vaccine, and that this candidate was regarded as highly promising in scientific circles, principles of public health preparedness would dictate that starting clinical trials and bringing the vaccine to regulators for review should have been a priority. Yet, as journalist Denise Grady put it during the large Ebola outbreak that took place from late 2013 to 2016 and ultimately resulted in over 11,000 deaths in eleven countries,[99] the world's leading Ebola vaccine candidate "sat on a shelf" for nine years.[100]

As seen in Chapter 2, the engagement of the private sector is typically necessary to bring pharmaceutical R&D into the resource-intensive stages of clinical trials. In

[92]   Centers for Disease Control & Prevention, "History of Ebola," note 91.

[93]   Centers for Disease Control & Prevention, "What Is Ebola Virus Disease?," (2021), www.cdc.gov/vhf/ebola/about.html.

[94]   Stephen M. Jones et al., "Live Attenuated Recombinant Vaccine Protects Nonhuman Primates against Ebola and Marburg Viruses" (2005) 11 *Nature Medicine* 786–90.

[95]   Recombinant Vesicular Stomatitis Virus Vaccines for Viral Hemorrhagic Fevers, Canada Patent No. WO 2004/011488 A2 (filed July 28, 2003).

[96]   Jones et al., "Live Attenuated Recombinant Vaccine," note 94.

[97]   Richard Knox, "Scientists Race to Find Vaccine for Ebola, Marburg" (June 6, 2005) *NPR*, www.npr.org/templates/story/story.php?storyId=4681932.

[98]   Denise Grady, "Ebola Vaccine, Ready for Test, Sat on the Shelf" (October 23, 2014) *New York Times*, www.nytimes.com/2014/10/24/health/without-lucrative-market-potential-ebola-vaccine-was-shelved-for-years.html.

[99]   US Centers for Disease Control and Prevention, "2014–2016 Ebola Outbreak in West Africa,"(2019), www.cdc.gov/vhf/ebola/history/2014-2016-outbreak/index.html.

[100]   Grady, "Ebola Vaccine," note 98.

spite of the promise shown by the Canadian Ebola vaccine candidate, private-sector companies had no interest in this particular line of R&D.[101] By 2011, public-sector scientists were still making the case that, in light of its efficacy profile, the Ebola vaccine candidate developed in Canada was "ready to be considered for investigational drug licensure."[102] That same year, the Canadian government finally found a private-sector player interested in licensing the vaccine: a small and virtually unknown American company based in Central Iowa, NewLink Genetics. At this point, six years had elapsed from the end of preclinical trials. NewLink was granted an exclusive license,[103] which effectively enabled it to become the sole manufacturer of this vaccine for the duration of the patent and any other legal protections surrounding the vaccine.

NewLink will feature prominently in another section of this chapter, which explains how intellectual property rights can be instrumentalized to monetize vaccine technology. But before turning to how patent rights were used after the onset of an epidemic altered demand for Ebola vaccines, it is important to note here that the licensure of the Ebola vaccine candidate did not solve the incentives problem that has historically characterized R&D in this area. By obtaining a license, NewLink gained the ability to use the relevant intellectual property to test and manufacture the vaccine. This particular license authorized the company to commercialize the vaccine, should it be approved by drug regulators, "for ... maximum commercial return" as a way to benefit "the Company and Canada." But instead of moving into the first stage of clinical trials after what was already a long period of R&D inaction, the vaccine was once again shelved.[104] For reasons never publicly disclosed – but likely related to projected limited revenue streams in the absence of an outbreak[105] – NewLink decided to maintain the vaccine candidate in its portfolio without developing it further.

A patent – and not merely the prospect of obtaining one – was therefore not sufficient an incentive for a relatively small private-sector player to perform R&D on a vaccine. As seen later, it would take another transfer of intellectual property rights, a major transnational Ebola outbreak, and several additional years for the vaccine to come to market.

3.3.2 *Insufficiencies at the Commercialization Stage: The Case of Lyme Disease Vaccines*

In some cases, eminently market-driven approaches to vaccine development – combined with reinvigorated problems of trust in vaccine technologies, which the

[101] Dan Lett, "Wanted: Manufacturer for Ebola and Marburg Vaccines" (2005) 173 *Canadian Medical Association Journal* 472; Grady, "Ebola Vaccine," note 98.
[102] Thomas W. Geisbert & Heinz Feldmann, "Recombinant Vesicular Stomatitis Virus-Based Vaccines against Ebola and Marburg Virus Infections" (2011) 204 *Journal of Infectious Diseases* S1075–S1081, 1079.
[103] Government of Canada, "Sole Licensing Agreement for Recombinant Vesicular Stomatitis Virus Vaccines for Viral Hemorrhagic Fevers," (2007), https://perma.cc/A7VJ-AA7U.
[104] Grady, "Ebola Vaccine," note 98.
[105] Francis A. Plummer & Steven M. Jones, "The Story of Canada's Ebola Vaccine" (October 30, 2017) 189(43) *Canadian Medical Association Journal* E1326–27.

book describes in Chapter 6 – may lead to situations in which there is a lack of commercialization of a vaccine that, unlike the case of the Ebola vaccine candidate, has been fully developed and has received approval from the relevant regulatory authorities. Consider now the case of the first vaccine developed to prevent Lyme disease.

Lyme disease is caused by several species of bacteria transmitted through the bite of ticks, small blood-sucking parasites.[106] Although it is now known to have affected humans for millennia, Lyme disease was not named until 1976, following reports of puzzling cases of what was initially presumed to be juvenile arthritis among several people in Lyme, Connecticut and surrounding areas.[107] Mild forms of Lyme disease may result in symptoms including skin rashes, fatigue, and fever. However, serious cases of the disease may result in cardiac, rheumatological, or neurologic problems.[108] And, unlike some diseases with markets primarily located in lower-income countries, Lyme disease is endemic to the United States, several European countries (in Northwest, Central, and Eastern Europe), and Asia.[109]

In the 1990s, SmithKline Beecham, a large pharmaceutical company that has since merged to form GlaxoSmithKline, developed a successful vaccine candidate against Lyme disease.[110] The FDA approved the vaccine in late 1998, at which point it entered the United States market under the name LYMERix.[111] The vaccine required two boosters, one at one month and the other after a year of administration of the first dose, raising some logistic and compliance issues, but it was shown to reduce cases of Lyme disease in adults by 80 percent.[112] A study conducted in 1999 found that administering the vaccine was cost-effective, saving an average of $4,466 per case of averted disease.[113] That same year, the Advisory Committee on Immunization Practices (ACIP) recommended the vaccine for individuals aged between fifteen and seventy years living in areas of the United States where Lyme disease is endemic.[114]

---

[106] US Centers for Disease Control and Prevention, "Lyme Disease: Transmission," (2020), www .cdc.gov/lyme/transmission/index.html.

[107] Andrea T. Borchers et al., "Lyme Disease: A Rigorous Review of Diagnostic Criteria and Treatment" (February 2015) 57 *Journal of Autoimmunity* 82–115.

[108] US Centers for Disease Control and Prevention, "Neurologic Lyme Disease," (2020), www.cdc.gov /lyme/treatment/NeurologicLyme.html; US Centers for Disease Control and Prevention, "Lyme Carditis," (2020), www.cdc.gov/lyme/treatment/lymecarditis.html.

[109] World Health Organization, "Lyme Borreliosis (Lyme Disease)," (2020), www.who.int/ith/diseases/ lyme/en/.

[110] L. E. Nigrovic & K. M. Thompson, "The Lyme Vaccine: A Cautionary Tale" (January 2007) 135(1) *Epidemiology & Infection* 1–8.

[111] Nigrovic & Thompson, "The Lyme Vaccine," note 110.

[112] Nigrovic & Thompson, "The Lyme Vaccine," note 110.

[113] Martin I. Meltzer et al., "The Cost Effectiveness of Vaccinating against Lyme Disease" (1999) 5 *Emerging Infectious Diseases* 321–28.

[114] Morbidity and Mortality Weekly Report, Recommendation Report: Recommendations for the Use of Lyme Disease Vaccine. Recommendations of the Advisory Committee on Immunization Practices (ACIP), (June 4 1999); 48(RR-7):1–17, 21–25.

In spite of the public health value of the vaccine, sales of LYMERix never soared. The vaccine faced "anti-vaccine sentiment and class action lawsuits, a complicated vaccine administration schedule, diminishing physician support for the vaccine, and low public demand for the vaccine."[115] By late 2001, it was selling 93,000 doses annually, with sales poised to further decline during the following year.[116] In February 2002 – less than four years after licensure – GlaxoSmithKline elected to stop manufacturing and selling the vaccine, indicating "poor market performance" as the main reason for its decision.[117]

At the same time, LYMERix was being developed and brought to market in the United States, another large pharmaceutical company, Pasteur Mérieux Connaught (now Sanofi Pasteur), developed its own Lyme vaccine candidate, ImuLyme.[118] Clinical trials for this vaccine candidate enrolled 10,305 volunteers from areas of the United States in which Lyme disease was endemic. Data showed that the efficacy rate of the vaccine was 68 percent after the administration of two doses, and that the number rose to 92 percent after the third and final dose was administered. In spite of these promising results, the company chose not to pursue regulatory approval of ImuLyme. While a contributing factor for this decision was related to undisclosed problems with some of the case reports generated in connection with phase 3 of the clinical trials, the decision was largely influenced by reasons tied to market and intellectual property considerations. First, the company deemed the market for Lyme disease vaccines "too small to make the vaccine profitable."[119] And second, there were concerns about components needed to make the vaccine that were likely covered by patents held by their competitor in this area (and the manufacturer of LYMERix) GlaxoSmithKline.[120]

The burden of Lyme disease has grown since these two companies made the choice, albeit for different reasons, not to commercialize a vaccine.[121] LYMERix illustrates how an R&D ecosystem structured around market demand may, in extremes cases, fail to supply the market even when there is a fully developed and approved vaccine. As physician Gregory Poland observed in connection with the withdrawal of LYMERix:

> This was the first time in the modern era that an FDA-licensed vaccine in the United States was withdrawn because of low public demand and class action

---

[115] Gregory A. Poland, "Vaccines against Lyme Disease: What Happened and What Lessons Can We Learn?" (2011) 52 *Clinical Infections Diseases* s253–58, https://academic.oup.com/cid/article/52/suppl_3/s253/444754.

[116] Poland, "Vaccines against Lyme Disease," note 115.

[117] Nigrovic & Thompson, "The Lyme Vaccine," note 110.

[118] Poland, "Vaccines against Lyme Disease," note 115.

[119] Poland, "Vaccines against Lyme Disease," note 115.

[120] Poland, "Vaccines against Lyme Disease," note 115.

[121] See US Centers for Disease Control and Prevention, "Lyme and Other Tickborne Diseases Increasing" (2019), www.cdc.gov/media/dpk/diseases-and-conditions/lyme-disease/index.html; Carnegie Mellon University "Lyme Disease Predicted to Rise in United States as Climate Warms" (November 1, 2018) *Science Daily*, www.sciencedaily.com/releases/2018/11/181101085246.htm.

lawsuits, despite the context of a high background rate of disease and a continuing, if not increasing, significant public health burden of morbidity (. . .) The consequence of this is that continuing significant morbidity and cost due to Lyme disease, both at the public health level and the individual level, continues to occur.[122]

But while LYMERix is not being commercialized, the patents that protect it remain in force. Even when intellectual property falls short of its role as an incentive to bring goods to market, it may still affect innovation elsewhere in the vaccine ecosystem. The exclusionary dimensions of a patent allow rightsholders to prevent competitors from coming to market altogether or, alternatively, subject the use of the patented technology to the payment of a royalty. In the case of ImuLyme, the cost of negotiating a license for the patented vaccine technology held by another firm, combined with the relative size of the market, acted as deterrents for late-stage development of another promising vaccine in an area of critical public health need.

3.3.3 *Instrumentalization of Intellectual Property in Tech Transfer: The Ebola Vaccine Race, Revisited*

As seen earlier in the chapter, spikes in funding for vaccine R&D triggered by infectious disease outbreaks are generally only available for short periods of time, corresponding to the height of concerns with the evolution of a pandemic or epidemic. Once the infection case count curve begins to bend downward – and considering that most public health crises are not of the magnitude of COVID-19 – funding for vaccine R&D quickly shrinks, sometimes to the point of nearly drying up. Given the restricted window of time available to R&D players to take advantage of these outbreak-induced funding spikes, it is desirable that any transfers of existing vaccine technology needed to enable or finalize research take place as quickly as possible.

Let us return to the case of the Ebola vaccine candidate developed and patented by the Canadian public sector, and then licensed to the small pharmaceutical company NewLink. Recall that NewLink licensed the intellectual property covering this vaccine candidate in 2011. At that point, this particular vaccine candidate was deemed one of the "most-promising strategies" in Ebola research.[123] In spite of this scientific promise, NewLink did not bring the vaccine into clinical trials or otherwise express interest in engaging with drug regulators and take steps to make the vaccine commercially available. Strikingly, the company's activity extended into the first months of the 2014 Ebola outbreak, even as the magnitude of this transnational public health crisis became apparent. The WHO declared the outbreak a Public Health Emergency in August. Even as multiple R&D partnerships entered the

---

[122]   Poland, "Vaccines against Lyme Disease," note 115.
[123]   Andrea Marzi et al., "Vesicular Stomatitis Virus-Based Ebola Vaccines with Improved Cross-Protective Efficacy" (2011) 204 *Journal of Infectious Diseases* s1066–74, at 1067.

Ebola vaccine race, NewLink did not move its vaccine candidate – at this point, a leading candidate in the Ebola vaccine race – into clinical trials. It quickly became clear that the company did not have the ability to test or manufacture the vaccine.[124] It also became clear that NewLink's endgame was to license the intellectual property covering the vaccine to a larger company. Facing increasing pressure from public health organizations and other institutional players, it finally did so in November – three months after the WHO declaration of a Public Health Emergency.[125]

The transfer of the relevant vaccine intellectual property from NewLink to a larger company – in this case, a large US pharmaceutical company, Merck – illustrates how patents can be instrumentalized in ways that no longer bear any connection with incentivizing productive R&D. NewLink had acquired the rights over the world's leading Ebola vaccine candidate from the Canadian public sector. Canadian research institutions, continuing work previously done by other scientists, were the players engaged in innovative R&D. NewLink acquired the rights over the resulting vaccine candidate in 2011 for US $205,000.[126] Having added nothing to the testing or development of this particular health good, the company then transferred the intellectual property to Merck for US $30 million in November 2014.[127] The transfer agreement further entitled NewLink to receive US $20 million at the beginning of clinical trials, as well as royalties from sales of the vaccine, should Merck obtain regulatory approval to commercialize it.

These transfers illustrate how intellectual property can be instrumentalized for monetization purposes, particularly against the backdrop of shifting market evaluations, such as those introduced by the onset of a large-scale public health crisis. This instrumentalization frustrates the patent bargain: No scientific or technical development occurred between licensure in 2011 and transfer of intellectual property in 2014. More importantly, in cases in which this instrumentalization occurs in connection with an underlying product that happens to be a health good, intellectual property can effectively be used in ways that are antithetical to the public health.

Moreover, from a legal perspective, licensure of patent-protected technology out of the public sector and into the private sector is subject to several requirements designed to further the public interest. These requirements include performing work on the patented invention. They applied in the case of the license governing the transfer of the intellectual property over the leading Ebola vaccine candidate from the Canadian public sector to NewLink.[128] Even though the licensing agreement included the obligation to submit and execute a business plan, there was no

---

[124] Amir Attaran & Jason W. Nickerson, "Is Canada Patent Deal Obstructing Ebola Vaccine Development?" (2014) 384 *Lancet* S61.

[125] Helen Braswell, "Canadian-Made Ebola Vaccine Gets Help from Merck" (November 24, 2014) *Toronto Star*.

[126] Lisa Schnirring, "NewLink, Merck Deal Boosts Prospects for Ebola Vaccine" (November 24, 2014) *Center for Infectious Disease Research and Policy*.

[127] Schnirring, "NewLink, Merck," note 126.

[128] Attaran & Nickerson, "Is Canada Patent Deal," note 124.

work on the vaccine until the intellectual property was transferred to Merck. Seventeen quarters went by between the start of the licensing agreement and the moment the vaccine finally entered clinical trials, now sponsored by a different company.[129]

Delays in the transfer of patented vaccine technology can have especially dire consequences during a public health crisis. The three months of inaction between the declaration of a Public Health Emergency and the transfer of intellectual property rights from NewLink to Merck might appear to be a relatively short period of time. However, inaction occurred precisely as both short-lived funding for Ebola vaccine R&D and Ebola infection rates were at their peak. The rights conferred under a branch of the law designed to promote innovation were thus used for rent-seeking purposes scarcely compatible with public health goals of bringing safe and effective vaccines to market as soon as possible.

3.3.4 *R&D Attrition: The Problem of Exclusive Licensing in the Zika Vaccine Race*

Another potential problem of intellectual property frameworks in the context of vaccine R&D is that they are sometimes implemented in ways that overly restrict the likelihood of multiple players entering the vaccine race. In cases like COVID-19, in which there is a plethora of competing vaccine R&D projects and a large number of players to populate the race, this may not be a concern. But most contemporary vaccine development does not take place as a global pandemic unfolds. If a vaccine R&D project led by a company fails or otherwise comes to a halt, the window of opportunity might have closed for another R&D player to enter the race.

Consider the case of the Zika vaccine race prompted by the 2015–2016 outbreak. As seen in the first section of this chapter, the US Army developed a leading vaccine candidate in record time, moving from R&D project design in January 2016 to clinical trials in November of the same year. In December 2016, the Army announced its intention to license the vaccine to a large French pharmaceutical company, Sanofi.[130] At this point, there were two known patent applications covering the vaccine, one for the "Zika virus vaccine and methods of production," and the other for the "Zika vaccine and methods of preparation."[131] The notice provided by the Army in the Federal Registry elucidated a few terms of the licensing agreement: The contract would grant Sanofi an "exclusive, royalty-bearing, revocable license" to the technology covered in the pending patent applications.

---

[129]   Attaran & Nickerson, "Is Canada Patent Deal," note 124.
[130]   "Intent to Grant an Exclusive License," note 26.
[131]   United States Provisional Patent Application 62/343, 315; United States Provisional Patent Application 62/370, 260.

Sanofi entered into a cooperative research and development agreement with the Walter Reed Army Institute of Research in July 2016.[132] While Walter Reed was able to conduct phase 1 clinical trials in partnership with the US National Institute of Allergy and Infectious Diseases (NIAID), Sanofi was brought in specifically to move the vaccine into the later stages of clinical trials and seek regulatory approval of the vaccine.[133] In September 2016, Sanofi received a US $43.2 million grant from the US Biomedical Advanced Research and Development Authority (BARDA) to pursue these goals. The grant provided a renewal option, which would give Sanofi an additional $130 million to support the manufacturing of vaccines for phase 2 testing.[134]

The US Patent Act allows federal agencies to grant exclusive licenses to their inventions under certain circumstances, all of which are designed to ultimately bring the product to market.[135] Section 209(a)(1) establishes that exclusive licenses can only be granted if exclusivity constitutes a "reasonable and necessary incentive" to secure the investment necessary to bring the invention to "practical application" or to "otherwise promote the utilization of the invention by the public." Section 209(a)(2) further conditions exclusive licenses to several other requirements, including a finding from the federal agency transferring the technology "that the public will be served by the granting of the license." Additional provisions require the potential licensee to commit to achieving practical application of the invention within a reasonable time frame, and that the exclusive license "will not tend to substantially lessen competition" or otherwise clash with antitrust law.[136]

Additionally, should a federal agency conclude that the grant of an exclusive license is appropriate to help bring the invention to market, the Patent Act establishes that the licensing agency must ensure that "the proposed scope of exclusivity is not greater than reasonably necessary to provide the incentive for bringing the invention to practical application."[137]

The Patent Act thus creates a technology transfer framework that limits the grant of exclusive licenses to cases in which exclusivity itself is necessary as a means to promote the public interest – namely, the interest of the public to have patent-protected inventions come to market. In the case of the Zika vaccine candidate developed by the Army, the public would potentially stand to benefit from the commercialization of a vaccine against a pathogen now known to pose much

---

[132] Sanofi Pasteur Press Release, "BARDA Grants $43.2 Million USD to Sanofi Pasteur for Zika" (September 26, 2016), www.news.sanofi.us/press-releases?item=137143.
[133] Sanofi Pasteur Press Release, "BARDA Grants," note 132.
[134] Knowledge Ecology International, "Timeline of US Army & Sanofi Zika Vaccine Collaboration," (2017), https://perma.cc/2U8U-8S33.
[135] 35 US Code § 209(a).
[136] 35 US Code § 209(a)(2)(3). § 209(a)(5) further governs cases in which there is a patent issued by a foreign patent office, in which case exclusivity must "enhance" the interests of the US government or of US-based industry.
[137] 35 US Code § 209(a)(2).

more severe problems to public and individual health than previously thought. This framework explicitly aligns the technology transfer of federally funded inventions with the incentives function of the patent system.

It is impossible to ascertain whether the intended licensure of the Zika vaccine candidate as announced in the Federal Registry in late 2016 configured a case in which exclusivity was necessary. This is primarily due to the fact that current practices surrounding the notice of intended licensure of federally funded inventions disclose very little information to the public.[138] As noted earlier, the notice provided by the Army only informed the public of the existence of two patent applications covering a vaccine candidate until then funded and developed by the US public sector and described the intended license with three attributes: "exclusive," "royalty-bearing" and "revocable." There was nothing atypical in this disclosure: No laws or regulations presently mandate that federal agencies provide a justification to the public of their reasons to license technology, not even when exclusive licenses are selected as the intended contractual framework for these transfers. I argued in an essay published in 2018 that, although not violative of any legal provisions, current notice practices are bound to translate into bad public policy.[139] Weak disclosure requirements enable negotiating strategies that may ultimately result in limited availability or unaffordability of much-needed health goods. By not prompting agencies to fully describe and justify the licensing profile of a transfer, the system creates opportunities for licenses to be granted in ways that may actually decrease prospects of commercialization of the technology, lead to affordability problems, or both. These problems are particularly acute in the case of exclusive licenses, as there will be no alternative R&D player or manufacturer readily available should any problems arise. The example of the Army Zika vaccine candidate illustrates these concerns, particularly when the justifications for exclusivity – a contractual option that the Patent Act clearly delineates as a second-best to nonexclusive licensure – remain undisclosed.

An issue that immediately arises when public-sector technology is licensed on an exclusive basis is that exclusivity may help prolong, rather than alleviate, the market failure that the public sector is trying to address. What if the only company licensed to use a technology somehow faces hurdles in testing and manufacturing, or changes its R&D priorities and decides to allocate resources elsewhere?

The Army gave notice that it would license a leading candidate to Sanofi to ensure late-stage development and manufacturing of the vaccine, and thus bolster the chances of bringing it to patients in need. In August 2017, in light of the dwindling effects of the Zika outbreak, BARDA – one of the federal funders of Zika-related R&D, which had already awarded Sanofi a US $43.2 million grant to work on the Army's Zika vaccine candidate – redirected resources from Zika R&D to Zika

---

[138]   35 US Code § 209(e).
[139]   Ana Santos Rutschman, "Vaccine Licensure in the Public Interest: Lessons from the Development of the US Army Zika Vaccine" (2018) 127 *Yale Law Journal Forum* 651–66.

surveillance.[140] This strategic reorganization meant that Sanofi would be unable to obtain further grant funding from BARDA. The company immediately decided to stop working on the Zika vaccine candidate.[141] At that point, the licensure of the vaccine had not been completed, and the company declined to pursue it further. Having taken an all-eggs-in-one-basket approach, the Army was left without the private-sector partner it needed, and R&D on this Zika vaccine candidate came to a halt. While in this particular case the transfer of vaccine technology was not completed, the potential drawbacks of exclusivity become apparent. In addition to raising concerns about the prices at which the vaccines will be commercialized – a topic explored in Chapter 4 – exclusivity may in some cases limit the R&D options left to an agency, should the exclusive partner stop work on the vaccine.

These concerns are especially heightened if vaccine R&D occurs in response to the availability of outbreak-spiked funding, as was the case of Zika vaccine R&D. In most cases, funding made available during the early or peak stages of the outbreak will wane quickly. Even though the 2015–2016 outbreak unveiled the link between Zika disease and major effects on public and individual health, by 2017 funding for Zika R&D had declined globally. A 2020 study published in the journal *Vaccine* described the situation as follows:

> A sustained source of support for the development of vaccines should be identified/maintained in the face of a waning epidemic. This has been a serious concern with ZIKV [Zika virus] vaccine development projects. When a sudden and significant outbreak of an epidemic occurs that threatens public health, emergency funding from governments becomes readily available, only to dry out later as the epidemic wanes, leaving the vaccine development projects incomplete.[142]

The same study also found that the remaining Zika vaccine R&D projects now face several hurdles, including a pervasive lack of R&D funding.[143] As of mid-2021, there is no approved Zika vaccine.

This is not to say that, in the context of the transfer of vaccine technology from the public to the private sector, exclusive agreements are always unwarranted. But they involve risk – and potential long-term costs to public health – that have remained underappreciated by federal agencies in the United States. At a minimum, granting exclusive licenses for the use of patented vaccine technology without evaluating the potential effects of exclusivity as mandated by the Patent Act practices constitutes bad innovation policy.

---

[140] Sanofi Pasteur Press Release, "Sanofi Statement on Zika Vaccine License" (September 1, 2017), www .news.sanofi.us/Sanofi-Statement-on-Zika-Vaccine-License.
[141] Sanofi Pasteur Press Release, "Sanofi Statement," note 140.
[142] Pattnaik et al., "Current Status of Zika Virus Vaccines," note 113.
[143] Pattnaik et al., "Current Status of Zika Virus Vaccines," note 113.

3.3.5 *Beyond Patents: Proprietary R&D through Secrecy*

As seen earlier, there are several components in a single vaccine that may qualify for patent protection, should they meet the requirements established in the domestic laws of the country or countries where a patent application is sought. These components include both physical elements (which are protectable through product patents) and methods (which are protectable through method patents). Product patents may, for instance, cover active ingredients like antigens (substances introduced in the human body in order to elicit a reaction from the immune system), inactive ingredients like adjuvants (substances that help enhance the body's immune response, such as oil-in-water emulsions), and stabilizers (substances that help maintain the potency of the vaccine, such as sugars), and the vaccine delivery mechanism.

In addition to patents, it is also possible – in fact, probable – that some components of vaccine development and production may escape disclosure through a patent application and be kept from competitors for potentially lengthy periods of time. Consider the case, for instance, of the existence of, and details about, an aspect of a process used in vaccine manufacturing that is not yet known at the time the patent application is filed. In other cases, a company or other entity may decide not to seek patent protection for a product or process that would in likelihood be deemed patentable for strategic reasons. Recall that, as biologics, vaccines are relatively complex technologies highly dependent on specific manufacturing practices. Precisely because vaccines and vaccine manufacturing cannot be easily reverse-engineered by competitors as is the case with conventional drugs, a company may forego the opportunity to obtain a patent as a way to avoid sharing some knowledge about the vaccine.

The type of knowledge that can be kept secret in vaccine manufacturing includes know-how and technical expertise held by the vaccine manufacturer. This knowledge can be transferred to others, but it is not readily apparent absent voluntary teaching from the original manufacturer. In some cases, this knowledge may be formally protected under a branch of law distinguishable from intellectual property, albeit closely related – trade secrecy.[144]

In the United States, the Uniform Trade Secrets Act defines trade secrets as follows:

> information, including a formula, pattern, compilation, program, device, method, technique, or process that: 1) derives independent economic value, actual or

---

[144] For the regulation of trade secrets in the United States, see generally Uniform Trade Secrets Act (amended 1985); US Patent & Trademark Office, "Trade Secret Policy," (2021), www.uspto.gov /ip-policy/trade-secret-policy. For the regulation of trade secrets in Europe, see generally Directive (EU) 2016/943 of the European Parliament and of the Council (June 8, 2016) on the protection of undisclosed know-how and business information (trade secrets) against their unlawful acquisition, use and disclosure, https://eur-lex.europa.eu/legal-content/EN/TXT/ PDF/?uri=CELEX:32016L0943&rid=4 (providing the legal framework for trade secrecy in the European Union). For the international legal framework, see TRIPS Agreement, article 39.

potential, from not being generally known to, and not being readily ascertainable by proper means by, other persons who can obtain economic value from its disclosure or use; and 2) is the subject of efforts that are reasonable under the circumstances to maintain its secrecy.[145]

Trade secrecy law operates in markedly different ways from the intellectual property system. Unlike patents, trade secrecy does not create a right to prevent competitors from entering the marketplace. It focuses instead on protecting the information that qualifies as a trade secret, preventing its illegitimate acquisition, use or spread. Moreover, and in sharp contrast with the twenty-year patent term, trade secrecy can last potentially forever – or at least for as long as the parties that benefit from it manage to keep it secret.

The contrast between the inner workings of trade secrecy and patents is often illustrated by alluding to the Coca Cola example. The recipe for making this popular drink was created in 1866 by pharmacist John Pemberton.[146] Pemberton later sold the recipe to Asa Chandler, who went on to promote and distribute the product widely while keeping the recipe secret. To this day, many have managed to approximate the recipe – take the case of Pepsi – but no one has successfully reverse-engineered the recipe and produced a perfect replica of Coca Cola. A patent would have protected Coca Cola from competition for a relatively short period of time; once the patent term expired, anyone could lawfully use the information disclosed in the patent application to produce the drink. Trade secrecy, on the other hand, has lasted for over a century with Coca Cola.

In the case of biologics, and vaccines in particular, the problem of replicating the reference product is complicated by the fact that there is not merely a choice between a patent and secrecy. A vaccine consists of an amalgamation of technologies. In the current patent-intensive culture, several components in this amalgamation are bound to be protected by patents – and some knowledge about the vaccine will be shared with the scientific community and competitors this way. At the same time, several other components, which intertwine with practical aspects of vaccine manufacturing, are bound to be kept secret for competitive reasons.

As discussed in Chapter 5, one proposal made during the COVID-19 pandemic to ameliorate the problem of global vaccine scarcity was a temporary waiver of patent rights. However, even if patent rights were not a factor during a vaccine race, the technological complexity of vaccines and vaccine manufacturing inevitably leads to a scenario in which enabling others to replicate a much-needed health good ultimately hinges on a voluntary collaboration from the original vaccine manufacturer. It is also important to note that, as of mid-2021, no patent waiver has ever been approved for the production of pharmaceutical products – and should one be

---

[145]   Uniform Trade Secrets Act (1985).
[146]   Coca Cola, "History" (2012), https://cocacolaunited.com/wp-content/uploads/2012/03/CLICK-HERE-FOR-HISTORY-OF-SAVANNAH-COCA-COLA1.pdf.

approved, it is likely to remain a seldom-used tool in the global political economy. Therefore, in virtually every single instance of vaccine production, enabling second-comers to replicate a vaccine will require both the sharing of explicit knowledge through the licensing of intellectual property proper *and* the transfer of secret knowledge such as informal know-how and trade secrets.

While operating in intrinsically different ways, both patents and secrecy contribute to the privatization of scientific knowledge and commodification of health goods. In this chapter, the book has explained how legal theory and practice have attempted to reconcile these phenomena with public interest goals: By pitting exclusionary rights as *necessary* tools to catalyze investment in areas of R&D that would otherwise fail to attract commercial interest. As seen throughout the chapter, this premise does not hold particularly well in the case of most vaccines against emerging pathogens, and it contributes to imposing severe burdens on public and individual health. The book now turns to further implications of the ingrained reliance of contemporary legal systems on innovation policies that accentuate exclusionary modes of R&D, moving the narrative from the development of vaccines (or lack thereof) to the moment in which vaccines do become available and enter the market.

4

Access to Vaccine Technology

A vaccine that overcomes scientific, funding, and R&D constraints and enters the market may still not become available to everybody who needs it. The public health goal of preventing or lessening disease through the administration of vaccines is not fulfilled at the point of market entrance. Rather, it requires that populations indicated for a particular vaccine are able to receive it. A separate dimension of investigating how well the vaccine innovation ecosystem functions is thus the problem of *access* to existing vaccines.

As seen in the previous chapters, a significant component of the issues encountered during the pre-market stages derives from subjecting vaccine development and production to legal and policy frameworks that were designed to reward market-driven players across all fields of science and technology. By treating vaccines in much the same ways in which they treat other commodities, pre-market dynamics of vaccine production are often at odds with public health goals. This chapter now shows how the laws, policies, and practices at play once vaccines enter the market largely perpetuate the same proprietary or otherwise exclusionary approaches that characterize the pre-market dynamics.

While enormous strides have occurred from the mid-twentieth century onward – particularly with regard to the availability of childhood vaccines in both the Global North and the Global South – significant gaps in vaccine access continue to persist. The chapter examines two different types of recurring hurdles in this area. First, it focuses on situations in which vaccine supply is plentiful but market entrants have the ability to set prices in ways that may effectively exclude lower-income populations from accessing an existing vaccine. And second, it considers situations in which vaccine supply is limited and the allocation of vaccines is skewed toward wealthier populations, thus compromising access to vaccines by populations in lower-income countries.

4.1 THE FLIPSIDE OF THE COIN: PROPRIETARY RIGHTS AND PRICING CONSIDERATIONS

Vaccine sponsors who obtain a green light from a drug regulator typically enter markets where competition is limited – or outright inexistent. As seen in Chapter 3, these sponsors control the intellectual property that surrounds a particular vaccine, with the consequence that others are not allowed to compete for the duration of patent protection, unless authorized by the patent holders. Whether entering the market alone, or allowing others to license its vaccine technology, the patent holder has the ability to influence the price at which a vaccine will be commercialized.

Property rights give patent holders a monopolist-like position in the market. That position enables them to set prices as high as the market will sustain – which may be, and often is, a different calculation from the one made by a player whose scope is to make the vaccine available to as many indicated people as possible. Proprietary frameworks once again subordinate the vaccine ecosystem to market-driven considerations that do not necessarily align with the public health imperative of broad access to vaccines.

Importantly, even though a rightsholder has the ability to set prices, there are forms of regulation extrinsic to intellectual property that can be deployed to nudge a vaccine manufacturer to commercialize a vaccine at affordable prices. Given the non-commodifiable value that public health attaches to vaccines, a government may intervene and set price controls. Yet, that is not always the case.

Early in the COVID-19 pandemic – when the potential toll and duration of the outbreak had not yet been fully grasped by many – the US Secretary of Health and Human Services was asked if COVID-19 vaccines would be priced affordably. The Secretary answered, "(W)e [the US government] can't control that price, because we need the private sector to invest. Price controls won't get us there."[1] Although not explicitly linked to intellectual property, the Secretary's answer directly echoes notions of the incentives function of the patent system. Without strong incentives, the answer implies, we may alienate collaboration from market-driven players in a future public health crisis. Nothing in the patent bargain suggests that society benefits from exempting rightsholders from price controls on patented goods, but current discourses on many critically needed health goods, including vaccines, often leave that aspect of the bargain underexplored.

At the time of writing of this book, the COVID-19 pandemic has not yet ended but there has not been an actual problem with the affordability of newly developed vaccines – although there were other types of vaccine access problems rooted in proprietary legal frameworks, as seen in the second half of the chapter. Consider, however, that COVID-19 has taken an abnormally high toll on public health, prompting markets and non-market players alike to respond in extraordinary ways. Most public health crises do not acquire pandemic proportions, and hopefully crises of the magnitude of COVID-19 will remain the exception rather than the rule. Accordingly, most public debates about vaccines do not generate the same type of traction in the public opinion and pressure on law- and policymakers as has COVID-19. As such, access to vaccines can be compromised by excessive pricing,

---

[1] Nicole Wetsman, "Health Secretary Alex Azar Won't Promise that a Coronavirus Vaccine Would be Affordable" (February 27, 2020) *Verge*, www.theverge.com/2020/2/27/21155879/alex-azar-coronavirus-vaccine-affordable-insurance.

as patent holders commercialize their vaccines with wealthy markets in mind and (some) governments fail to intervene in pricing debates. The following sections describe recent or ongoing situations in which access to newly developed vaccines may be limited by affordability problems.

4.1.1 *Uncertainty about Vaccine Affordability: The Zika Vaccine Race, Revisited*

Recall that the intended licensure of the Zika vaccine candidate developed by the US Army happened against a backdrop of limited information about the terms governing the transfer of vaccine technology from the Army to French pharmaceutical Sanofi. A licensing culture in which there is little disclosure of licensing terms – including those that may directly address pricing issues – can easily lead to contractual agreements that do little to curb the excessive overpricing of critically needed health goods.

During the attempted licensure of the Army's Zika vaccine candidate, several commentators made the case that the licensing agreement should contain a clause requiring Sanofi to sell the vaccine at affordable prices. For example, the nongovernmental organization Knowledge Ecology International asked that the Army "describe and provide any provisions" regulating the prices of the vaccine in the United States, as well as "affordable access in developing countries."[2] In response, the Army answered that "[t]he US Army lacks the means, expertise, and authority to define, implement, and enforce 'affordable prices' or to set price controls for a potential vaccine that will require great investment and face high risk of failure."[3]

The Army's position appears to indicate that great emphasis was placed on incentives-related aspects of vaccine R&D: The public sector's lack of resources to see the vaccine through the later stages of R&D and the consequent need for a private-sector partner willing to take the scientific and financial risks associated with bringing the vaccine to market. However, as seen earlier, the Patent Act does not direct funding agencies to base their licensing decisions solely on the need for a commercial partner. Rather, it directs them to balance that need against the need to choose the appropriate means to further the public interest while designing the licensing agreement. An exclusive license, such as the one the Army intended to grant Sanofi, cannot constitute the default response to R&D and market needs. It is only appropriate *if* exclusivity is necessary to ultimately make the invention available to the public. The Patent Act prescribes that federally funded inventions be made available to the public "on reasonable

---

[2] Letter from James Love, Knowledge Ecology International, to Command Judge Advocate, US Army Medical Research and Materiel Command (December 21, 2016).

[3] Letter from Barry M. Datloff, Chief, US Army Medical Research and Materiel Command, to James Love, Knowledge Ecology International (April 21, 2017).

terms."[4] Allowing for the licensure of a vaccine without imposing any sort of contractual requirements with regard to pricing seems ill-advised – the more so in situations in which the licensee will become the sole source of the good. The Army's lack of involvement in pricing negotiations – if nothing else at a minimal level through the inclusion of an affordability clause in the license – enables economic behaviors aimed at maximizing profit. The licensing framework for the Zika vaccine candidate shows how legal instruments can be used in ways that accentuate the commodification of vaccines, failing to account for their public health value and the specific characteristics that render vaccines a poor fit for market-driven bargaining.

This posture of the public sector on pricing issues related to vaccines is not unique to the case of Zika, as evidenced by the position of the US government on the possibility of regulating the price of COVID-19 vaccines. While it is true that the private sector has played and will likely continue to play a crucial role in vaccine R&D, it does not immediately follow that incentive-driven considerations should be the *only* driving forces of vaccine R&D policy. At a systemic level, a disproportionate emphasis on incentives to the private sector risks hindering the public interest in having access to vaccines at affordable prices. The troubling element in recent interactions between the public and private sectors in the United States has been the lack of consideration given to the impact of adopted licensing frameworks on the availability and affordability of newly developed vaccines – and which, in the case of exclusive licenses, the Patent Act demands.

Even when alluding to the need to provide incentives to attract private-sector interest to late-stage vaccine R&D, representatives of the public sector in the United States are often silent on monetary incentives offered before the licensure stages. In the case of the Army's Zika vaccine candidate, recall that Sanofi had already received public-sector funding in order to perform R&D on the vaccine. Such a grant (US $43.2 million) had at least mitigated some of the financial risk associated with committing time and resources to this particular R&D project. Federal funding had thus supported a significant amount of work on this vaccine candidate, first through R&D performed directly by the Army, and then through the grant made to a partner in the private sector. In addition to this monetary type of incentive, Sanofi also stood to benefit from a license that would put it in sole control of the intellectual property generated by work partly performed by the Army – subject to the payment of royalties, but unrestricted in terms of the prices the company could charge for the vaccine. Yet, these factors were not taken into account when the Army decided to pursue exclusive licensure of vaccine technology without subjecting its commercialization to any kind of reasonable or affordable pricing principles. Similarly, during COVID-19, the vaccine candidate usually credited solely by Moderna but which was actually developed by the company through a collaboration with United States public-sector

---

[4]   35 USC § 201(f).

scientists, received US $483 million from BARDA in April 2020, followed by US $472 in July of the same year.[5] The incentives narrative must therefore be refined to account for these multiple incentive entry points into the R&D process. Recent licensing practices in the United States public sector fail to do so.

In the case of this particular vaccine candidate, the price point at which a Zika vaccine will be commercialized – if fully developed and approved – is not yet known. As noted earlier, R&D on Zika vaccines has remained globally underfunded since the 2015–2016 Zika outbreak began waning. The way in which the US public sector has shied away from pricing negotiations when it transfers vaccine technology to the private sector raises questions about the affordability of vaccines developed outside the context of a global pandemic, where inordinate demand for vaccines and public pressure drive vaccine commercialization under exceptional circumstances. Vaccine licensure practices have thus opened the door to scenarios in which vaccines may become commercially available and yet prices may be set at levels that not everybody who needs a vaccine may be able to meet. The following case, revisiting commercially available vaccines, shows how this problem acquires even more troubling contours with regard to populations in lower-income countries.

4.1.2 *Vaccine Unaffordability and the Global South/North Divide: The Case of HPV Vaccines*

In Chapter 3, the book referenced vaccines against certain strains of the human papillomavirus (HPV) in the context of the proliferation of patents covering multiple technological components of a vaccine.[6] There, as here, the book was agnostic on the price at which these vaccines are commercialized in the United States (US $300), as the scope of the book is to probe the legal and policy frameworks that enable certain market behaviors, encompassing excessive pricing – rather than provide a case-by-case evaluation of specific vaccine pricing points, a task it leaves to commentators with the requisite analytical tools for such a determination. But the book does pause to consider how the market position of patent holders based in higher-income countries may affect access to newly developed vaccines by populations in lower-income countries. As a caveat, the pathogens targeted by HPV vaccines are distinguishable from the ones causing the emerging infectious diseases surveyed so far. This section uses the example of these vaccines strictly to illustrate the interplay between markets in lower- and higher-income countries – and how the fact that HPV vaccines are commercially

[5]   Judy Stone, "The People's Vaccine – Moderna's Coronavirus Vaccine Was Largely Funded by Taxpayer Dollars" (December 3, 2020) *Forbes*, www.forbes.com/sites/judystone/2020/12/03/the-peoples-vaccine-modernas-coronavirus-vaccine-was-largely-funded-by-taxpayer-dollars/?sh=26c7d7476303.

[6]   Padmanabhan et al., "Intellectual Property," note 76.

available does not automatically translate into indicated populations being able to access these vaccines.

A study published in *Nature Biotechnology* has shown that, while commercialized in the United States for US $300, HPV vaccines have been acquired through private markets in several lower-income countries for even higher prices, in excess of US $500.[7] These prices make the vaccines unaffordable to many of the indicated populations in the Global South.

Compounding this problem is the fact that, for more recently developed vaccines covered by a plethora of patents, as is the case of the HPV vaccines *Gardasil* and *Cervarix*, there might not be an effective work-around method available to researchers wishing to develop lower-cost versions of the original vaccine. Unlike some of the basic vaccines developed in earlier periods, these vaccines were developed as high-tech products from the beginning, with little room for incremental low-cost innovation.

These combined features – high prices and difficulties in work-around strategies – have consequences to public health that are both detrimental and paradoxical. One type of cancer targeted by *Gardasil* and *Cervarix*, cervical cancer, is among the leading causes of female cancer mortality and it disproportionately affects women in lower-income countries, where screening services are not widely available. At the time of the *Nature Biotechnology* study, around 80 percent of deaths associated with cervical cancer occurred precisely in these impoverished parts of the world.[8] The vaccines available to populations in higher-income countries – albeit at a high cost for the respective health systems – have been shown to be effective in preventing approximately 70 percent of HPV-related disease.[9] Yet, they were and remain unavailable to most women in the places where the disease burden is the greatest.

Vaccine commercialization may thus lead to limited public health gains if the populations that need a vaccine the most experience a de facto lack of access. In the case of HPV vaccines, these limitations are tied to pricing considerations. In the scenarios surveyed in the following section, access is constrained by a different set of market – and legal – forces.

4.2 EQUITY IN TRANSNATIONAL ALLOCATION OF VACCINES

Producing and distributing vaccines according to proprietary paradigms is anchored on laws, policies – and worldviews – that artificially draw lines across market players. These lines signify ownership of vaccine technology and enable rightsholders to exclude others from using their products. The consequences of this line of demarcation are similarly artificial when considered from the perspective of allocating the resulting health goods, as the exclusionary powers enshrined in a patent or a contract licensing vaccine technology allow a manufacturer to provide vaccines according to

---

[7] Padmanabhan et al., "Intellectual Property," note 76, at 671.
[8] Padmanabhan et al., "Intellectual Property," note 76, at 671.
[9] Padmanabhan et al., "Intellectual Property," note 76, at 671.

principles that do not mirror public health needs. Pathogens spread across physical, sovereign, and market lines. By contrast, players with unrestricted allocative power may choose to allocate vaccines precisely within these artificial lines, even if they do not coincide with the locales that public health approaches would prioritize.

The COVID-19 pandemic provided a somber illustration of this problem, which acquires dire contours in situations of severe product scarcity. The allocation of limited doses of vaccines to certain markets in higher-income countries has become known as "vaccine nationalism," which the book proceeds to describe.

4.2.1 *The Problem of "Vaccine Nationalism"*

As seen in Chapter 3, large-scale public health crises may temporarily eliminate the incentives problem for vaccines targeting the pathogen at the root of an outbreak. As different groups of players rush to develop a vaccine, some research projects quickly distance themselves from the pack, by showing greater promise, moving more rapidly into clinical trials, or both. In the recent history of vaccine races, leading candidates have appeared within a few months from the beginning of the outbreak.

When the response to a particular public health crisis unfolds globally or quasi-globally, the identification of leading vaccine candidates may in turn trigger a parallel race to secure the earliest possible access to the first batches of emerging vaccines. Although dependent on the outcomes of vaccine development and manufacturing efforts, this secondary race seeks to affect the distributive stages of a vaccine race. Because newly developed vaccines – particularly if targeting an emerging pathogen – will at first be in short supply, players with the ability to guarantee access to first batches of vaccine will move quickly to do so through the use of advance purchase agreements.

Typically, this allocative game is played through bilateral channels, featuring a country or international actor on the demand side, and a pharmaceutical company or other type of vaccine manufacturer on the supply side. The legal tool that allows a party to reserve early access to emerging vaccines is a set of contractual mechanisms enabling the purchase of a certain number of vaccine doses even before they have been made commercially available, manufactured, or even fully developed.[10] Knowing which vaccine candidates are leading the R&D race and thus more likely to enter the market first enables affluent purchasers to place orders with one or more vaccine suppliers ahead of purchasers with lesser economic and bargaining power.

Orders placed early in the vaccine race normally condition the (future) purchase of vaccines to regulatory approval by the relevant drug regulation agencies. Once a vaccine is approved or authorized for use in a particular country or geographical area, the obligation to buy the preestablished amount of vaccine becomes effective. Because negotiations for this purchase have already taken place, negotiating delays

[10] See Ana Santos Rutschman, "The Reemergence of Vaccine Nationalism" (July 3, 2020) *Georgetown Journal of International Affairs Online*. https://gjia.georgetown.edu/2020/07/03/the-reemergence-of-vaccine-nationalism/.

at this point are virtually eliminated. Logistic details can be worked out in advance and vaccine suppliers can transfer vaccine doses to purchasers as quickly as their infrastructure permits.

From the perspective of the purchaser, there is some degree of risk associated with the placement of advance orders. Picking the wrong candidate – for instance, by pre-committing resources to a vaccine that fails to gain market approval – can set back a country's response to an outbreak as the first batches of vaccines available through other suppliers are allocated elsewhere. The wealthiest purchasers can nonetheless offset this risk by placing orders for multiple leading vaccine candidates. Moreover, evidence from recent vaccine races suggests that countries engaging in advance purchase of in-development vaccines make accurate predictions about leading candidates – something made less arduous because the number of players in the field in also relatively limited.

Importantly, these agreements also improve the position of vaccine suppliers. Faced with the many unknowns surrounding outbreaks of infectious diseases – duration, impact, pathogen mutation – a pharmaceutical company may hesitate to enter a vaccine race or take a cautious business approach and plan to commit a relatively limited set of resources to R&D on an emerging pathogen. Advance orders create a market early on in the vaccine race for this otherwise risky R&D endeavor. As long as the vaccine is approved or authorized for commercialization, companies have minimum demand for their product that they can count on, even if the circumstances of the outbreak begin to change.

Advance orders thus split the risk – even if unevenly – between different players in the vaccine ecosystem, performing a signaling function in terms of market demand and greatly reducing bargaining processes at the moment of vaccine allocation. As such, they are becoming an emerging tool for the creation of a better global system for vaccine development, stockpiling and allocation, which the book explores in Chapter 5. For the time being, however, their primary use during large-scale public health crises has taken place at the bilateral level, with higher-income countries negotiating directly with private-sector companies, and often reserving the bulk of initial batches of newly developed vaccines.

4.2.2 *Vaccine Nationalism in the 2009 Swine Flu Pandemic*

In the two most recent pandemics – COVID-19 and the swine flu in 2009 – wealthier countries resorted to the advance purchase model to place orders with suppliers of all the leading vaccine candidates, reserving either the totality of projected initial doses of vaccines or the ability to purchase additional doses of vaccines ahead of first-time buyers who had not placed advance orders.[11] This type of country-driven

---

[11] David P. Fidler, "Negotiating Equitable Access to Influenza Vaccines: Global Health Diplomacy and the Controversies Surrounding Avian Influenza H5N1 and Pandemic Influenza H1N1" (May 4, 2010) *PLOS Medicine*, https://journals.plos.org/plosmedicine/article?id=10.1371/journal.pmed.1000247

strategy, which skews the allocation of a public health good needed transnationally, is now commonly described as "vaccine nationalism."

In 2009, a novel influenza A (H1N1) virus first detected during spring in North America spread quickly around the world,[12] prompting the WHO to declare a pandemic in June, when seventy-four countries and territories had reported cases of infection.[13] This became known as the swine flu pandemic – the second known pandemic linked to the H1N1 influenza virus, following the 1918 Spanish flu pandemic – and it lasted until August 2010, affecting over 200 countries and territories or communities and causing 18,449 officially reported deaths worldwide.[14] Several estimates suggest that unreported deaths were considerably higher. The US Centers for Disease Control and Prevention, for instance, have calculated that the global death toll in the first year of the pandemic may have been at least 151,700 people and possibly as high as 575,400.[15]

A race to develop a vaccine targeting this new strain of the H1N1 virus began even before the WHO declaration of a pandemic. By May 2009, several high-income countries had placed advance orders to such an extent that all the vaccine supply that could reasonably be expected to be made available under existing manufacturing conditions had been effectively allocated to a restricted number of developed countries.[16] This strategy illustrates how the use of bilateral contracts can lead to extremely disproportionate imbalances in the global allocation of vaccines. The United States alone entered into agreements with four vaccine suppliers, reserving the ability to buy at least 600 million doses of emerging H1N1 vaccines.[17] At that point in time, the global vaccine manufacturing capacity during a pandemic was deemed to be somewhere between one and two billion vaccine doses.[18] Should actual capacity hold closer to lower-end projections, the United States would therefore have reserved more than half of the initial supply of vaccines. It was also confirmed that several other high-income countries had also placed advance vaccine orders by May 2009, although the total number of reserved vaccine doses was

[12] US Centers for Disease Control and Prevention, "2009 H1N1 Pandemic (H1N1pdm09 virus)," www .cdc.gov/flu/pandemic-resources/2009-h1n1-pandemic.html; US Centers for Disease Control and Prevention, "Outbreak of Swine-Origin Influenza A (H1N1) Virus Infection – Mexico, March– April 2009," www.cdc.gov/mmwr/preview/mmwrhtml/mm58d0430a2.htm.

[13] US Centers for Disease Control and Prevention, "WHO Pandemic Declaration," www.cdc.gov /h1n1flu/who/; World Health Organization, "What Is the Pandemic (H1N1) 2009 Virus?," www .who.int/csr/disease/swineflu/frequently_asked_questions/about_disease/en/.

[14] World Health Organization, "Pandemic (H1N1) 2009 – Update 112" (August 6, 2010), www.who.int /csr/don/2010_08_06/en/.

[15] US Centers for Disease Control and Prevention, "2009 H1N1 Pandemic," note 12.

[16] Jeanne Whalen, "Rich Nations Lock in Flu Vaccine as Poor Ones Fret" (May 16, 2009) *Wall Street Journal*, www.wsj.com/articles/SB124243015022925551.

[17] David Brown, "Most of Any Vaccine for New Flu Strain Could Be Claimed by Rich Nations' Preexisting Contracts" (May 7, 2009) *Washington Post*, www.washingtonpost.com/wp-dyn/content/ article/2009/05/06/AR2009050603760.html.

[18] Brown, "Most of Any Vaccine," note 17.

not disclosed.[19] Lower-income countries rightly worried at the time that their response to the pandemic would be hindered by a de facto unavailability of vaccines to their populations. The Pan American Health Organization (PAHO) characterized these approaches to vaccine allocation as a "restriction to equitable access" to vaccines at the global level, with particularly burdensome effects on developing countries seeking to respond to the pandemic.[20]

Unlike the COVID-19 pandemic, the global vaccine manufacturing infrastructure was not fully put to an extreme test during the swine flu pandemic. Initially feared to turn into a prolonged event of catastrophic consequences, the spread of the virus began decreasing in 2009. Interest in vaccines started to wane accordingly. After research indicated that a single dose of the vaccine would be enough to trigger protective immunity,[21] countries that had guaranteed early access to H1N1 vaccines announced they would donate part of their supply (around 10 percent) to lower-income countries.[22] These donations, which were largely cast as evidence of goodwill on the part of the donating countries, do not lessen the fact that the global allocation of a public health good periodically needed can easily be captured by a limited number of wealthy players yielding nearly unfettered bargaining power in the geoeconomic chessboard. Moreover, reliance on a donation model – at least one as unstructured as this one – reinforces the position of dependency of lower-income countries vis-à-vis wealthier countries on matters of public health and by extension of economic and social policy.

4.2.3 *Vaccine Nationalism in the COVID-19 Pandemic*

Vaccine nationalism flared up once again during the COVID-19 vaccine race – although the pandemic also bred a rudimentary structure for the procurement and transnational allocation of pandemic vaccines, a public–private partnership called Covax, which the book analyzes in Chapter 5, suggesting that it should be formalized into a more permanent and robust organization.

Global vaccine manufacturing capacity increased between the H1N1 and the COVID-19 vaccine races. A study conducted in August 2020 estimated that the overall manufacturing capacity for COVID-19 vaccines between then and the end of 2021 would range from two to four billion doses.[23] Estimates from November 2020

---

[19]   Brown, "Most of Any Vaccine," note 17.
[20]   Brown, "Most of Any Vaccine," note 17.
[21]   US Centers for Disease Control and Prevention, "Vaccine against 2009 H1N1 Influenza Virus," www
       .cdc.gov/h1n1flu/vaccination/public/vaccination_qa_pub.htm.
[22]   Kaiser Health News, "Nine Countries Pledge H1N1 Vaccine Donations to Developing Countries"
       (September 18, 2009), www.kff.org/news-summary/nine-countries-pledge-h1n1-vaccine-donations-to-
       developing-countries/.
[23]   CEPI, "CEPI Survey Assesses Potential COVID-19 Vaccine Manufacturing Capacity" (August 5,
       2020), https://cepi.net/news_cepi/cepi-survey-assesses-potential-covid-19-vaccine-manufacturing-
       capacity/.

placed that number slightly higher, at over five billion vaccine doses, with additional capacity in localized low-income areas, including India.[24] While an improvement over previous benchmarks, these projections still left the global community facing the likelihood of vaccine scarcity once the first vaccine candidates were approved by regulatory authorities – especially because all the vaccines poised to gain the earliest regulatory approval required the administration of two doses per person.

Echoing what happened during the 2009 pandemic, high-income countries moved quickly to place advance orders of vaccines with suppliers working on leading candidates.[25] Months before the first COVID-19 vaccines were approved, thirty-two high-income countries had reserved more than half of the projected global supply of vaccines. This group included the European Union member-states and five other countries (Canada, the United States, the United Kingdom, Australia, and Japan). Even though the group appropriated the majority of vaccine supply, these countries accounted for just about 13 percent of the world's population.

Some of these countries reserved vaccine doses that far exceeded their likely needs even when factoring in the required two-dose regimen. The most prominent example was Canada, which preordered over eight doses per person.[26]

A study released by the Duke Global Health Institute in November 2020 – a few weeks before the United States and Europe began vaccinating their populations against COVID-19 – estimated that, given the limited vaccine supply and its skewed global allocation, most populations in low-income countries would have to wait until 2024.[27]

Vaccine suppliers took some steps to improve access to emerging vaccines in lower-income countries, which nonetheless left the lopsided allocative effects of nationalism largely unaddressed. For instance, AstraZeneca, a British pharmaceutical company developing a leading COVID-19 vaccine candidate, pledged to make the vaccine available at no-profit prices to low- and middle-income countries. While affordability of vaccines is critical for health systems and populations in these countries, it does not solve the problem of delayed access to vaccines as batches are first allocated to wealthier countries – a problem that precedes matters of affordability.

To be sure, nationalistic approaches operationalized through bilateral contractual mechanisms are not the only reason populations in lower-income countries are not able to access newly developed vaccines in a timely fashion during a pandemic. Even if a more globally equitable approach to vaccine distribution had been in place during the COVID-19 pandemic, there were severe shortages of vaccines during the

[24] Asher Mullard, "How COVID Vaccines Are Being Divvied up around the World" (November 30, 2020) *Nature*, www.nature.com/articles/d41586-020-03370-6.
[25] Mullard, "How COVID Vaccines Are Being Divided," note 24.
[26] Mullard, "How COVID Vaccines Are Being Divided," note 24.
[27] Duke Global Health Institute, "Will Low-Income Countries Be Left Behind When COVID-19 Vaccines Arrive?" (November 9, 2020), https://globalhealth.duke.edu/news/will-low-income-countries-be-left-behind-when-covid-19-vaccines-arrive.

months that followed the approval or authorization of the first vaccines. These shortages largely had to do with the gaps in the global infrastructure for manufacturing and distributing vaccines, which was not prepared to face the exponential increase in the demand for vaccines triggered by the spread of COVID-19.

Moreover, lower-income countries often face infrastructural problems that may further delay the distribution of vaccines – even when the global supply becomes less limited. In the case of the COVID-19 pandemic, the fact that one of the first vaccines to come to market required the maintenance of ultra-cold transportation and storage temperatures rendered its deployment in many geographical areas of the Global South virtually impossible.

In addition to the split between lower- and higher-income countries, the most disadvantaged communities in lower-income countries are also likely to be disproportionately affected by the redistributive effects of nationalism. As the first batches of COVID-19 vaccines were being administered to priority patients, refugees and internationally displaced people were among the groups that were most adversely affected by the combination of vaccine nationalism and shortages of vaccine doses. In January 2021, the International Rescue Committee pointed out that neglecting expeditious administration of the vaccine to people in conflict-afflicted areas and to people fleeing from conflict would likely result in additional spread of COVID-19.[28] This possibility unfolded on the heels of a series of historic increases in the number of refugees and displaced people. The United Nations High Commissioner for Refugees – the U.N. agency dedicated to refugees, forcibly displaced communities and stateless people[29] – has characterized the period between 2010 and 2019 as "a decade of displacement"[30] and calculated in 2020 that around 1 percent of the world's population is currently displaced.[31]

Finally, from a global perspective – the only one compatible with the spread of pandemic pathogens – predominantly country-based approaches to vaccine allocation may in the long run harm populations in the wealthiest countries that are able to guarantee early access to vaccines through advance orders. If largely detached from cooperative efforts at the international level to coordinate vaccine allocation, the prioritization of domestic public health strategies by individual countries may delay the end of the pandemic itself. This, in turn, temporally extends risks to global and national public health, the individual health of citizens of lower- and higher-income

---

[28] International Rescue Committee, "Billions Will Not Receive a COVID-19 Vaccine in 2021" (January 12, 2021), www.rescue.org/press-release/billions-will-not-receive-covid-19-vaccine-2021.

[29] United Nations High Commissioner for Refugees, "About Us," (2021), www.unhcr.org/en-us/about-us.html.

[30] United Nations High Commissioner for Refugees, "Global Trends: Forced Displacement in 2019," (2020), www.unhcr.org/globaltrends2019/.

[31] United Nations High Ccommissioner for Refugees USA, "1 Per Cent of Humanity Displaced: UNHCR Global Trends Report," (2020), www.unhcr.org/en-us/news/press/2020/6/5ee9db2e4/1-cent-humanity-displaced-unhcr-global-trends-report.html.

countries alike, national and regional economies impaired by the public health crises, international trade and the global economy, and the social fabric of populations around the globe.

While seemingly an extension of contemporary notions of sovereignty, vaccine nationalism clashes with the global public nature of health goods needed in the prevention of, and response to, pandemics and large-scale public health crises. When applied to vaccine allocation, predominantly nationalistic behaviors accentuate systemic inequalities between higher- and lower- income countries. It is likely counterproductive from a global public health perspective, as pandemic and epidemic diseases pose borderless challenges. And, ultimately, it may disadvantage some of the populations that higher-income countries were trying to protect in the first place.

5

Aligning Vaccine Innovation with Public Health Needs

So far, the book has explored different problems in the life cycle of a vaccine. First, it surveyed the pathways to bring new vaccines to market against a backdrop of weak incentives to R&D, in spite of the recognized public health value of vaccines and the widespread use of intellectual property rights as an incentive to vaccine R&D. Second, it examined the allocative disparities that result from the commodification of vaccines, especially in situations of product scarcity, in which lower-income populations often face considerable hurdles in obtaining access to vaccines. This section examines possible solutions to alleviate these problems. It considers proposals that would take effect at the incentives level, by increasing funding for vaccine-related R&D work; proposals that would operate at a transactional level, facilitating the transfer of vaccine technology through the use of patent pools and patent pledges; and proposals to expand and fine-tune the role of vaccine-dedicated public–private partnerships as instruments for the promotion of equitable access to vaccines by populations irrespective of their socioeconomic status.

5.1 ADDRESSING COMMODIFICATION PROBLEMS THROUGH NON-IP INCENTIVES FRAMEWORKS

There is a persistent misalignment between the legal regimes currently in place to incentivize costly and risky R&D and the public health for sustained and robust financial commitments to vaccine R&D. While the premier legal regime for promoting these goals is the patent system, there are other types of incentives worth considering.

These types of incentives are often called nonintellectual property (IP) incentives, and they have long attracted scholarly and, to a lesser extent, policy attention.[1] Many of these incentives embody efforts to promote selected types of R&D with less

---

[1] Amy Kapczynski, "The Cost of Price: Why and How to Get Beyond Intellectual Property Internalism" (2012) 59 *UCLA Law Review* 970–1026; Daniel J. Hemel & Lisa Larrimore Ouellette, "Beyond the Patents-Prizes Debate" (2013) 92 *Texas Law Review* 303.

reliance on market-driven considerations compared to those on which intellectual property is structured around.

To be sure, intellectual property and other types of R&D incentives are not mutually exclusive. For instance, in his influential analysis of the patent system, economist Fritz Machlup noted that "(p)roposals for systems of prizes and bonuses to inventors, as alternatives to patents, are almost as old as the patent system."[2] Yet, non-IP incentives have consistently remained marginal in the policy landscape when compared to intellectual property.

The following sections provide a cursory overview of how these incentives work, noting both their potential advantages and their inherent limitations under current economic models of production.

5.1.1 Ex Ante *Incentives to Vaccine R&D: The Case of Grants*

One of the most common forms of attracting R&D attention to a particular field of science or technology is through grants. Grants provide funding for work on a specific project or set of projects, often in areas of basic research traditionally overlooked in private-sector R&D agendas.[3]

Grant funding is especially important in the context of R&D in the life sciences. The US National Institutes of Health (NIH), an agency within the US Department of Health & Human Services, is the world's largest public-sector funder in this area. As of mid-2021, the NIH has spent over US $32 billion per year supporting biomedical R&D.[4]

In the case of vaccine R&D, public-sector grants have long played an important role in catalyzing research. In the United States, the National Institute of Allergy and Infectious Diseases (NIAID), which operates under the umbrella of the NIH, is especially active in this area. As of mid-2021, thirty-six of the 176 funding opportunities sponsored by the NIAID were for vaccine-related work.[5]

In an ecosystem in which market forces tend to drive much of the R&D activity, grants can be a useful tool to promote vaccine R&D, especially at the early-stage level. The awarding of a grant is based on scientific or technical promise of a project, rather than projected or potential market results. Nevertheless, studies about the role of grants in innovation policy often point out that the ex ante nature of grant funding is precisely the Achilles' heel of the grant system.[6] Unlike incentives mechanisms in which an award is made after some measurable result has been achieved, a grant may result in an R&D failure – even though research failures are valuable from

---

[2] Machlup, "An Economic Review," note 50, at 15.
[3] W. Nicholson Price II, "Grants" (2019) 34 *Berkeley Technology Law Journal* 1–89, at 5–6.
[4] US National Institutes of Health, "Grants & Funding" (2021), www.nih.gov/grants-funding.
[5] US National Institute of Allergy and Infectious Diseases, "Opportunities & Announcements" (2021), www.niaid.nih.gov/grants-contracts/opportunities?search=vaccine.
[6] See generally Price, "Grants," note 3, at 9–16.

a scientific perspective, contributing knowledge about R&D pathways that do not work or approaches that need refining.

By contrast, intellectual property is theoretically designed to reward some degree of innovative activity and does not reward R&D failures. As seen in Chapter 3, in order to attain patent protection, all domestic intellectual property laws require that an invention meet the cumulative criteria of novelty, inventiveness, and susceptibility of industrial application. In evaluating a patent application against these threshold requirements, examiners in patent offices around the world subject the invention to a "quality check," ensuring that no duplicative products or processes (and products or processes only trivially different from existing ones) are protected by a patent. And while sometimes patents are improperly issued, this quality check provides some degree of screening – although it is worth noting here that, as documented by economist Bhaven Sampat and political scientist Kenneth Shadlen, the aggressive patenting culture within the pharmaceutical industry has often resulted in the issuance of poor-quality patents.[7]

On balance, grants and patents operate in differentiated ways and cater to different segments of the R&D time line. Under current economic models, a robust system to incentivize vaccine R&D will likely rely on both, with grants playing an especially important role in the production of foundational knowledge. However, in light of the severe dearth of funding for R&D on vaccines against emerging pathogens – and given the particular issues that arise in vaccine intellectual property, as detailed in previous chapters – policymakers should consider strengthening the vaccine grant system. Doing so comes necessarily at a cost, implicating the commitment of financial and administrative resources, and tapping into polarizing political economy debates. But virtually any interventions to correct the current shortcomings in the vaccine R&D landscape are likely to entail these types of costs. Maintaining the status quo, on the other hand, will likely magnify costs to public health, in the form of lacking preparedness frameworks to prevent and respond to outbreaks of infectious diseases.

5.1.2 Ex Post *Incentives to Vaccine R&D: The Case of Prizes*

Concerns with ex ante allocation of funding resources, associated with the need to create incentives to late-stage R&D, have led several commentators to focus on sets of non-IP incentives that operate ex post, through the provision of a monetary or potentially monetizable reward once some measurable R&D is achieved.

One of the most discussed frameworks for incentivizing R&D using ex post mechanisms is through prizes. Prizes link the disbursement of funds (or the

---

[7]   Bhaven N. Sampat & Kenneth C. Shadlen, "Secondary Pharmaceutical Patenting: A Global Perspective" (2017) 46 *Research Policy* 693–707.

awarding of a nonmonetary reward) to successful completion of a task or challenge set out by the prize administrator and evaluated according to preestablished metrics. At the same time, proponents of the increased adoption of prize-based models note that, unlike the patent system, prizes enable policymakers to de-link the price at which a drug or vaccine is sold from the profits its manufacturer makes upon entering the market.[8] Patents artificially suppress competition, thereby allowing patent holders to charge supra-competitive prices. Under a prize model, innovators are compensated when they succeed in producing a drug or vaccine (or a component thereof), not if they succeed on the market. Monetization of R&D thus occurs through the prize, potentially associated with commercialization of the drug or vaccine at lower prices than under a patent-driven model. If only patent rights are at play, prices are bound to be higher, as they are the only tool available to innovators to recoup R&D costs and make a profit.

Economist Alberto Galasso and colleagues have theorized that, in general, prizes incentivize better innovation, whereas intellectual property, in its race-to-patent format, incentivizes speedy innovation.[9] Some commentators have argued that monetary prizes would be especially useful in the area of pharmaceutical R&D. For example, James Love and Tim Hubbard – the director of the nongovernmental organization Knowledge Ecology International and a professor of bioinformatics, respectively – have described several theoretical models for implementing "mega cash prizes" designed specifically for the development of drugs and vaccines.[10] In the most sweeping version of their proposal, a prize system would replace patent rights in these areas – a solution that, as seen in Chapter 3, would likely implicate major changes to both domestic and international intellectual property frameworks, as well as to the business model the pharmaceutical industry has long operated by.

Prizes have also been proposed at smaller scales. For instance, early in the COVID-19 pandemic, legal scholars Daniel Hemel and Lisa Larrimore Ouellette suggested that a tailored prize could assuage then-growing concerns that COVID-19 vaccines would be priced unaffordably. They suggested the implementation of a "large cash prize for any firm that develops a successful coronavirus vaccine. The prize would be payable only on the condition that the firm makes the vaccine available to patients at low or zero cost."[11] Similarly early in the pandemic, business scholar Chris Callahan proposed the establishment of a large prize – in the realm of "many billions of pounds" – for the expedited

---

[8]   James Love, "De-Linking R&D Costs from Product Prices" (April 6, 2011), www.who.int/phi/news/phi_cewg_1stmeet_10_KEI_submission_en.pdf.
[9]   Alberto Galasso et al., "A Theory of Grand Innovation Prizes" (2018) 47(2) *Research Policy* 343–62.
[10] James Love & Tim Hubbard, "Prizes for Innovation of New Medicines and Vaccines" (2009) 18 *Annals of Health Law* 155–86, 156.
[11] Daniel Hemel & Lisa Larrimore Ouellette, "Want a Coronavirus Vaccine, Fast? Here's a Solution" (March 4, 2020) *Time*, https://time.com/5795013/coronavirus-vaccine-prize-challenge/.

development of COVID-19 vaccines.[12] The prize would be funded through contributions solicited and administered by the WHO or the United Nations.

While prizes might offer some comparative advantages, they are not without drawbacks. Even though prizes are awarded ex post, the framework for the reward is set before commercialization, which limits the information available to price-setters about market demand for the goods in question. A government, or other prize-setter, may thus undervalue or overvalue a prize, or otherwise tailor it inadequately to the goal it seeks to achieve. Moreover, as with grants, greater reliance on prizes to incentivize R&D would entail increasing prize budgets in ways never before seen in the contemporary economy, as well as expanding the administrative apparatus that supports their administration.

Even if confined to the area of vaccine R&D, expanding the footprint of prize funding constitutes a monumental endeavor. Within the spectrum of non-IP incentives, the grant system has long absorbed more funding and policy preferences. While prizes remain an option for policymakers to consider, they are better understood as complementary to other incentives rather than as substitutes.

5.1.3 *Industry-Specific Incentives Available to Vaccine R&D: The Case of Regulatory Exclusivities and Insurance*

Scholars of innovation policy have progressively identified certain types of incentives available to R&D players working specifically in the pharmaceutical arena. Albeit with some variation, patents, grants, and prizes are available to both pharmaceutical and non-pharmaceutical innovation. Pharmaceutical products, including vaccines, may also qualify for additional incentives, often in nonmonetary forms, that are not available to other types of technologies.

One particular set of such incentives consists in *regulatory exclusivities*, also known as "data" or "market" exclusivities.[13] Legal scholar Yaniv Heled has defined these exclusivities as "competitive advantages resulting from statutory bars on regulatory action where such action is otherwise mandated and would have taken place but for the triggering of the bar."[14] If a regulatory exclusivity applies, the law precludes a drug regulator from reviewing or approving applications to bring competing products to market for a certain period of time. In practice, this means that the sponsor of a vaccine that might succeed in gaining regulatory approval on the merits of its product may nonetheless have to wait out an artificially imposed period of time in which no one competing with the reference product is allowed to come to market.

---

[12]   Chris Callaghan, "Would a Longitude Prize Speed Production of a COVID-19 Vaccine?" (March 28, 2020) *World University Rankings*, www.timeshighereducation.com/blog/would-longitude-prize-speed -production-covid-19-vaccine.
[13]   Yaniv Heled, "Regulatory Competitive Shelters" (2015) 76 *Ohio State Law Journal* 299–356.
[14]   Heled, "Regulatory Competitive Shelters," note 13, at 305.

These exclusivities are not rooted in intellectual property rights, and operate independently from patents. However, in deliberately restricting competition between drug and vaccine manufacturers, they have effects that are similar to the ones triggered by the application of intellectual property rules: Even without a patent, or while having one, an R&D player can get another legal entitlement to operate on the market without competition. The justification for creating yet another layer of rights that results in delays to the commercialization of health goods has long been anchored in discourses about incentives to R&D. Because pharmaceutical R&D is seen as particularly risky and costly, policymakers have responded to requests to increase incentives specific to pharmaceutical R&D, and one way in which they have done so has been through the creation of this additional layer of exclusionary rights. Hence, in some cases, drug regulators in several countries, including the United States and European jurisdictions, are barred from reviewing or approving drug and vaccine applications for certain periods of time – for reasons completely extraneous to the purposes of drug regulation, and instead formally rooted in innovation policy.

Regulatory exclusivities arise when the sponsor of a drug or vaccine obtains approval to commercialize a product that is the first to enter the market in its category. There is a broad range of qualifying products. To give but a few examples, if a sponsor obtains regulatory approval for a new chemical compound, a product that is the first to treat an orphan disease or a new biologic product, a regulatory exclusivity applies. The time during which a drug regulator is subject to the bar varies according to the type of product, and also from country to country. For example, in the case of biologics – the category vaccines belong to – the corresponding regulatory exclusivity is set for a period of twelve years in the United States, while in Canada it is set at eight years.

A vaccine sponsor thus benefits from an additional system of incentives that is specific to pharmaceutical technology – and which, at a given point in time, may be hard to reconcile with the public health need for the robust supply of health goods under competitive conditions, which tend to lower price points for consumers. Heled, who has argued that these exclusivities function as de facto "regulatory competitive shelters," has emphasized the duplicative nature of exclusivities in their mirroring of the artificial market scarcity already created by the patent system.[15]

Regulatory exclusivities are not the only policy levers that afford vaccines and other pharmaceutical products forms of legal protection not available to other types of innovation. Recent work by legal scholar Rachel Sachs has highlighted the fact that *insurance* mechanisms can be viewed as a form of incentive for R&D players to bring products to market:

> Prescription drug insurance may be broadly understood as a "pull" mechanism of the type articulated by economists in the global health literature. It is a reward

---

[15]   Heled, "Regulatory Competitive Shelters," note 13. See also Yaniv Heled, "Patents v. Statutory Exclusivities in Biological Pharmaceuticals – Do We Really Need Both" (2012) 18 *Michigan Telecommunications & Technology Law Review* 419–79.

provided ex post, after the development of a successful technology. And although patients may be charged small amounts for any given prescription, drugs are paid for in large part not by the users of the technology, but by a much broader segment of the population (...) Like most other consumer goods, the size of the reward a pharmaceutical company receives will largely be determined by how their drug performs in the market, primarily measured in this case by the amount of times it is prescribed and the price of each prescription.[16]

Sachs' work has explained how Medicaid reimbursement, or prospect thereof, should be regarded as yet another incentive for R&D players to invest in certain types of pharmaceutical R&D, and work by legal scholars Mark Lemley, Lisa Larrimore Ouellette, and Sachs has further explored this mechanism in the context of Medicare.[17]

In the United States, the Affordable Care Act (ACA) mandates insurance coverage for vaccines recommended by the Centers for Disease Control and Prevention's Advisory Committee on Immunization Practices (ACIP), which translates into most patients with private insurance not having to incur cost-sharing expenses when receiving routine vaccines.[18] During the COVID-19 pandemic, Congress passed the Coronavirus Aid, Relief, and Economic Security (CARES) Act, which added to the ACA framework by mandating similar coverage of COVID-19 vaccines.[19] Insurers were required to cover ACIP-recommended COVID-19 vaccines fifteen days after a favorable recommendation was made.

For some types of vaccines, insertion into insurance schemes can thus function as another ex post incentive, as it removes some of the financial hurdles in vaccine access that a person indicated for a vaccine might otherwise have to bear. By making vaccines available to patients who do not have to incur an ad hoc payment that could otherwise dissuade them from seeking administration of the vaccine, insurance helps maintain a market for covered vaccines. Admittedly, this type of incentive may remain a relatively marginal policy lever in the case of vaccine markets, but it nonetheless adds to the roster of features that contribute to lessen the economic risk traditionally associated with engaging in vaccine R&D. Moreover, in the case of vaccines developed in response to an emerging pathogen, legislative action may be required to implement insurance coverage, as was the case in the United States during the COVID-19 pandemic.

[16]   Rachel Sachs, "Prizing Insurance: Prescription Drug Insurance as Innovation Incentive" (2016) 30 *Harvard Journal of Law & Technology* 153–208.

[17]   Mark A. Lemley et al., "The Medicare Innovation Subsidy" (2020) 95 *New York University Law Review* 75–129.

[18]   US Department of Health and Human Services, "Where and How to Get Vaccines," (2021), www .hhs.gov/ash/oah/adolescent-development/physical-health-and-nutrition/vaccines/where-and-how-to-get-vaccines/index.html.

[19]   Public Law No: 116–136 (March 27, 2020). Coronavirus Aid, Relief, and Economic Security Act or the CARES Act.

5.1.4 *Limitations of Non-IP Incentives*

This brief incursion into the landscape of non-IP incentives shows that intellectual property is far from being the sole instrument in the modern innovation policy tool kit. But while the book has repeatedly underscored the insufficiencies of our collective over-reliance on intellectual property – and adjacent legal frameworks anchored primarily on market-driven models of vaccine development and allocation – it is important to note that increasing the footprint of non-IP incentives alone is a hard task and one that is unlikely to solve the overall problem of funding scarcity for vaccine R&D.

First, non-IP incentives need to be understood in their relative dimension. Incentives offered through the models surveyed earlier – or complementary modes such as philanthropy or R&D tax credits – pale when compared to the amount needed for vaccine R&D. To date, existing non-IP incentives, and especially those providing direct funding such as grants and prizes, have been used sparingly. Recall the R&D Blueprint released by the WHO in 2016, reporting a "lack of R&D preparedness" affecting vaccines needed to combat emerging pathogens.[20] The Blueprint provided a holistic overview of lacking R&D pipelines – one in which IP and non-IP incentives alike were failing. As such, while policymakers should consider which non-IP incentives are worth bolstering in the vaccine R&D space, under current economic models these incentives are better understood as complementary rather than substitutive of other means of funding vaccine development.

Second, calling for greater use of non-IP incentives – and in particular those resulting in direct monetary awards – necessarily implicates finding the budgetary room for this increase. As seen in Chapter 2, public-sector funding for scientific and technical R&D has been shrinking over the past decades. This does not mean that these types of incentives cannot play an important role in vaccine innovation policy, but any proposals must at a minimum incorporate a pathway for sourcing these funds, a formidable task.

Third, not all non-IP incentives are created equal. Under circumstances of enriched funding streams, greater use of prizes and grants may be desirable from a policy perspective *and* consistent with public health goals of populating vaccine R&D pipelines. By contrast, continued expansion of other types of non-IP incentives may be at odds with the adoption of innovation policies designed to further public health goals. Analytical work done by Heled and several other scholars suggests that regulatory exclusivities disproportionately exacerbate exclusionary and anti-competitive market dynamics without increasing actual incentives to R&D in discernible ways.[21]

Lastly, creating more incentives to vaccine R&D in non-patent forms does not automatically exclude the application of intellectual property rules or market-driven

---

[20] World Health Organization, "R&D Blueprint," note 8.
[21] Heled, "Regulatory Competitive Shelters," note 13, and "Patents v. Statutory Exclusivities," note 15.

approaches to vaccine innovation. Deploying one or more of the incentives surveyed earlier means that an innovation lever other than intellectual property is being used, but tells us nothing about concomitant applications of intellectual property. Adopting a policy of bolstering grants or prizes for vaccine R&D, for example, presumably results in more funding being available for vaccine-related work. But if the contractual frameworks governing the awarding of grants or prizes allow for the unbridled propertization of that R&D, the same problems identified throughout the book are still likely to emerge. For instance, a grant recipient may still price the resulting R&D product unaffordably, unless prevented from doing so – either by the contract that governs the grant or by extrinsic motivations. An approach to vaccine innovation policy in alignment with public health needs would thus dictate that increasing non-IP incentives be linked to requirements that further the goal of increasing access to vaccines – in all its components, from equitable allocation to affordability – once a vaccine enters the market.

5.2 COLLABORATIVE SOLUTIONS WITHIN INTELLECTUAL PROPERTY REGIMES: PATENT POOLS

A completely different set of tools that can help mitigate some of the drawbacks of overly market-driven modes of vaccine development and production is available within intellectual property itself. This section introduces the first of two legal structures aimed at facilitating the sharing of patent-protected technologies: patent pools. It begins by describing their general characteristics, advantages, and limitations; it then examines the experience of a patent pool created for the cross-licensure of technology during the COVID-19 pandemic; and it concludes by proposing the creation of a permanent vaccine-dedicated patent pool.

5.2.1 *Patent Pools in Context*

As seen in Chapter 3, the existence of multiple layers of proprietary rights covering different components of a vaccine may pose challenges at the transactional level. An R&D player willing and able to develop or manufacture a vaccine may not have all the relevant patents in its portfolio. Negotiating the transfer of the relevant vaccine technology often entails overcoming some degree of initial uncertainty about the potential licensure of patented components; a period of time- and resource-consuming negotiations between licensor and licensee; and other transaction costs, including royalties associated with the use of the patented technology. If these negotiations unfold during a pressing public health crisis, they also face the same type of compressed timelines under which pandemic and epidemic vaccine R&D occurs. At a time when funding streams are typically at their highest, the transfer of vaccine technology should ideally happen under conditions that minimize uncertainty, negotiating delays and transaction costs – and, in extreme cases, delays attributable to rent-seeking behavior as was the case with NewLink during the Ebola vaccine race.

A possible way of mitigating some of these hurdles to timely collaborations during the onset of a public health crisis is through the formation of patent pools. These pools can also be used outside the context of pandemics and epidemics, to jumpstart or maintain a relatively unencumbered licensing framework for technology needed among parties working on similar or complementary R&D areas.

Patent pools are contractual mechanisms that allow multiple patent holders to license their intellectual property to one another, as well as to parties outside the pool.[22] Patent holders with interests in similar or complementary areas of technology may decide to pool a subset of their patents as a way to gain access to a wider variety of patented technologies while potentially monetizing their own intellectual property, within a system that condenses bargaining processes and reduces both uncertainty and transaction costs. The pool is formed through a contract (or series of contracts) establishing the terms of licensure of predetermined patents belonging to the pool members. Each patent in the pool becomes available for others to use, provided that they comply with the licensing agreement, which typically requires the payment of a fee.[23]

Patent pools can be useful to remove or lessen different types of transactional hurdles, particularly in complex areas of technology. There are several efficiency arguments in favor of pooling intellectual property.[24] First, pools perform an important signaling function by removing uncertainty as to the status of a product or method, as well as the rightsholder's willingness to license it. In turn, this indirectly reduces the probability of litigation arising with regard to pooled patents. Moreover, pools eliminate the need for individualized negotiations. The contractual structure in place provides access to multiple patents – as many as a licensee may deem of interest within the pool. Rightsholders rely on that same contractual structure to market their technology and create an avenue to receive compensation for uses thereof. Collectively, these features help reduce bargaining and transaction costs. A licensee must have the economic means to pay the licensing fee, but the other

---

[22] World Intellectual Property Organization, "Patent Pools and Antitrust – A Comparative Analysis" (2014), www.wipo.int/export/sites/www/ip-competition/en/studies/patent_pools_report.pdf, at 3.

[23] See generally Jorge L. Contreras, "Intellectual Property Pools and Aggregation," in *Intellectual Property Licensing and Transactions: Theory and Practice*, Jorge L. Contreras, eds. (Cambridge University Press, forthcoming 2022); Robert P. Merges, "Institutions for Intellectual Property Transactions: The Case of Patent Pools," in *Expanding the Boundaries of Intellectual Property, Innovation Policy for the Knowledge Society*, Rochelle Cooper Dreyfuss et al., eds. (Oxford University Press, 2001).

[24] World Intellectual Property Organization, "Patent Pools and Antitrust," note 22, at 9 (describing the pro-competitive effects of patent pools).

constraints and costs normally associated with using patented technologies disappear or are significantly reduced.

Patent pools can be especially useful in areas in which R&D tends to occur in siloed models, as they create a pathway that facilitates the licensure of complementary or blocking patents. If different firms hold relevant patents necessary to produce a single vaccine, R&D is largely contingent on cooperation between parties who operate on a daily basis as competitors in pharmaceutical markets. Under a pool model covering the relevant patents, vaccine development is no longer contingent on the firms' willingness to cooperate – nor the delays caused by time and cost associated with intellectual property negotiations. Legal scholar Daniel Crane once described this function of patent pools as "a form of intra-industry social contract permitting the emergence from this Hobbesian war of each against all."[25]

Finally, the literature on patent pools also notes that the sheer availability of technology under certain and a simplified contractual frameworks is expected to lead to follow-on innovation that results in the public ultimately benefiting from the offering of better or more varied products, or both.[26]

Patent pools have been in use since the mid-nineteenth century, with the first known case in the United States involving patents covering sewing machine technology.[27] Since then they have been documented across different technological sectors, including, more recently, health-related technologies[28] – the most well-known example being that of the Medicines Patent Pool, which was founded in 2010 and has since negotiated licenses for the commercialization of drugs needed for the treatment of HIV/AIDS, hepatitis C, and tuberculosis drugs needed in lower-income countries.[29] In March 2020, the Medicines Patent Pool announced that it would also be temporarily active in the negotiation of COVID-19 drugs.[30] At the time of writing, negotiations were ongoing for a license covering molnupiravir, an antiviral that was entering phase 3 clinical trials as a potential treatment for COVID-19.

---

[25]   Daniel A. Crane, "Patent Pools, RAND Commitments, and the Problematics of Price Discrimination," in *Working within the Boundaries of Intellectual Property: Innovation Policy for the Knowledge Society*, Rochelle C. Dreyfuss et al., eds. (Oxford University Press, 2010).
[26]   See e.g. Erik Hovenkamp & Herbert Hovenkamp, "Patent Pools and Related Technology Sharing," in *Cambridge Handbook of Antitrust, Intellectual Property, and High Tech*, Roger D. Blair & D. Daniel Sokol, eds. (Cambridge University Press, 2017).
[27]   Adam Mossoff, "The Rise and Fall of the First American Patent Thicket: The Sewing Machine War of the 1850s" (2011) 53 *Arizona Law Review* 165–211.
[28]   See generally Esteban Burrone, "Patent Pooling in Public Health," in *The Cambridge Handbook on Public–Private Partnerships, Intellectual Property Governance, and Sustainable Development*, Margaret Chon et al., eds. (Cambridge University Press, 2018).
[29]   Medicines Patent Pool, "About Us," (2021), https://medicinespatentpool.org.
[30]   Medicines Patent Pool, "Disease Areas," (2021), https://medicinespatentpool.org/what-we-do/disease-areas#pills-COVID-19.

5.2.2 *Limitations of Patent Pools: The Case of the COVID-19 Technology Access Pool*

In March 2020, Costa Rica submitted a proposal to the WHO for the formation of a COVID-19 patent pool. The proposal was designed to cover a wide array of technologies:

> This pool, which will involve voluntary assignments, should include existing and future rights in patented inventions and designs, as well rights in regulatory test data, know-how, cell lines, copyrights and blueprints for manufacturing diagnostic tests, devices, drugs, or vaccines. It should provide for free access or licensing on reasonable and affordable terms, in every member country.[31]

One reason that Costa Rica specifically invoked a proposal for a pandemic pool was due to the concern with the affordability of emerging drugs and vaccines, particularly with regard to populations in less affluent countries.[32] The WHO echoed these concerns, noting that the "COVID-19 pandemic has revealed the fallibility of traditional ways of working when it comes to equitable access to essential health technologies," and framing the patent pool as a mechanism that "sets out an alternative, in line with WHO's efforts to promote global public health goods, based on equity, strong science, open collaboration and global solidarity."[33]

The proposal resulted in the swift creation of the COVID-19 Technology Access Pool (C-TAP), which was launched in May 2020.[34] In addition to Costa Rica, forty countries joined the pool as sponsors. While C-TAP has been hailed as a groundbreaking achievement, it nonetheless failed to attract the commitment of any technology in the months after it was launched – a situation that stretched into 2021, with the pool remaining unpopulated at the time of writing.[35] Public health advocate Ellen 't Hoen has labeled this utter lack of pooling activity as "the elephant in the room" in conversations across the international community about collaborative responses to the pandemic.[36]

---

[31] Letter from Costa Rica to the WHO, Knowledge Ecology International (March 23, 2020), www .keionline.org/wp-content/uploads/President-MoH-Costa-Rica-Dr-Tedros-WHO24March2020.pdf.

[32] Ed Silverman, "WHO is Asked to Create a Voluntary Intellectual Property Pool to Develop COVID-19 Products" (March 24, 2020) *Stat*, www.statnews.com/pharmalot/2020/03/24/covid19-coronavirus-costa-rica-intellectual-property/.

[33] World Health Organization, "Solidarity Call to Action: Making the Response to COVID-19 a Public Common Good," (2021), www.who.int/initiatives/covid-19-technology-access-pool/solidarity-call-to-action.

[34] World Health Organization, "COVID-19 Technology Access Pool,"(2021), www.who.int/emergen cies/diseases/novel-coronavirus-2019/global-research-on-novel-coronavirus-2019- ncov/covid-19-technology-access-pool.

[35] Michael Safi, "WHO Platform for Pharmaceutical Firms Unused since Pandemic Began" (January 22, 2021) *Guardian*, www.theguardian.com/world/2021/jan/22/who-platform-for-pharmaceutical-firms-unused-since-pandemic-began.

[36] Ellen 't Hoen, "The Elephant in the Room at the WHO Executive Board" (January 22, 2021) *Medicines Law & Policy*, https://medicineslawandpolicy.org/2021/01/the-elephant-in-the-room-at-the-who-executive-board/.

The irresponsiveness of vaccine patent holders to C-TAP is hardly surprising, and it provides a window into some of the inherent limitations of collaborative models based on patent pooling. As was the case with C-TAP during COVID-19, patent pools have historically failed to attract inherently uncooperative players. In areas where innovation processes carry heightened risk and cost, firms with strong intellectual property portfolios are likely to privilege approaches that maximize the prospect of economic revenue through in-house development of technology, acquisition of smaller companies, or highly selective licensure of their technology. The voluntary nature of patent pools thus often translates into limitations in the quantity and heterogeneity of participants, pooled patents, and use made thereof.

In spite of these challenges, patent pools remain underexplored as a policy tool in the context of vaccine innovation policy. The chapter now turns to an illustration of how such pools can be structured, advocating for the creation of a patent pool tailored to vaccine technology.

5.2.3 *The Case for Vaccine Patent Pools*

Policymakers should consider the formation of a pool dedicated to vaccine technology needed for R&D on emerging infectious disease pathogens. While there are several drawbacks to the use of pooling mechanisms – and the experience with C-TAP does not appear auspicious in the case of pandemic or epidemic health goods – this section makes the case that a vaccine-dedicated patent pool would constitute a strategic addition to the vaccine innovation ecosystem.

In the space of public health-oriented patent pools, there are already several cases of disease-specific pools. The Medicines Patent Pool, as noted earlier, focuses on three diseases and temporarily expanded its mandate to cover COVID-19. Legal scholars Dianne Nicol and Jane Nielsen have documented the formation of a patent pool dedicated to technology targeting a specific disease (SARS) caused by an emerging pathogen (the coronavirus known as SARS-CoV).[37] Rather than focusing on a disease or set of diseases, the model proposed here would focus on a set of technology – vaccine technology.

Although tailored to technologies needed for pandemic and epidemic preparedness, the proposed pool would differ from the C-TAP model by creating a permanent pooling structure developed ahead of a specific public health crisis. In short, the pool would be designed according to a three-part formula: technology specificity, ex ante formation, and adoption of rules imposing equitable pricing and allocation obligations on participants in the pool.

---

[37]   Dianne Nicol & Jane Nielsen, "Opening the Dam: Patent Pools, Innovation and Access to Essential Medicines," in *Incentives for Global Public Health: Patent Law and Access to Essential Medicines*, Thomas Pogge, Matthew Rimmer, & Kim Rubenstein, eds. (Cambridge University Press, 2010), 232–62.

Technology specificity allows policymakers conceiving and negotiating a pool to pay attention to the idiosyncrasies of vaccines as health technologies produced primarily through market-driven models. One aspect that the book has sought to emphasize is the fact that, even though vaccines against emerging infectious diseases are not the only type of underfunded or inequitably allocated health technology, they share characteristics and face market dynamics that set them apart from other types of pharmaceutical products. As such, it is worth considering the adoption of policies and legal solutions catering to the specificities of vaccines, as well as vaccine markets, producers, and consumers – while this section focuses on patent pools, the following sections will adopt similarly vaccine-tailored approaches when making other policy and legal recommendations.

A vaccine-dedicated pool is nonetheless compatible with technological heterogeneity. As seen in Chapter 1, there are multiple types of commercially available vaccines and several other types are being researched and tested. The COVID-19 pandemic underscored the fact that it is possible to develop safe and effective vaccines targeting an emerging pathogen using radically different types of technology: some of the first vaccines to enter the market were based on mRNA technology (the Pfizer-BioNTech, and Moderna vaccines), while others were based on viral vector technology (the Johnson & Johnson and AstraZeneca vaccines). A vaccine-specific pool can capture patents relating to different technological approaches to vaccine R&D.

Conversely, it is important to recognize that, given the voluntary nature of commitments to a patent pool, holders of especially valuable or otherwise strategic intellectual property will be less likely to commit those segments of their patent portfolio. Consider the case of mRNA technology. COVID-19 accelerated the testing and commercialization of vaccines based on this type of technology, which is also being tested in a variety of non-vaccine applications, ranging from cancer immunotherapy to R&D on rare genetic diseases. A cutting-edge technology that can serve as an R&D platform for multiple purposes tends to be more valuable and strategically more important than older-type or single-purpose technologies. Holders of patents on platform technology in the vaccine space are therefore less likely to make those technologies available through a pool.

A vaccine-dedicated pool can and should thus be understood strategically, and designed with the deliberate goal of attracting some vaccine intellectual property, but not all types of vaccine technology. A means to achieving this goal is by linking certain incentives to the commitment of technology to the pool: policymakers may award a prize to entities contributing a patented component or process; or a portion of grants available for vaccine R&D can be linked to the obligation of making the resulting technology available through the vaccine-specific pool. Moreover, these incentives can be customized. For example, entrance prizes can be set higher for some vaccine components, reflecting either their functional value or their relative scarcity within the pool.

Unlike the approach adopted in the formation of C-TAP, a vaccine patent pool as proposed here would be less diffuse in scope. It would enable policymakers to target a smaller number of R&D players – including, potentially, less established players in the vaccine R&D space for whom the combination of institutional networking, the possibility of an entrance prize, and the prospect of royalties might be appealing.

In order to further strategic design, a vaccine pool should be negotiated outside the context of large public health crises. C-TAP was formed under quick-shifting public health, economic, and business conditions. By contrast, the model proposed here would be created ex ante, in the sense that it would not be designed in response to an ongoing event, but rather in furtherance of public health notions of preparedness. Given the knowledge that epidemic and pandemic outbreaks of emerging infectious diseases will continue to occur, the inevitability of future vaccine races is apparent. Reactive solutions are warranted as needed, but the vaccine ecosystem – and, more generally, the public health ecosystem – lack proactive intellectual property strategies. A vaccine patent pool would be one step toward the development of such strategies.

Keeping in line with the need for tailorable solutions, a vaccine patent pool could also be structured in a two-tier format. One tier would be open for the pooling of vaccine-related technology at any time, while the other would only become active in the event of a large-scale public health crisis. The "open tier" would essentially function as a regular patent pool. The "restricted tier" would consist of committed technology that would become available for licensure according to predetermined contractual frameworks at the beginning of a pandemic or epidemic. The trigger for the restricted tier to become active should be designated in advance and clearly identifiable: for example, a declaration of Public Health Emergency of International Concern by the WHO.

Finally, it is important to recognize that, while the creation and use of a patent pool may facilitate the use of patented vaccine technology, it might still not move the needle on issues related to access to goods developed through the use of pooled technology. A contractual framework regulating interactions within a pool typically covers issues such as permitted uses of patented technology and licensing fees, but may be silent on the downstream cost imposed on consumers of the resulting technology. As such, the distribution and pricing of a health good developed through the use of pooled technology may still occur under inequitable circumstances. These may include unaffordable prices, preferential allocation of initial units to a restricted number of wealthier consumers, or allocation according to geographical patterns that do not align with public health needs. In this sense, while pools can be instrumental in promoting collaborative R&D, they do not automatically eliminate the most concerning traits of proprietary modes of R&D. As such, a vaccine pool should be structured so that it imposes contractual obligations that go beyond the regulation of interactions between participants – for instance, by imposing an obligation that resulting health goods be commercialized at price points that consumers are able to afford in their respective geoeconomic markets.

5.3 FORMALIZATION OF SOFT LEGAL APPROACHES: THE CASE OF PATENT PLEDGES

This section explores the concept of the patent pledge, a mechanism that shares a key feature with patent pools, in that it signals a permissive stance of the patent holder toward the use of technology covered by intellectual property rights. There are nonetheless significant differences between pledges and pools, which this section surveys before setting forth a proposal for the creation of a vaccine-specific patent pledge for R&D on pandemic and epidemic vaccines.

5.3.1 *Pledges of Non-Assertion in Context*

Intellectual property gives patent holders an essentially negative right, conditioning the use of patented technologies to licensure or other mechanisms signaling authorization for others to use the patented product or process.

As seen earlier, patent pools signal the availability of proprietary technologies for licensure, likely against the payment of a royalty. While referring to technologies with a similar proprietary status, patent pledges revolve around a promise to limit the enforcement of one or more patents. The bundle of rights conferred by the patent remains in full force, but the patent holder self-limits their exclusionary powers by indicating to the public at large that the patent will not be asserted for the duration of the pledge.[38]

For some reason – whether altruistic or strategic – a rightsholder decides to inform the public that the patent will not be enforced. As a consequence, parties who have never entered into a contractual agreement with the patent holder are able to use the patented technology without having to negotiate a license or seek any other type of permission from the rightsholder. Moreover, no direct payment or other form of consideration is required.[39] The diffuse nature of the promise, combined with the absence of consideration, differentiates pledges from pools.

While pledges are often made through language that appears to be so diffuse as to target the general public, in practice they tend to be directed at the R&D actors in technical and scientific fields similar to, or overlapping with, the ones in which the patent holder operates. For instance, one of the most well-publicized patent pledges was made in 2014 by Tesla, a California-based manufacturer of electric vehicles, and read "Tesla will not initiate patent lawsuits against anyone who, in good faith, wants to use our technology."[40] Although the pledge was seemingly made to the public at large, only players in areas connected to Tesla's have the ability to take advantage of the pledge from an R&D perspective.

---

[38] Jorge L. Contreras, "Patent Pledges" (2015) 47 *Arizona State Law Journal* 543–608, 546.
[39] Contreras, "Patent Pledges," note 38, at 546.
[40] Elon Musk, "All Our Patent Are Belong to You" (2014), www.tesla.com/blog/all-our-patent-are-belong -you (the title of the article pledging Tesla's patents is a play on an internet meme).

Some pledges make this distinction explicit. In October 2020, the pharmaceutical company Moderna – which produced the second mRNA COVID-19 vaccine to enter the US market – announced that "while the pandemic continues, Moderna will not enforce our COVID-19 related patents against those making vaccines intended to combat the pandemic."[41] The company's promise is thus targeted to R&D players who are Moderna's direct competitors and who, absent the pledge, would infringe on Moderna's intellectual property if they used the patented technology without obtaining authorization from the company, and likely paying for it. In addition to publicizing the pledge on their website, Moderna published a representative list of patents covering its COVID-19 vaccine.[42] Both the pledge and the listing of the patents were made available even before Moderna's COVID-19 vaccine was authorized for emergency use by the FDA emergency use authorization in December 2020.

Moderna's pledge exemplifies a case of a temporally limited pledge, even though the sunset date was unknown at the time the promise was made. Tesla's, by contrast, contained no language limiting the duration of the company's pledge.

By notifying interested parties of a self-limitation on the part of the patent holder, pledges can perform a valuable notice function,[43] paving the way for technology held under proprietary frameworks to be used by others, even if for a limited period of time. The pledge format can therefore be particularly useful in cases in which R&D processes unfold under compressed timelines and in response to heightened social needs, as is the case with a vaccine race during a pandemic or epidemic. Yet, both within and outside the context of pharmaceutical R&D, the use of patent pledges has historically been marginal and often plagued by uncertainty.

5.3.2 *Limitations of Pledges*

As was the case with the formation of patent pools, a pledge depends entirely on a voluntary gesture of the patent holder. However, unlike a pool, a pledge typically excludes or severely limits the possibility of monetization of the patented invention in the short-term. In the current patent-intensive R&D culture, pledges do not comport well with the pressures imposed by R&D models that default to exclusionary frameworks. As such, their adoption remains episodic.

Additionally, several ongoing or past pledges are shrouded in uncertainty, with commentators questioning whether the promises made by a given pledgor are legally enforceable. As legal scholar Jorge Contreras has explained, "(i)n order for a corporate pledge to be actionable, it should be of a type that would reasonably

---

[41] Moderna, "Statement by Moderna on Intellectual Property Matters during the COVID-19 Pandemic" (October 8, 2020), https://investors.modernatx.com/news-releases/news-release-details/statement-moderna-intellectual-property-matters-during-covid-19.

[42] Moderna, "Program Patents," (2021), www.modernatx.com/patents.

[43] Contreras, "Patent Pledges," note 38, at 595–96.

be assumed by the pledgor to induce action or forbearance in the pledgee."[44] Nonetheless, some of the most prominent pledges of non-assertion have been made in ways that may fall short of meeting this threshold. Consider, for instance, the promise made by Tesla ("Tesla will not initiate patent lawsuits against anyone who, in good faith, wants to use our technology"). The pledge was made through a website announcement, with no contractual framework developing the terms of the promise, and adopting porous language. As a rule, courts are reluctant to protect vague promises – especially those in which no consideration is offered.

Relatedly, the porosity of the language used in the Tesla pledge is problematic for reasons beyond enforceability. No definition of "good faith" or "use" was provided, even though the former limits the scope of permissible acts, and the latter refers to the material actions allowed under the pledge. As such, a party relying on Tesla's promise faces additional uncertainty stemming from the lack of definitional clarity: until there is a judicial challenge or Tesla provides more information, no one knows what the actual scope of permissible acts under the pledge might be.

Against this backdrop of uncertainty, taking the pledge at its face value may entail a great deal of risk. If a given pledge is found unenforceable and the patents at stake have not been invalidated, an R&D actor who used the underlying technology may come to face time- and resource-consuming litigation.

Albeit narrower in its framing, Moderna's pledge ("Moderna will not enforce our COVID-19 related patents against those making vaccines intended to combat the pandemic") is detached from any other applicable contractual or interpretive framework and raises similar questions to the ones explored in connection with the Tesla pledge. For example, even though a determinable duration is provided, what is the meaning of "vaccines *intended* to combat the pandemic"? As worded, the promise does shed light on what kinds of vaccine R&D would qualify as meeting this threshold – for instance, does the pledge cover only late-stage R&D, or would more basic research be permissible as well, as long as it is tied to the development of a pandemic vaccine? If the resulting vaccine does not obtain FDA authorization or approval, is the requirement of intent satisfied? And, perhaps even more critical, how will royalties and other licensing terms be calculated and implemented the moment the pandemic ends?

As seen in Section 5.4 of this chapter, the uncertainty surrounding Moderna's pledge with specific regard to mRNA vaccine technology is likely to matter more from a legal interpretive perspective than from a practical viewpoint. Because the technology in question is especially complex, it is doubtful that an mRNA vaccine – and likely other types of vaccines – can be developed based exclusively on the information disclosed by patents. If the originator company, such as Moderna in this case, does not transfer additional knowledge on practical aspects of vaccine manufacturing, second-comers are likely to face unsurmountable challenges in

---

[44] Contreras, "Patent Pledges," note 38, at 594.

replicating the vaccine. The following timeline helps illustrate this problem: Moderna's pledge was made before any COVID-19 vaccines were authorized or approved by drug regulators; in December 2020, the first vaccine doses entered the market, when it was already apparent that the global supply of authorized COVID-19 vaccines was manifestly insufficient to meet pandemic needs; during the first half of 2021, pleas for increased manufacturing of COVID-19 vaccines increased; nevertheless, by mid-2021, no single entity had availed itself of Moderna's pledge and replicated its vaccine.

In spite of these legal and practical shortcomings, steps taken during the COVID-19 pandemic have shown that pledges can be used in productive ways. The chapter now explores how the uncertainty inherent to pledging as it is often practiced can be reduced through the "formalization" of patent pledges – their inscription into preexisting, yet malleable, contractual frameworks.

5.3.3 *Formalizing Pledges: The Open COVID-19 Pledge*

Early in the COVID-19 pandemic, a group led by legal scholars Jorge Contreras and Mark Lemley, and lawyers Diane Peters and Mark Radcliffe, developed a framework for a patent pledge covering technologies related to COVID-19 and implemented it in collaboration with colleagues across other disciplines.[45] The purpose of the Open COVID-19 Pledge was to attract commitments "by holders of intellectual property to share their intellectual property for the purposes of ending and mitigating the COVID-19 Pandemic."[46]

Instead of merely inviting pledgors to make a statement about not enforcing their intellectual property during the pandemic, the Open COVID-19 Pledge directed interested parties to adopt a set of contractually binding frameworks. This feature set it apart from the cases described in Section 5.3.2 in two ways. First, a party could only join the Pledge by agreeing to a tailorable license recognized by the Pledge as meeting its requirements: The pledgor was free to choose the contractual terms that better suited its altruistic or strategic purposes (or both), and uncertainty about the enforceability of the promise was eliminated. Second, the Open COVID-19 Pledge functioned as a centralized venue, congregating pledging activity and information about pledged COVID-19 technologies. The website of the Pledge included a searchable database through which interested parties could look for other COVID-19-related technologies also committed through the Pledge.

The contractual frameworks offered by the Pledge ranged from different standard licenses made available for adoption "as is" to Pledge-compatible licensing formats and "alternative" licenses.[47] Standard licenses gave pledgors several choices on how

---

[45] Jorge L. Contreras et al., "Pledging Intellectual Property for COVID-19" (2020) 38 *Nature Biotechnology* 1146–49.

[46] Open COVID-19 Pledge, "Frequently Asked Questions," (2021), https://opencovidpledge.org/faqs/.

[47] Open COVID-19 Pledge, "About the Licenses," (2020), https://opencovidpledge.org/licenses/.

to self-limit their rights. These licenses covered only five core contractual areas, matching the bare essentials of most technology transfer agreements: grant and scope; time limitation; regulatory exclusivity; defensive suspension; and the inexistence of a warranty.[48] The Pledge offered three types of standard licenses, two of which cover both patent and copyright issues, and one covering patents alone.

In addition to standard licenses, the Pledge allowed for the use of custom licenses, as long as the licensing terms were deemed compatible with a set of minimum standards established by the Pledge.[49] Compatible licenses were defined as those originally drafted by sources external to the Pledge, which were prescreened by the Pledge and labeled as meeting its requirements, or licenses reviewed on a case-by-case basis and found to meet the same requirements. Examples of compatible licenses included the MIT license and the Apache 2.0 license, two of the most well-known and used licenses developed in other fields of technology.[50]

The third option was for pledgors to also adopt "alternative" licenses. These were defined as licensing frameworks that, albeit not fitting the other two categories, were nonetheless "consistent" with the Pledge.[51] Examples included a license developed by Creative Commons to promote the use of creative works,[52] and GNU's General Public License, a type of license developed to enable a wide range of uses of software.[53]

One advantage of providing a range of licensing options is that it allows participants to tailor the permissions they wish to give to possible uses of their intellectual property during a limited period of time. For instance, even aspects like the duration of the non-assertion period can be approached in ways that reflect different approaches to the temporal uncertainties posed by a pandemic. One standard license, for example, provided a framework that was in effect "until one year after WHO declares the COVID-19 Pandemic to have ended."[54] Other standard licenses were set to expire in January 2023, absent an explicit extension provided by the pledgors before the term runs out.[55] Similarly, while standard licenses did not address the issue of indemnification, custom licenses may require "the licensee to indemnify the licensor for liability directly attributable to the licensee's actions."[56]

---

[48] See e.g. Open COVID-19 Pledge, "OCL-PC v1.0 License," (2020), https://opencovidpledge.org/v1-0/.

[49] Open COVID-19 Pledge, "About the Licenses," note 47.

[50] See Open Source Initiative, "The MIT License," (2021), https://opensource.org/licenses/MIT; Apache, "Apache License, Version 2.0," (2021), www.apache.org/licenses/LICENSE-2.0.

[51] Open COVID-19 Pledge, "About the Licenses," note 47.

[52] Creative Commons, "Attribution-ShareAlike 4.0 International (CC BY-SA 4.0)," (2021), https://creativecommons.org/licenses/by-sa/4.0/.

[53] GNU Operating System, "GNU General Public License," (2020), www.gnu.org/licenses/gpl-3.0.en.html.

[54] See e.g. Open COVID-19 Pledge, "Open COVID License 1.0 March 31, 2020," (2020), https://opencovidpledge.org/v1-0/.

[55] See e.g. Open COVID-19 Pledge, "OCL-PC v1.1," (2020), https://opencovidpledge.org/v1-1-ocl-pc/.

[56] Open COVID-19 Pledge, "About the Licenses," note 47.

The Open COVID-19 Pledge was launched in March 2020. Founding adopters included large private-sector companies operating across a wide spectrum of non-medical areas of technology – Facebook, Amazon, Intel, IBM, Microsoft, and Hewlett Packard; Unified Patents, a California-based organization coordinating interventions to diminish the number of entities that improperly assert intellectual property rights; Fabricatorz Foundation, a Missouri-based nonprofit organization working with individuals and entities developing creative technologies; Apheris AI, a German company working in the data privacy space; and the Sandia National Laboratories, one of the three R&D laboratories run by the National Nuclear Security Administration, an agency under the US Department of Energy.[57]

The Pledge was able to collect a large patent portfolio from pledgors across the world within weeks. Among the early pledgors, there were large institutions in both the private and public sector. For instance, NASA pledged a patent covering 3D-printed respirators, Fujitsu pledged a patent covering disease diagnosis through automated software, and Facebook pledged a patent covering systems and methods for the detection of contextual information indicative of misinformation.[58]

In addition to its quick implementation against the backdrop of a severe public health crisis, the formation of the Open COVID-19 Pledge was noticeable for creating a licensing framework that was both structured and flexible. From a contractual perspective, it provided exemplificative legal frameworks, which can be especially useful for first-time pledgors or patent holders with limited licensing experience. Simultaneously, it provided a set of minimum standards that could be built on by those wishing to further customize their promise of nonenforcement. These features combined to provide a mechanism to incentivize the licensure of technology while significantly reducing transaction costs and uncertainty at a time when expedited R&D was critical for pandemic response.

From a technological perspective, the Pledge was designed to cover a broad array of products and methods that may be relevant in the development of products needed to respond to a specific public health crisis. While it attracted a robust number of patent pledges, the pledged technologies did not relate to vaccine development and manufacturing. I ran searches using the Pledge's search function in late 2020 and throughout the first half of 2021[59] and had informal conversations on this topic with some of the creators of the Pledge. This absence does not detract from

---

[57] Open COVID-19 Pledge, "Make the Pledge to Share Your Intellectual Property in the Fight against COVID-19," (2021), https://opencovidpledge.org (last visited August 30, 2020).

[58] Open COVID-19 Pledge, "NASA-JPL-3D Printed Respirators" (May 20, 2020), https://opencovid pledge.org/2020/05/20/nasa-jet-propulsion-laboratory/; Open COVID-19 Pledge, "Fujitsu – Faster Disease Diagnosis Using Computer Software" (June 3, 2020), https://opencovidpledge.org/2020/06/03/fujitsu-faster-disease-diagnosis-using-computer-software/; US Pat. 20200118682, Medical Diagnostic Aid and Method; Open COVID-19 Pledge, "Facebook – Combating the Spread of COVID-19 Related Misinformation" (August 11, 2020), https://opencovidpledge.org/2020/08/11/facebook-combating-the-spread-of-covid-19-related-misinformation/; US Pat. 20190163794, Contextual Information for Determining Credibility of Social-Networking.

[59] Open COVID-19 Pledge, "Featured IP," (2021), https://opencovidpledge.org/partner-ip/.

the remarkable achievements of the Pledge – which was not designed specifically to attract vaccine technology – but rather highlights the fact that policies designed to promote collaborative R&D and technology transfer in the field of vaccines may warrant supplemental interventions, such as the one proposed in Section 5.3.4.

5.3.4 *The Case for a Vaccine Technology Pledge*

The Open COVID-19 Pledge can be regarded as a natural experiment in the formalization of patent pledges in the context of a major public health crisis. The book uses the word "formalization" to emphasize the creation of structures, both legal and organizational, that support the creation and management of a pledge. Crucially, these structures help instill definitional and operational clarity into the pledge's framework, which has been one of the most severe limitations of many pledges, especially those made by prominent corporations to a diffuse audience. In so doing, these structures also help guarantee the enforceability of pledges, especially if they rely on recognizable licensing instruments, as was the case of the Open COVID-19 Pledge.

The highly structured and pliable contractual frameworks offered by the Open COVID-19 Pledge can be used as a blueprint for the creation of future pledging frameworks tailored to different public health needs, technologies – and, potentially, even permanent pledging structures. Using the Pledge as a starting point, this section makes the case for the creation of a formalized, permanent, and technology-specific patent pledge. The pool would cover vaccine-related technology, with a focus on vaccines needed for pandemic and epidemic prevention and response. In addition to formalization and permanency, the pool would offer the possibility of license customization modeled after the Open COVID-19 Pledge, and borrow several other structural features of the Pledge, including its centralizing function and online presence. Furthermore, the proposed pledge could be coupled with non-IP incentives aimed at attracting participation, the sharing of non-patent information, or both.

With regard to the scope of the vaccine pledge, the proposal once again calls for a distinction between different types of vaccine technology. As noted in connection with the proposal for a vaccine patent pool, holders of patents covering platform technology – which can be used to develop different types of products, including in some cases vaccine and non-vaccine products – are generally less likely to respond to this type of technology transfer framework. Rather, such rightsholders will typically elect to perform R&D on their own, or in collaboration with a small number of close partners, often repeat players to whom the technology is licensed on an individual basis. A vaccine-dedicated patent pool would thus be designed to attract primarily pledges covering relatively simpler vaccine components and vaccine-related processes. In addition to making a centralized pledging structure available, as done by the Open COVID-19 Pledge, one way to achieve this goal would be by offering incentives to long-term participation in the vaccine pledge. For instance, holders of non-platform technology who pledge a patent for a fixed number of years would be entitled to a monetary prize. The list of technologies eligible for this or another non-IP incentive would be set in advance and revised periodically to reflect changing needs and the status quo of vaccine R&D.

There are additional ways to customize the scope of the pledge. A more atomic version of the pledge could focus solely on some types of vaccine-preventable diseases and concentrate efforts – and funding – on attracting vaccine technology in these areas. This narrower version of the proposal could be useful if the pledge-cum-incentives model is adopted and funding is limited; if policymakers wish to experiment with an initial pledge model covering diseases that take a particular toll on certain geographical areas; or if they wish to focus on diseases deemed by public health experts as likely to cause a significant outbreak in the short- or medium-term – using a model reflective of, or similar to, the WHO's R&D Blueprint.

On the opposite side of the spectrum from a funding and design perspective, another possibility would be to create enhanced prizes for the pledging of vaccine-related technology deemed especially valuable from an R&D perspective, which could include platform technology, if any were to be pledged.

Yet another way of populating a vaccine pledge would be by tying some non-IP incentives available to vaccine R&D to a requirement of participating in the pledge. For instance, policymakers in the public sector could designate a portion of the existing grant funding for vaccine-related work as reserved for applicants who agree to a contractual obligation of pledging any resulting patentable vaccine technology. A variation of this model, described later in the text, would consist in tying the non-IP incentive to the obligation of pledging resulting vaccine-related intellectual property, but the pledge would only produce effects if and when there was a declared pandemic or epidemic.

The vaccine pledge would employ the same versatile approach to licensing that was used by the Open COVID-19 Pledge. Standard licenses would regulate a core set of contractual domains, while additional licenses reflecting tried-and-tested approaches in other fields of technology would be screened and made available to pledgors of qualifying vaccine technology where appropriate.

While the Open COVID-19 Pledge was more successful in attracting participants than the C-TAP patent pool, both mechanisms constituted a reaction to an ongoing public health crisis of extraordinary magnitude. By contrast, the proposed vaccine pledge would be created as a permanent institution. However, as was the case with the vaccine patent pool proposed earlier, there could be a two-tiered structure. The first tier would be active at all times and comprise pledges made with no temporal contingencies. The second would be formed by pledges of non-assertion that would only become active in the event of a formally declared outbreak, be it a pandemic or epidemic. The types of formal declaration qualifying as triggering the activation of this tier of the pledge would be determined in advance and could once again be a declaration of Public Health Emergency of International Concern or a pandemic declaration by the WHO.

As with all patent pledges, the one proposed here would still be constrained by voluntarism and strategic, market-driven behaviors that lead some R&D players away from non-exclusionary modes of managing their intellectual property portfolio. Moreover, if implemented in connection with prizes or other non-IP incentives awarded to encourage participation, the pledge would need to source monetary contributions in a funding climate marked by relatively few resources allocated to vaccine R&D – at least absent a considerable public health crisis.

Nevertheless, there is an argument to be made that voluntarism (coupled with funding needs, should funding be required at all) may present advantages worth considering. Operating from a perspective of searching for room within existing intellectual property frameworks to promote less exclusionary forms of R&D, voluntarism does not disrupt the status quo in the way compelled transfers of intellectual property do – as seen in Section 5.4. Therefore, policymakers should seriously consider incentivizing the creation and adoption of voluntary mechanisms such as patent pledges and patent pools. If treated strategically and incentivized properly, these mechanisms can be especially useful in an area such as vaccine R&D on emerging pathogens, which absent an outbreak is often relegated to the backburner of pharmaceutical R&D.

Finally, if participation in the pool were incentivized indirectly – such as in the case of making a portion of existing grant funding conditional on participation in the pledge – the resources consumed by the pledge would be minimal, as no new resources would need to be committed to the incentive. If policymakers chose instead to implement a direct monetary award to attract participants (or a segment thereof) the creation of a vaccine pledge would consume a nonnegligible amount of resources. That being said, the cost of a narrow intervention such as the funding of awards for a vaccine-specific pledge or pool is bound to be far less than for other types of interventions, and may help change, however slowly, the exclusionary R&D culture that currently permeates the development of vaccines against emerging pathogens.

5.4 RECONSIDERING "FORCED" COLLABORATIONS IN VACCINE R&D

Having explored different voluntary mechanisms to promote the transfer of vaccine technology, the book now considers the role of nonvoluntary forms of technology transfer. International and domestic legal regimes have long contemplated the possibility of forced licensure of patented goods – most notably through compulsory licensing, which has been successfully deployed in past epidemics by lower-income countries facing difficulties in accessing patented pharmaceutical products. The COVID-19 pandemic brought to the forefront proposals for a different type of legal intervention, which had never been used or received serious political or policy consideration: A waiver of intellectual property rights covering COVID-19 vaccines and other health goods needed to respond to the pandemic. The waiver was widely promoted as a tool that would help increase the production and distribution of vaccines, particularly across lower-income countries. In a departure from previous stances on intellectual property, the United States government endorsed the proposal in May 2021, even though several higher-income countries like Germany opposed it.

This section examines the waiver in the context of the COVID-19 pandemic, and makes the case that, even though it would seemingly lessen exclusionary frameworks and promote technology transfer, it did not tend to the specific characteristics of vaccines as products of biotechnology. While powerful as a statement against the market-driven vaccine R&D status quo, the waiver would not solve the replicability problems that are a hallmark of biological products like vaccines. Unlike previous interventions compelling the sharing of patented pharmaceutical products, the proposed waiver was an example of a mismatch between a pressing public health need and the legal tool chosen to address it.

5.4.1 *Patent Waivers and Compulsory Licensing in Context*

In October 2020, India and South Africa submitted a proposal to the World Trade Organization (WTO) for a waiver of intellectual property rights covering technologies needed for the "prevention, containment or treatment of COVID-19."[60] As worded, the proposal would apply to a broad range of health goods: The drafters specifically highlighted the heightened public health need for diagnostics, personal protective equipment, ventilators, vaccines, and drugs.[61] For an intellectual property waiver to produce legal effects, it must be approved by the WTO's General Council – which had not happened at the time of writing, as of mid-2021. If adopted as proposed, the waiver would remain in effect "until widespread vaccination is in place globally, and the majority of the world's population has developed immunity."

From a legal perspective, a waiver upends the usual dynamics of the TRIPS Agreement. Ordinarily, the Agreement allows signatories to challenge countries that violate TRIPS provisions through specialized dispute settlement procedures at the WTO.[62] The waiver requested by the governments of India and South Africa would establish that countries granting compulsory licenses on products related to COVID-19 would not be held in violation of any intellectual property rules, preventing these WTO-based challenges from occurring.

---

[60]   Communication from India and South Africa, Waiver from Certain Provisions of the TRIPS Agreement for the Prevention, Containment and Treatment of Covid-19 (October 2, 2020), https://docs.wto.org/dol2fe/Pages/SS/directdoc.aspx?filename=q:/IP/C/W669.pdf.

[61]   Communication, note 60.

[62]   TRIPS Agreement, article 64.

The TRIPS Agreement gives countries the ability to issue compulsory licenses on patented goods in cases of need.[63] The WTO defines compulsory licensing as instances in which "a government allows someone else to produce a patented product or process without the consent of the patent owner or plans to use the patent-protected invention itself."[64] These licenses are issued by national governments and are generally subject to a requirement that an attempt be made to obtain a voluntary license from the patent holder. In situations of "extreme urgency," as is the case of a large public health crisis, this requirement can be waived.[65] Early in the COVID-19 pandemic, several countries – including high-income countries such as Germany, France, and Canada – amended their domestic laws to facilitate the grant of compulsory licenses.

Originally, the TRIPS Agreement restricted compulsory licensing by preventing countries from issuing licenses for patented pharmaceutical products meant primarily for export to other countries. This prohibition was highly detrimental to lower-income countries, most of which lack the manufacturing capacity necessary to produce these products in the first place. Legal scholar Jerome Reichman labeled article 31 of TRIPS "an empty gesture" toward these countries.[66]

Article 31(f) still establishes that compulsory licensing should "be authorized predominantly for the supply of the domestic market" of the country issuing the license. However, building on the 2001 Doha Declaration on TRIPS and the Public Health, a waiver to article 31(f) was introduced to allow lower-income countries to import pharmaceutical products under a compulsory license. The waiver, which is only applicable to pharmaceuticals that lower-income countries cannot produce themselves, became effectively a permanent part of TRIPS in 2017 as article 31bis. By the time the COVID-19 pandemic began most, but not all, TRIPS signatories had ratified this amendment to the Agreement.[67]

The different type of waiver proposed in 2020 by India and South Africa would go beyond the cases contemplated by the TRIPS compulsory licensing architecture. First, while compulsory licensing is restricted to patents and very limited cases in copyright law, the COVID-19 waiver would apply broadly to cover "patents, industrial designs, copyright and protection of undisclosed information." Second, compulsory licensing as allowed by TRIPS occurs on a country-by-country and product-by-product basis. By contrast, the COVID-19 waiver would suspend the enforcement of intellectual property rights, and in so doing it would eliminate the need for a patchwork approach to compulsory licensing, effectively

---

[63] TRIPS Agreement, article 31.
[64] World Trade Organization, "Compulsory Licensing of Pharmaceuticals and TRIPS," (2021), www .wto.org/english/tratop_e/trips_e/public_health_faq_e.htm.
[65] TRIPS Agreement, article 31.
[66] Jerome H. Reichman, "Compulsory Licensing of Patented Pharmaceutical Inventions: Evaluating the Options" (2009) 37 *Journal of Law, Medicine and Ethics* 247–63, at 248.
[67] World Trade Organization, "Amendment of the TRIPS Agreement," (2021), www.wto.org/english/ tratop_e/trips_e/amendment_e.htm.

creating a temporary blanket umbrella for the exercise of compulsory licensing with regard to any COVID-19-related products.

5.4.2 *The COVID-19 Vaccine Waiver*

The proposal for such a broad waiver in the context of COVID-19 was motivated by concerns with obstacles created by intellectual property rights to the development of pandemic health goods. As the drafters explained, they were moved by "several reports about intellectual property rights hindering or potentially hindering timely provisioning of affordable medical products to the patients."[68]

The reports referenced in the text of the proposal related to non-vaccine technologies, such as ventilators and personal protective equipment. For instance, one report cited in the waiver proposal referred to the case of N95 respirators, a type of face mask widely regarded as an industry standard in situations involving the spread of pathogens causing transmissible respiratory disease.[69] The N95 respirators were in high demand during the pandemic and several countries faced difficulties in their procurement. In April 2020, the Governor of Kentucky called on the main US distributor of N95 respirators – M3, a US-based multinational company – to "provide (the patents covering N95 respirators) to the nation under a license for this period of time."

As seen throughout the book, vaccines present considerably more significant manufacturing and replicability challenges than personal protective equipment like N95 respirators. Yet, the epicenter of the proposal submitted to the WTO quickly became the waiving of patent rights covering COVID-19 vaccines. For months after it was made, the proposal was discussed primarily in specialized circles and opposed by a substantial number of higher-income countries. As the May 2021 meeting of the WTO General Council approached, discussions about the waiver increasingly focused on the suspension of vaccine-related intellectual property rights.

On May 5, a little over six months after the proposal was originally made, the United States announced its support of the proposal. To some extent, the announcement marked a departure from previous US external intellectual property policy, which has long been known as disfavoring compulsory licensing of pharmaceutical products, or any other interventions that may lessen the exclusionary dimension of patent rights covering pharmaceuticals.[70]

In this sense, the statement of support for the waiver made by the US Trade Representative introduced a different tone to the country's pharmaceutical patent policy: "The administration believes strongly in intellectual property protections,

---

68 Communication, note 60.
69 Morgan Watkins, "Kentucky Gov. Andy Beshear Calls on 3M to Release Patent for N95 Respirator amid Pandemic" (April 3, 2020) *Louisville Courier Journal*. : www.courier-journal.com/story/news/2020/04/03/beshear-calls-3-m-release-patent-n-95-respirator-amid-pandemic/5112729002/.
70 Sapna Kumar, "Compulsory Licensing of Patents during Pandemics," at 14 (manuscript on file with author). Volume number: 54, 2022, *Connecticut Law Review*.

but in service of ending this pandemic, supports the waiver of those protections for Covid-19 vaccines."[71]

The announcement received considerable praise. The Director of the WHO hailed the position taken by the United States as a "historic decision for vaccine equity."[72] Activists in the public health space and many commentators in the United States and abroad responded in a similarly enthusiastic ways to the news. At the same time, the waiver was criticized by many others. The editorial board of the *Wall Street Journal* labeled the US endorsement of the waiver a "vaccine patent theft," framing it as an instance in which "the White House helps other governments steal."[73] The pharmaceutical industry condemned the shift in US policy in less inflammatory language, but underscored its opposition to the waiver.[74] A point of quasi-agreement for competing views on the waiver was that the position adopted by the United States was, by and large, surprising in light of its longstanding intellectual property policy. The day after the US Trade Representative's announcement, an article in *Nature* carried the headline *In Shock Move, US Backs Waiving Patents on COVID Vaccines*.[75]

Even after the United States supported the waiver, most other high-income countries continued to oppose it. In mid-May, the G20 Group met in Rome for a summit on global health. G20 is an international forum convening meetings of government representatives of the twenty largest economies of the world.[76] The following countries are permanent members: Argentina, Australia, Brazil, Canada, China, France, Germany, Japan, India, Indonesia, Italy, Mexico, Russia, Saudi Arabia, South Africa, South Korea, Turkey, the United Kingdom, the United States, and the European Union. Spain participates as a permanent guest, and additional guest countries and organizations are invited each year. Even though the original proponents of the waiver (India and South Africa) and the United States are permanent members of G20, the May 2021 Summit ended with a declaration that rejected the adoption of a waiver of patent rights for COVID-19 vaccines.[77] While

[71] Office of the US Trade Representative, "Statement from Ambassador Katherine Tai on the COVID-19 Trips Waiver" (May 5, 2021), https://ustr.gov/about-us/policy-offices/press-office/press-releases/2021/may/statement-ambassador-katherine-tai-covid-19-trips-waiver.

[72] World Health Organization, "WHO Director-General Commends United States Decision to Support Temporary Waiver on Intellectual Property Rights for COVID-19 Vaccines" (May 5, 2021), www.who.int/news/item/05-05-2021-who-director-general-commends-united-states-decision-to-support-temporary-waiver-on-intellectual-property-rights-for-covid-19-vaccines.

[73] Editorial Board, "Biden's Vaccine Patent Theft" (May 5, 2021) *Wall Street Journal*, www.wsj.com/articles/bidens-vaccine-patent-theft-11620255362.

[74] Jonathan Gardner & Ned Pagliarulo, "Pharma Erupts as Biden Administration Backs Waiver of Vaccine Patent Rights" (May, 6, 2021) *BioPharma Dive*, www.biopharmadive.com/news/biden-vaccine-patent-waiver-pharma-opposition/599704/.

[75] Amy Maxmen, "In Shock Move, US Backs Waiving Patents on COVID Vaccines" (May 12, 2021) 593 *Nature* 173, www.nature.com/articles/d41586-021-01245-y.

[76] G20, "About the G20," (2021), www.g20.org/about-the-g20.html.

[77] Francesco Guarascio, "G20 Snubs COVID Patent Waiver, Waters down Pledge on WHO's Funding" (May 18, 2021) *Reuters*, www.reuters.com/business/healthcare-pharmaceuticals/exclusive-g20-snubs-covid-patent-waiver-waters-down-pledge-whos-funding-draft-2021-05-18/.

this declaration has no binding force on the WTO, it is highly indicative of the lack of broad international support for the waiver at a time when the pandemic raged throughout the Global South.

5.4.3 *The Case against Vaccine Patent Waivers*

The events described earlier provide a glimpse into the political economy surrounding the COVID-19 patent waiver. But while the waiver proposed during the COVID-19 pandemic was met with support from an unlikely source and opposition from most of the Global North, a separate question remains: Absent (considerable) impediments posed by the political economy, are waivers of intellectual property rights a viable tool for promoting the transfer of vaccine technology in a future vaccine race?

The book answers that question predominantly in the negative.

Vaccines belong to a group of technologies that are especially hard to replicate. As biologics, they are virtually impossible to fully reverse-engineer. If someone who was not involved in the development process for a conventional drug or an N95 respirator wishes to replicate it, it is usually possible to do so. The process for producing copies of the drug or respirator does not have to squarely match the one employed by the originator, and departures from the originator's manufacturing process do not affect the end product in significant ways. In fact, when the United States faced a shortage of N95 respirators and the company controlling the intellectual property on this particular good was not able to ramp up production, the US government invoked the Defense Production Act – a law – and directed a different company working in related areas of filtration technology, Hollingsworth & Vose, to produce N95 respirators, as well as N95 ventilator filters.[78]

Vaccines, by contrast, are so highly manufacturing-dependent that attempting to replicate them by using a slightly different process is likely to compromise the efficacy of the final product. Significant amounts of relevant manufacturing information are held by vaccine manufacturers in forms other than a patent. These forms range from trade secrets to know-how shared among those who work for or partner with the company, but not with third parties. Once patents (or patent applications) are published, anyone can locate their full text through a simple online search – in addition to electronic tools made available to specialized audiences, anyone can use Google's search engine for patent-related content, Google Patents, to read a published patent or patent application.[79] The information contained in the

---

[78]   US Department of Defense, "DoD Announces Defense Production Act Title 3 COVID-19 PPE Project: $2.2 Million Investment Will Increase U.S. Domestic Production of N95 Mask Respirator and Mask Ventilator Filter Production by Over 30 Million Combined Over the Next 120 Days," (May 28, 2020), www.defense.gov/News/Releases/Release/Article/2200654/dod-announces-defense-production-act-title-3-covid-19-ppe-project-22-million-in/.

[79]   Google Patents, https://patents.google.com.

patents, however, is generally far from sufficient for a third party to manufacture a vaccine without some collaboration from the original manufacturer.

Domestic patent laws mandate that the invention be described in the text of a patent. This description functions as a set of instructions to replicate the product or process covered by the patent. With complex forms of technology such as vaccines, putting together the instructions provided by all relevant patents does not teach a third party all the steps required to manufacture a vaccine. Consider the following analogy: A culinary recipe in a restaurant cookbook teaches readers – who probably did not receive any direct instruction from the person who made the original dish – how to navigate a multistep, multi-component process to replicate a product. Yet, home cooks who have scrupulously followed recipes sometimes discover that the final product does not quite taste like or even resemble the original dish. If the recipe writer omitted a "secret ingredient" (anchovies that melt into a sauce leaving no visible trace but adding a type of flavor undiscernible to the untrained palate) or a technique (whisking in a particular way to aerate the batter and give a cake a certain structure), recipe readers may approximate the original products but not be able to fully replicate it.

Pharmaceutical companies routinely use knowledge that is never shared through a patent. In some cases, a "secret ingredient" may even be listed in the composition of the product, but not highlighted in any particular way in the patent instructions, and competitors will not immediately realize the heightened importance of that component – hence failing to fully replicate the process-dependent good generated by the patent holder. In the discussions leading up to the US support for the waiver, vaccine manufacturers made it clear that they did not expect that competitors would be able to replicate a vaccine without the transfer of information not taught by patents. For instance, a representative of Bharat Biotech, an Indian company manufacturing a COVID-19 vaccine, stated that "Vaccine manufacturing is not just in the patents [. . .] If I give that to just anybody, I don't think they'll be able to do anything about it. They need know how and expertise . . . It's needed in a package."[80]

Recall that the proposed waiver would cover "patents, industrial designs, copyright and protection of undisclosed information."[81] The two relevant areas for enabling the manufacturing of a vaccine by a third party are patents and the type of information not taught by patents referenced earlier in the text, which would fall under the bracket of "undisclosed information." By suspending patent protection, the waiver would allow these third parties to act on patent-covered information in ways they normally cannot under the duration of the patent. However, even though the waiver proposed to suspend protection of non-patent information, there are no legal or practical mechanisms that would force companies to transfer knowledge

---

[80] Ed Silverman, "Millions Sign Petitions Urging the US to Back a WTO Proposal for Greater COVID-19 Vaccine Access" (April 23, 2021) *Stat*, www.statnews.com/pharmalot/2021/04/23/covid19-coronavirus-vaccine-wto-biden-intellectual-property/.

[81] Communication, note 60.

that is not codified in repositories accessible by others. Tricks of the trade and other key information would not automatically be disclosed to third parties should the waiver come into effect.

Therefore, although a waiver may be helpful in addressing some of the issues that other legal tools cannot address – such as fragmentation problems in the case of compulsory licensing – it would still be insufficient to enable third parties to replicate COVID-19 vaccines without some cooperation from the original manufacturers. This is yet another reason why it is important to understand vaccines in their technological dimension. Compelled transfers may work in other areas of technology – including pharmaceutical technologies – but likely not in the realm of biologics.

This is not to say the proposed waiver is devoid of value. Epidemiologist Gregg Gonsalves highlighted the "domino effect" of the US support for the proposal, prompting other countries and institutional actors to also express favorable views of the waiver.[82] In embodying a non-absolutist view of intellectual property, it signaled the need for the implementation of intellectual property frameworks that better align with the pursuit of public health goals. In this sense, the proposal for a waiver operated as a tool in the international relations space in much more pronounced ways than it did in the technological field.

An underappreciated point during public debate about the waiver, however, was the fact that lower-income countries spent political capital mustering support for the adoption of a legal tool unlikely to solve the technological problem at the heart of vaccine scarcity. It remains to be seen what the long-term consequences of support by countries like the United States will truly mean. During the first decade of the twenty-first century, countries in the Global South successfully resorted to compulsory licensing (or the threat thereof) to lower the price at which HIV/AIDS drugs were being commercialized.[83] Unlike vaccines, these were conventional drugs that could be reverse-engineered by competitors and replicated without cooperation of the original manufacturers. In this sense, the legal tool used by these countries – compulsory licensing – was an effective and needed means to achieve a public health goal.

Even though the use of tools such as compulsory licensing is lawful under the TRIPS Agreement, countries like the United States have long been known to attempt to discourage lower-income countries from lawfully using intellectual property mechanisms to promote goals that further their domestic public health agendas. As legal scholar Sapna Kumar has put it:

> For the past several decades, the US government has treated its anti-compulsory licensing stance for pharmaceuticals as a form of moral high ground. Under both Republican and Democratic administrations, the US Trade Representative has

---

[82]   Gregg Gonsalves, "The COVID-19 Vaccine Patent Waiver: A Crucial Step Towards a 'People's Vaccine'" (2021) 373 *British Medical Journal* n1249–50; Gavin Yamey, 108: 110–19.

[83]   World Health Organization, "Access to Affordable Medicines for HIV/AIDS and Hepatitis," (2014), https://apps.who.int/iris/bitstream/handle/10665/204741/B5144.pdf.

threatened trade sanctions against countries that utilize it, maintaining that it undermines TRIPS' minimum protections. US pharmaceutical companies have also found ways to directly retaliate when a country issues a license on one of their drugs.[84]

The US trade representative – the same institutional representative who announced support for the COVID-19 waiver proposal – regularly spearheads the negotiation of bilateral trade agreements between the United States and lower-income countries under which the latter are granted trade benefits on the condition of agreeing to more stringent forms of intellectual protection than those imposed by the TRIPS Agreement. Legal scholar Ruth Okediji has observed that this "new intellectual property bilateralism" helps the United States and other high-income countries "secure strong global intellectual property rights" in the long-term.[85]

It remains to be seen at what cost, if any, US support of the proposed waiver will come. Given the fact that the waiver would not have solved the technological problems of replicability that it was intended to address, further exploration in years to come of the long-term consequences of its proposal is warranted.

Finally, it is also worth keeping in mind the practical limitations of waiver models when vaccine technology is at stake. These limitations underscore the need for collaborative technology transfer frameworks to be negotiated – and preferably memorialized through contractual agreements – *ahead* of highly disruptive public crises, instead of being discussed in the volatile climate of pandemics and epidemics. In addition to being subject to a multitude of immediate constraints, this climate may all too easily disguise long-term agendas of some countries.

5.5 THE EXPANDING ROLE OF PUBLIC–PRIVATE PARTNERSHIPS

The previous sections have advocated for voluntary R&D collaborations wherever possible. These collaborations are especially needed against the backdrops of product and infrastructure scarcity, as was the case during the COVID-19 vaccine race. The book now turns its attention to a particular mode of cooperation between multi-sector players in the vaccine R&D ecosystem – through the formation of public–private partnerships. Although not new, these structures have gained momentum in recent years as a way to overcome some of the recurring problems hindering the development of vaccines against emerging pathogens in the pronounced market-driven climate of modern-day pharmaceutical R&D. During the COVID-19 pandemic, the public–private partnership format was also used as an attempt to mitigate some of the allocative imbalances experienced in the distribution of limited doses of vaccines.

---

[84] Kumar, "Compulsory Licensing," note 70, at 14.
[85] Ruth Okediji, "Back to Bilateralism? Pendulum Swings in International Intellectual Property Protection" (2004) 1 *University of Ottawa Law & Technology Journal* 125, at 142.

This section examines the emergence of public–private partnerships in the public health space, as well as their growing role at both the beginning and tail end of the vaccine R&D pipeline. The partnerships surveyed later – and especially those solely focused on vaccines – provide actual examples of the technology-specific type of approach that the book has argued for. Moreover, because many public–private partnerships in this area are formed with some degree of permanency, insights distilled from ongoing experiences are also of interest to policymakers searching for long-term models of bolstering vaccine R&D, promoting equitable distribution of vaccines or both.

5.5.1 *Public–Private Partnerships in Context*

While there is no universal definition of "public–private partnership," the expression typically refers to a contractually based, long-term collaboration between parties in the public and private sectors. The PPP Knowledge Lab – an online resource made available by the World Bank Group in collaboration with several multilateral development agencies – defines a public–private partnership as "a long-term contract between a private party and a government entity, for providing a public asset or service, in which the private party bears significant risk and management responsibility, and remuneration is linked to performance."[86]

Focusing on public–private partnerships operating in the health-related areas, the WHO offers the following definition:

> Public-private partnerships are seen as an effective way to capitalize on the relative strengths of the public and private sectors to address problems that neither could tackle adequately on its own, in particular in respect of diseases that particularly affect developing countries where research by the private sector is deemed insufficient. Thus the public sector contributes both basic science and funding, and the private sector has strengths in drug discovery and bringing candidate drugs through the trials process to regulatory approval.[87]

The bioethicist Jonathan H. Marks, who studies public–private partnerships in the context of the provision of health-related goods, has provided an exemplificative list of "public partners" as encompassing "a government agency or official, an academic research institution, a non-governmental organization, and an international non-governmental organization among others"; and "private partners" as encompassing "corporations, trade associations, and other organizations that represent industry interests."[88]

---

[86] PPP Knowledge Lab, "PPP Reference Guide: Introduction," (2021), https://pppknowledgelab.org /guide/sections/1-introduction.

[87] World Health Organization, "Public–Private Partnerships (PPPs)," www.who.int/intellectualprop erty/topics/ppp/en/.

[88] Jonathan H. Marks, "What's the Big Deal? The Ethics of Public–Private Partnerships Related to Food and Health," Edmond J. Safra Center for Ethics, Harvard University, Working Paper, No. 11 (May 2013), http://ssrn.com/abstract=2268079, 5.

Within the umbrella of formalized relationships between actors in different sectors, the concept of public–private partnerships includes collaborative arrangements structured in markedly different ways. For instance, some partnerships may be designed to jumpstart the processes leading to the development or production of certain types of goods, while others may be designed with the objective of acquiring and distributing those goods. Based on this distinction, public–private partnerships are often categorized as *product development* partnerships or *access* partnerships, a taxonomy the book adopts when discussing existing partnerships involved in vaccine R&D and allocation.[89]

Product development partnerships often operate at the beginning of the R&D pipeline, seeking to attract resources to catalyze the development or production of a predefined good or set of related goods. This type of partnership has come to play an important role in areas entailing relatively high investment costs and risk, and is often overlooked by funders and R&D players – as is the case with historically neglected areas of pharmaceutical R&D.

Access partnerships operate predominantly at the tail end of the R&D pipeline. They seek to bring together resources to enable the purchase and distribution of products deemed necessary or beneficial for a variety of socio-economic reasons.

From the early 2000s onward, the number and scope of public–private partnerships operating in health-related fields grew exponentially. During the late 1990s, the number of new partnerships becoming active in this area ranged from one (1995, 1996) to four (1997) per year.[90] In 2001, seven new partnerships were launched, and the number of new entrances per year started climbing steadily from 2005 onward: in 2006, eighteen new partnerships were launched; three years later the number had doubled to thirty-six; in 2012, a total of sixty-three partnerships became active. Until 2003, most new entrants were partnerships based in North America. After that, and especially from 2008 onward, the majority of new partnerships were based in Europe, with Asia occupying a distant third place after North America.

Existing health-oriented public–private partnerships vary significantly in size and scope. For example, the Innovative Medicines Initiative (IMI), the largest public–private partnership in the life sciences in the world, was broadly designed as a product development partnership between the European Union and EFPIA (the European Federation of Pharmaceutical Industries and Associations), which represents thirty-three countries and forty pharmaceutical companies.[91] In the first ten years (2008–2018), IMI garnered €5.3 billion in funding (approximately USD

[89] Jon F. Merz, "World Health Organization, Intellectual Property and Product Development Public/ Private Partnerships" (May 16, 2005) Final Report to the World Health Organization Commission on Intellectual Property Rights, Innovation and Public Health, 17.

[90] See Mark D. Lim et al., "Consortium Sandbox: Building and Sharing Resources" (June 25, 2014) 6 (242) *Science Translational Medicine* 1–2.

[91] IMI, "IMI Mission and Objectives," (2021) www.imi.europa.eu/about-imi/mission-objectives.

6.46 billion per mid-2021 conversion rates).[92] Launched in 2008 with the objective of improving "health by speeding up the development of innovative medicines, particularly in areas where there is an unmet medical or social, public health need," IMI funds the development of pharmaceutical products across a wide spectrum.[93] As of 2021, IMI is involved in 171 discrete projects, covering disparate areas ranging from digital pathology to R&D on respiratory syncytial virus, a common pathogen that can trigger serious symptoms among very young and older populations.[94] An overview of the "health priorities" set by IMI is telling of the breadth of the partnership. Its strategic agenda for 2014–2020 lists the following priority areas: osteoarthritis, cardiovascular diseases, diabetes, neurodegenerative diseases, psychiatric diseases, respiratory diseases, immune-mediated diseases, ageing-associated diseases, cancer, rare and orphan diseases, and vaccines.[95]

By contrast, other public–private partnerships focus on much narrower sets of diseases or medical problems, or on specific types of health-related technologies.[96] An example of the former is the Drugs for Neglected Diseases Initiative (DNDi), created in 2003 as a product development partnership to spur the development of "urgently needed treatments for neglected patients" at affordable prices.[97] DNDi concentrates its work on a selected number of diseases, all of which are prevalent in lower-income countries: Chagas disease, cutaneous and visceral leishmaniasis, river blindness hepatitis C, mycetoma, pediatric HIV, and sleeping sickness.[98] Between 2003 and 2021, DNDi helped fund and develop eight new treatments for diseases in its area of action. Starting in 2020, in response to the extraordinary public health challenges posed by the COVID-19 pandemic, DNDi temporarily broadened its scope to include work related to coronaviruses.[99]

Another example of a narrowly focused public–private partnership is the Combating Antibiotic-Resistant Bacteria Biopharmaceutical Accelerator (CARB-X), launched in 2016 with the goal of "investing in the development of new antibiotics and other life-saving products to combat the most dangerous drug-resistant bacteria."[100] Instead of tailoring its activity to one or more diseases,

92 IMI, "10 Years of Transforming Medical Research," (2021), www.imi.europa.eu/news-events/10-years-transforming-medical-research.
93 IMI, "How IMI Works," (2021), www.imi.europa.eu/about-imi/how-imi-works.
94 IMI, "Project Factsheets," (2021), www.imi.europa.eu/projects-results/project-factsheets.
95 IMI, "Strategic Research Agenda" (2021), www.imi.europa.eu/about-imi/strategic-research-agenda.
96 See e.g. Frederick M. Abbott, "Public–Private Partnerships as Models for New Drug Development: The Future As Now," in *Public–Private Partnerships, Global Intellectual Property Governance and Sustainable Development*, Ahmed Abdel-Latif, Margaret Chon, & Pedro Roffe, eds. (Cambridge University Press, 2018), 33–34.
97 Drugs for Neglected Diseases Initiative, https://dndi.org.
98 Drugs for Neglected Diseases Initiative, "Diseases," (2021), https://dndi.org/diseases/.
99 Drugs for Neglected Diseases Initiative, "COVID-19," (2021), https://dndi.org/diseases/covid-19/.
100 Combating Antibiotic-Resistant Bacteria Biopharmaceutical Accelerator (CARB-X), https://carb-x.org.

CARB-X focuses on a growing medical problem, antimicrobial resistance, which happens when pathogens mutate and pharmaceuticals previously effective in the prevention or treatment of a disease cease to work. CARB-X finances the development of different types of products relevant in this, including antibiotics and vaccines. Between 2016 and 2021, the partnership provided USD 333.6 million in funding to eighty-nine R&D projects.[101]

These examples point to the growing footprint of public–private partnerships operating in different corners of global health. Before turning to the narrower universe of vaccine-dedicated partnerships – and arguing, that in spite of their flaws, they should be expanded further – the book pauses to examine some of the drawbacks of public–private partnership models in general.

5.5.2 *Shortcomings of (Over)Reliance on Public–Private Partnerships*

Multi-stakeholder, large-scale partnerships bring resources and expertise to the concentrated, underfunded market of vaccine R&D. Yet, they do not cure all of the underlying shortcomings of vaccine R&D, and they leave unanswered the question of how to support vaccine R&D more generally. For instance, rare diseases and unknown pathogens[102] are unlikely to be the primary focus of attention of transnational collaborations equipped with massive funding, legal and bureaucratic structures.

A first line of arguments cautioning against excessive reliance on public–private partnerships stems from their intrinsic nature. In a world of limited resources, R&D approaches based on partnerships are sectoral by definition, even within subfields of pharmaceutical research. As with other types of ad hoc initiatives, they do not overcome the problem of fragmentation: internally, they create a consolidated R&D space, but they do not solve external fragmentation and potentially add to it.[103]

The sheer scale of well-funded, multiplayer collaborations entails the development of a decision-making and management apparatus that renders the creation of partnerships a protracted process. They thus constitute a slow form of responding to emerging health problems.

If one advantage of public–private partnerships is to bring together actors from different sectors that would otherwise operate independently, the corresponding disadvantage is that the interests of diverse actors may not align. Within a partnership, asymmetries between partners may also result in imperfect

---

[101]   CARB-X, note 100.
[102]   See World Health Organization, "R&D Blueprint," note 8 (adding an "unknown pathogen" to the list of diseases likely to trigger outbreaks in the foreseeable future).
[103]   CEPI, "Preliminary Business Plan 2017–2021" (2016), https://perma.cc/FU2R-HJNG, at 15 ("Ad-hoc initiatives for vaccine development are fragmented and unpredictable").

coordination[104] or dominance of one party's agenda over the public interest.[105] Legal scholar Margaret Chon has noted that:

> The heterogeneity of PPPs is also their all-too-obvious Achilles heel. As hybrid actors, PPPs attempt to accommodate both commercial and non-commercial interests, directly raising the question of whether public interest norms in IP can be expressed when hybrid actors are motivated instrumentally for profit in addition to social mission within networks consisting of simultaneous instrumental and epistemic exchange. Similar questions have been asked of purely commercial actors in the corporate social responsibility (CSR) context.[106]

Even in cases of convergence of interests, a partnership alone may not be able to bridge the gap between the early development stages of a product and the later ones, including commercialization. The common split between product development and access partnerships means that the divide between preclinical development and later stage R&D might not always be bridged.[107]

A related aspect of multiparty coordination relates to the assumption that partnerships reduce transaction costs in R&D, therefore increasing the opportunities for collaborative innovation. This might not necessarily be true.[108] Prior to the beginning of the collaboration, parties who have never worked together may estimate costs differently or, given the uncertainties associated with biopharmaceutical research and regulatory review, transaction cost may change as R&D moves forward.[109]

Although partnerships like CEPI have relatively flexible approaches to the allocation and management of proprietary rights, this is also not a guarantee that all parties in a project will be rewarded equally. As legal scholar Liza Vertinsky has put it:

> Patents are likely to systematically over-reward the private sector participants, who tend to engage in later stage developments that are more readily patented. Conversely, they are likely to under-reward the public-sector participants, who are concentrated in upstream areas of early stage research that is often either

---

[104] National Academies Press, "The Role of Public–Private Partnerships in Health Systems Strengthening: Workshop Summary" (hereinafter "NAP Workshop Summary") (2016), at 42 (examining the relationship between corporate and noncorporate partners).

[105] But see Peter K. Yu, "Intellectual Property, Human Rights and Public–Private Partnerships," in *Public–Private Partnerships*, note 96, at 398 (calling for public–private partnerships to abide by a human rights-enhancing framework).

[106] Margaret Chon, "PPPs in Global IP" [Public–Private Partnerships in Global Intellectual Property], in *Methods and Perspectives in Intellectual Property*, Graeme B. Dinwoodie, ed. (Edward Elgar, 2014), 269.

[107] Merz, "World Health Organization," note 89, at 15 (noting that some product development partnerships reported being forced to engage in late-stage clinical R&D before being able to secure a commercial partner).

[108] See Jens K. Roehrich et al., "Are Public–Private Partnerships a Healthy Option? A Systematic Literature Review" (2014) 113 *Social Science & Medicine* 110, 113.

[109] Roehrich et al., "Are Public–Private Partnerships a Healthy Option?," note 108.

freely shared or licensed to the private sector on terms favorable to the private sector.[110]

Additional criticism of public–private partnerships has included observations directed at the substitution effect of partnerships for the role of states and transnational institutions like the United Nations[111] and the WHO.[112]

Perhaps the most striking downside of public–private partnerships in health-related areas is concerning the sustainability of funding models.[113] CEPI benefits from a broad network of funders that enables the partnership to support long-term R&D projects. However, that is not the case with most partnerships. In a survey conducted by the WHO in 2014, "nearly all" respondents indicated concerns with the "sustainability of their efforts" and their ability to "ensur[e] continuity of funding."[114]

Finally, many types of pharmaceutical R&D – including vaccine R&D – depend heavily on philanthropy. Currently, reliance on funding from the Gates Foundation is so overwhelming that an undisclosed respondent to the WHO survey stated that "but for Gates, we'd be dead."[115]

These overarching constraints inform the dynamics of the universe inhabited by public–private partnerships in the specific areas of vaccine R&D and vaccine procurement, to which the book now turns.

5.5.3 *The Role of Vaccine-Focused Public–Private Partnerships*

The following section surveys examples of partnerships dedicated to a specific type of technology – vaccines. As seen earlier, there are public–private partnerships that, although not presenting themselves as vaccine-dedicated, fund R&D on vaccines. The cases that the chapter now turns to are relevant to the themes explored in the book not only because of their vaccine-centric nature, but also because these partnerships are technology-specific. Each one of them was created in direct response to the particular challenges long experienced in the development and distribution of new vaccines: The underfunding of socially valuable R&D, and the equitable allocation of vaccine doses, especially to populations in need in lower-income countries.

---

[110] Liza Vertinsky, "Boundary-Spanning Collaboration and the Limits of Joint Inventorship Doctrine" (2017) 55 *Houston Law Review* 401, 426–27.

[111] See Kenny Bruno & Joshua Karliner, "Tangled Up in Blue: Corporate Partnerships at the United Nations" (September 1, 2000) *CorpWatch*, https://corpwatch.org/article/tangled-blue.

[112] Kent Buse & Amalia Waxman, "Public-Private Health Partnerships: A Strategy for WHO" (2001) 79 (8) *Bulletin of the World Health Organization: The International Journal of Public Health* 748–54.

[113] See Merz, "World Health Organization," note 89, at 14 (describing the phenomenon of "donor fatigue"). But see NAP Workshop Summary, note 104, at 57 (discussing the role of public–private partnerships as a sustainable financing mechanism for health systems).

[114] NAP Workshop Summary, note 104.

[115] NAP Workshop Summary, note 104.

There are now vaccine-dedicated partnerships at both ends of the R&D pipeline. The book provides an overview of two partnerships created in direct response to shortcomings in the reaction to recent public health crises: CEPI, formed in the wake of the 2014–2016 Ebola outbreak, and Covax, which came quickly together in the early stages of the COVID-19 pandemic.

5.5.3.1 The Coalition for Epidemic Preparedness Innovations (CEPI)

The Coalition for Epidemic Preparedness Innovations (CEPI) was launched at Davos in 2017 "to accelerate the development of vaccines against emerging infectious diseases and enable equitable access to these vaccines for affected populations during outbreaks."[116] The partnership was formed in response to faltering funding and support for R&D on vaccines needed to prevent or respond to outbreaks caused by emerging pathogens. In this sense, it operates as a product development partnership, seeking to attract monetary commitments from different sectors, and coordinating the development – and to some extend the distribution – of vaccines. The partnership describes its role as both a funder and facilitator of vaccine R&D and distribution: "We focus on vaccine development, licensure, and manufacturing while supporting the efforts of our partners in vaccine discovery and delivery."[117]

In addition to responding to a long-felt need in vaccine R&D, CEPI was created in the wake of the 2014–2016 Ebola outbreak. One reason a vaccine-dedicated product development partnership was able to attract the necessary support at that point in time was precisely due to the failures and delays in the commercialization of Ebola vaccines that were made apparent during the outbreak, as recounted in Chapter 3. To this day, CEPI's website and documentation reference the case of the Ebola vaccine candidate that could have come to market years before its launch date as indicative of the need for solutions to bolster vaccine R&D that are not predominantly market-based:

> Events like the devastating 2014/15 outbreak of Ebola in West Africa – which killed more than 11,000 people and had an economic and social burden of over $53 billion – showed us that very few vaccines are ready to be used against these threats.
>
> The world's response to this crisis fell tragically short. A vaccine that had been under development for more than a decade was not deployed until over a year into the epidemic. That vaccine was shown to be 100% effective, suggesting that much of the epidemic could have been prevented.[118]

While conceived as vaccine-specific, CEPI does not operate in all fields of vaccine R&D. Given its focus on emerging infectious diseases, the partnership has

---

[116]   CEPI, "Why We Exist," (2021), https://cepi.net/about/whyweexist/.
[117]   CEPI, "Why We Exist," note 116.
[118]   CEPI, "Why We Exist," note 116.

narrowed its list of "priority diseases" to selected areas, matching the pathogens identified in the 2016 WHO Blueprint as likely to cause outbreaks in the near future, and for which R&D has long remained underfunded: Ebola viruses, Lassa virus, Middle East Respiratory Syndrome coronavirus (MERS), Nipah virus, Rift Valley Fever virus, and Chikungunya virus.[119] Like several other public–private partnerships, in early 2020 CEPI added COVID-19 to the roster of diseases it provides funding and other support for.

Conversely, even though CEPI's approach is technology-specific in the sense that its sole focus is on vaccine-related technology, the partnership funds and helps develop vaccines produced through multiple technological approaches. To give but a few examples, at the time of writing CEPI is funding recombinant and live attenuated vaccines against COVID-19, inactivated vaccines against Chikungunya, and recombinant viral vector vaccines against the Lassa, MERS, and Nipah viruses.

Moreover, the partnership is also funneling resources toward the development of vaccine platform technology, which it describes as "platform technologies that can be used for rapid vaccine development against unknown pathogens (Disease X)."[120] As explored in Chapter 3, the unpredictably of which pathogens will cause significant outbreaks in the near- and medium-term, allied to the possibility of the emergence of a new pathogen, has long been one of the contributing factors to lukewarm investment in the field of vaccines against emerging pathogens.

The initial five-year budget for CEPI was calculated at between USD 600 million and 1 billion.[121] A year into its existence, CEPI has received USD 625 million from donors.[122] The largest donors are the governments of Norway, Japan, and Germany, as well as the Bill & Melinda Gates Foundation and the Wellcome Trust, the fourth largest foundation in the world.

CEPI-funded vaccines are subject to a requirement described by the partnership as "equitable access." CEPI's 2017 Preliminary Business Plan provided an initial definition of the requirement, as an obligation that "[g]lobal access arrangements will be negotiated in contracts between CEPI and vaccine developers to ensure affordability and availability in Low and Middle Income Countries (LMICs)."[123] CEPI's Policy Documentation shed additional light on the meaning of "access" in this context by explaining that agreements should impose two conditions.[124] First, should an outbreak occur, recipients of CEPI funding must provide "access to investigational vaccine stockpiles for phase III trials and emergency deployment." And second, in the case of vaccines funded by CEPI that succeed in gaining

[119]   CEPI, "Our Portfolio," (2021), https://cepi.net/research_dev/our-portfolio/.
[120]   CEPI, "Our Portfolio," note 119.
[121]   CEPI, "Preliminary Business Plan," note 103, at 47.
[122]   Catherine Cheney, CEPI, "A Year In: How Can We Get Ready for the Next Pandemic?" (February 5, 2018) *DEVEX*, www.devex.com/news/cepi-a-year-in-how-can-we-get-ready-for-the-next-pandemic -91987.
[123]   CEPI, "Preliminary Business Plan," note 103, at 12.
[124]   CEPI, "CEPI Policy Documentation," (2017), https://perma.cc/YJS8-YBQL, at 4.

approval from a domestic drug regulator, "access to the licensed vaccine" means that it must be made available to the indicated population at affordable prices.

The CEPI enterprise is relatively young, and as such it is not possible to perform a meaningful assessment of the efficacy of the partnership's equitable access policy at the time of writing. However, it suggests that it is feasible from a practical perspective to include pricing considerations into the contractual frameworks that govern the development of new vaccines. Recall the statement by the US Secretary of Health and Human Services in the early stages of the COVID-19 pandemic, implying that at any attempts to impose affordability obligations on recipients of public-sector funding for vaccine R&D are bound to irreversibly lower incentives for companies to invest in future vaccine R&D.[125] CEPI was designed to provide funding that, under standard R&D funding models is lacking for vaccine work – as such, it creates the forward-looking incentives that opponents of affordability provisions appear to worry about, while *simultaneously* conditioning the funding incentive to the recipient's agreement to commercialize the resulting vaccine at affordable prices. This brings into alignment both the economic and public health dimensions of vaccine development. The public–private partnership provides a monetary incentive for work in a chronically underfunded area, but imposes conditions aimed at furthering the public health goal of making vaccines available to indicated populations – rather than only to those who can afford them.

Operating under this model, CEPI has entered into agreements with heterogen-ous players, including private-sector vaccine manufacturers. For example, it is currently funding Moderna for work on a vaccine candidate targeting the corona-virus that causes Middle East Respiratory Syndrome (MERS), as well as work targeting other pathogens performed by other well-known vaccine manufactures, such as Inovio (US), Novavax (US), CureVac (Germany), and Valneva (France). This suggests that there is not a profound incompatibility between attracting vaccine manufacturers and imposing affordability requirements. It is possible that some actors in the vaccine R&D ecosystem might shy away from vaccine-related work if the possibility of setting supra-competitive prices is not available to them; yet others are likely to accept a contractual imposition of affordable pricing.

In any event, it is useful to keep in mind that, unlike the earliest COVID-19 vaccines to enter the market, most vaccines against emerging pathogens are not typically moneymakers. Actors who are strongly driven by economic returns have much more profitable areas of pharmaceutical R&D available to them. CEPI's Preliminary Business Plan explicitly recognized this: "It is anticipated that vaccines developed with CEPI support will not be profitable."[126] Against this backdrop, ensuring that key public health tools like vaccines are made available to those who

---

[125] Wetsman, "Health Secretary," note 1.
[126] CEPI, "Preliminary Business Plan," note 103, at 12.

need them through affordability requirements is a much more modest ask for policymakers and funders to make than in other areas of pharmaceutical R&D.

Lastly, a related takeaway from the limited number of years in which CEPI has been operating concerns the cases in which vaccines do become profitable and reinforces the point that affordable commercialization of vaccines is not incompatible with intellectual property-driven models and profits. Immediately after stating the assumption that profitability would constitute the exception and not the norm, CEPI's Preliminary Business Plan added the following:

> In the event that a vaccine developed with CEPI support does develop economic value, agreements between CEPI and the vaccine developer will ensure either that CEPI's investment is reimbursed or that the economic value is shared through royalties or other risk sharing agreements. Any rewards that accrue to vaccine developers should be proportionate to the level of risk undertaken and to the nature of the R&D, infrastructure, IP or other contributions a developer has made.[127]

This policy underscores the idea that models of vaccine R&D that make use of intellectual property – which remain the overwhelmingly predominant status quo – are not automatically incompatible with the adoption of contractual frameworks that promote public health goals. Should a CEPI-funded vaccine turn a profit, both the R&D players and the public–private partnership are entitled to recover their investment in proportional ways. Moreover, CEPI is under the obligation of returning any profits to its funding pool.[128]

This articulation with intellectual property frameworks also gives parties contracting with CEPI the possibility of negotiating intellectual property provisions on an ad hoc basis.[129] This gives both the partnership and the funding recipient flexibility to adjust contracts to specific situations. As a default, CEPI does not acquire ownership of any patents or other intellectual property brought by the funding recipient or generated during work on a CEPI-funded vaccine.[130] This dissociates CEPI's funding and coordinating functions from the acquisition and management of intellectual property rights.

Importantly, CEPI policies, under the umbrella of prompting funding recipients to "foster broader research efforts and innovation of vaccines for emerging infectious diseases that lack market potential," requires that patent-protected vaccine technology be made available to third parties on a "non-exclusive, royalty-free, sub-licensable, worldwide license."[131] This approach contrasts sharply with the one taken by the US public sector, as seen in connection with the development of the US Army's Zika vaccine candidate, for which the funding entity proposed issuing an exclusive license.

---

[127] CEPI, "Preliminary Business Plan," note 103, at 12.
[128] CEPI, "CEPI Policy Documentation," note 124, at 8.
[129] CEPI, "CEPI Policy Documentation," note 124, at 10.
[130] CEPI, "CEPI Policy Documentation," note 124, at 3.
[131] CEPI, "CEPI Policy Documentation," note 124, at 10.

Finally, CEPI layers obligations of clinical trial data sharing on top of the requirements set forth in domestic laws, which as seen in Chapter 2 often go unmet. These requirements bind funding recipients to publish results – including negative results – in a timely fashion, free of charge, and through a publicly available platform.[132]

As a whole, this contractual framework balances the current preference for proprietary modes of R&D with public health imperatives of development and distribution of health goods, as well as with scientific precepts of knowledge dissemination and enablement of follow-on research. The book makes no pronouncement as to how well CEPI's policies have been implemented in practice, given the relative newness of this particular public–private partnership. Nonetheless, it notes that from a legal and policy perspective, CEPI's principles and contractual approach provide a blueprint that can serve as a starting point for ongoing and future efforts to inscribe vaccine R&D into frameworks that do not lose sight of public health needs.

5.5.3.2 The COVID-19 Vaccine Global Access Facility (Covax)

CEPI is a vaccine-dedicated product development public–private partnership. The first access partnership to focus exclusively on vaccines appeared much earlier. The Global Alliance for Vaccines and Immunizations (Gavi), was launched in 2000 "to "improv(e) access to new and underused vaccines" in lower-income countries.[133] Funded by donors and contributions from countries to which it provides vaccines, Gavi has become the epicenter of the procurement of childhood vaccines for the Global South. Currently, it has seventeen vaccines in its portfolio, covering areas that range from polio and cholera to measles and rubella.[134]

The strategy that Gavi pioneered in the field of vaccines is one that has long been deployed in local, regional, and international trade. After securing funding for a particular purpose – often one not attainable by most players in the field – a buyer places a high-volume order, which brings down the marginal cost of each item.[135] As an economic agent, Gavi secures funding for goods that, absent this drop in marginal cost, would be unaffordable to governments of lower-income countries negotiating on their own. By repeatedly spiking demand for childhood vaccines bound for lower-income markets, Gavi gives vaccine manufacturers in wealthier countries the incentive to manufacture doses of vaccine for markets that are normally neglected, and in doing so lowers the cost of vaccines for governments in these markets. Between 2000 and 2019, vaccines procured by Gavi were administered to over 822 million children in seventy-seven countries.[136]

[132] CEPI, "Preliminary Business Plan," note 103, at 3.
[133] Gavi, "About Our Alliance," (2021), www.gavi.org/our-alliance/about.
[134] Gavi, "Vaccine Support," (2021), www.gavi.org/support/nvs/.
[135] Danzon et al., "Vaccine Supply," note 9.
[136] Gavi, "Facts and Figures," (2021), www.gavi.org/programmes-impact/our-impact/facts-and-figures.

The basic strategy used by Gavi to help bring vaccines to countries that, on their own, have long been unappealing to most market-driven R&D players was also used during the COVID-19 vaccine race in response to escalating concerns with vaccine nationalism – the skewed allocation of emerging vaccines to higher-income countries, as described in Chapter 4. Also structured as a vaccine-specific access public–private partnership, the COVID-19 Vaccine Global Access Facility (Covax) was swiftly conceived and rolled out as a financing and procurement mechanism aimed at promoting the equitable distribution of vaccines across the globe.[137]

Covax is led jointly by CEPI, Gavi, and the WHO and works in partnership with UNICEF on vaccine delivery. Unlike most other access partnerships, COVAX was not designed as a standalone entity, being integrated into a larger institutional network – the Access to COVID Tools (ACT) Accelerator.[138] ACT-A was launched in April 2020 by the WHO, the European Commission, the government of France, and the Bill & Melinda Gates Foundation. It was created as a "support structure" for work in closely related areas, known as "pillars." ACT-A has three pillars – diagnostics, therapeutics, and vaccines – with a fourth, the health systems connector, intersecting with the previous three.

Covax is the vaccines pillar of ACT-A. It plays a role throughout the arc of vaccine development and distribution through three distinct organizations that focus on different stages of this arc. CEPI is involved in the funding, development, and manufacturing of vaccine candidates.[139] The WHO oversees policy issues related to emerging vaccines and the process of allocating doses as they become available. Finally, Gavi brings in its expertise at the procurement and vaccine delivery levels.

While Gavi's procurement work in the field of childhood vaccines is aimed only at lower-income countries, Covax is open to any country wishing to join, irrespective of income level. When Covax was launched in April 2020, all interested countries were invited to join. Countries that chose to participate in Covax's procurement system for COVID-19 vaccines were required to commit to purchase a certain amount of vaccine doses. At this point in time, there were several leading vaccine candidates being developed by pharmaceutical companies, but none had been authorized or approved. Placing vaccine orders was thus both necessary as countries needed to secure doses for administration as soon as the vaccines were green lighted by drug regulators, but also risky since it was impossible to know with certainty which vaccines would make it to market first, and which might encounter late-stage hurdles or possibly even fail unexpectedly.

The dynamics of Covax procurement diffused this risk to some extent. Because Covax negotiated with multiple private-sector vaccine manufacturers at the same

[137] Gavi, "Covax, the ACT-Accelerator Vaccines Pillar," (2020), www.gavi.org/sites/default/files/docu ment/2020/COVAX-Pillar-backgrounder_3.pdf.

[138] World Health Organization, "The Access to COVID-19 Tools (ACT) Accelerator," www.who.int /initiatives/act-accelerator.

[139] Gavi, "Covax," note 137.

time, a country that chose to join the procurement scheme would stand in line to receive vaccine doses from a pool of multiple vaccine candidates. Moreover, participating countries obtained these vaccine doses at a price previously negotiated between Covax and individual pharmaceutical companies. From the perspective of these companies, the commitments entered into by countries joining Covax functioned as "carrots" – incentives to start or continue producing vaccine doses at risk, with the assurance that, should their candidates receive market approval or authorization, those commitments represented monetizable orders. In the context of a raging global public health crisis and a volatile economy, Covax functioned as a risk-sharing and portfolio diversification mechanism while attempting to promote access to vaccines outside the nationalistic framework used by high-income countries.

In June 2020, Covax entered into its first procurement agreement, preordering 300 million doses of the vaccine candidate developed by British-Swedish pharmaceutical company AstraZeneca.[140] The vaccine was first authorized for emergency use in late December in the United Kingdom. Agreements with other vaccine manufacturers followed, and by mid-March 2021, Covax had shipped over twenty-nine million doses of COVID-19 vaccines to forty-six participants. It sourced three different vaccines: the vaccine manufactured by the Serum Institute in India, which became the first COVAX-supported vaccine to be administered, forty-three days after the beginning of COVID-19 vaccination in the United Kingdom; the AstraZeneca vaccine, manufactured by the South Korean pharmaceutical company SK-Bio; and the Pfizer-BioNTech vaccine, the first COVID-19 vaccine commercialized in the United States under an emergency use authorization. By late May 2021, the number of distributed Covax-procured vaccines had climbed to seventy-two million, distributed among 126 participants.[141]

A large and heterogeneous group of players thus managed to come together with remarkable rapidity as highly disruptive events unfolded, and procure some of the most sought-after and scarce commodities in the world at the time. In addition to the sheer speed with which the partnership was formed and began entering into binding agreements, another striking aspect of Covax was the fact that it squarely relied on the same contractual mechanism that is used to further vaccine nationalism – advance purchase orders.

As a purchaser, Covax did what individual high-income countries were already doing in the COVID-19 pandemic and had done in previous public health crises: It entered a race to acquire as many vaccine doses as possible given the resources and bargaining power at its disposal. But because Covax was bargaining and buying on behalf of countries straddling income levels, the partnership

[140]   Gavi, "Gavi Launches Innovative Financing Mechanism for Access to COVID-19 Vaccines" (June 4, 2020), www.gavi.org/news/media-room/gavi-launches-innovative-financing-mechanism-access-covid-19-vaccines.

[141]   Gavi, "Covax Vaccine Roll-Out" (May 27, 2021), www.gavi.org/covax-vaccine-roll-out.

functioned as a non-nationalistic actor on the demand side, capturing a portion of the limited supply globally available. In so doing, it adapted existing trade mechanisms and contractual frameworks to introduce a blueprint for the first truly global vaccine procurement scheme.

There were, however, aspects of the implementation of this scheme that were far from ideal and that once again worked to the disadvantage of lower-income countries. Some of these shortcomings were perhaps unavoidable, given the remedial nature of the intervention that led to the formation of Covax: However swiftly a global procurement structure may have come together, it was nonetheless negotiated and implemented during a highly disruptive crisis, when vaccine nationalism was already in full swing and considerable amounts of vaccine doses had already been reserved by high-income countries. The playing field was no longer level by the time Covax entered the vaccine acquisition race. It is therefore not surprising that the volume of vaccine doses that countries could obtain through Covax was relatively low – the partnership offered each participating country the possibility of signing up for enough doses to cover up to 20 percent of their population in the long-term.[142] This presents a quantitative problem. Given the much higher threshold projected for herd immunity against COVID-19 to occur, Covax procurement by itself was not enough to provide countries with as much vaccine required to meet public health needs. While higher-income countries might be able to cover this gap by contracting bilaterally with vaccine manufacturers, many lower-income countries could not afford that option, or could only afford it in much more limited terms than their counterparts in the Global North. Covax was thus able to lessen some of the effects of vaccine nationalism but did not eliminate the problem.

There were also qualitative problems in Covax's approach to vaccine allocation. The partnership was designed with the ultimate goal of providing equitable access to vaccines to all participants – a goal that is reflected in the proportional approach to vaccine allocation. Yet, there were differences in the policies applicable to lower- and higher-income countries. These differences derived from the use of two types of financing mechanisms to secure advance purchase orders: some countries self-financed their own orders, while others received financial assistance in order to enter into the Covax procurement scheme. The self-financing group was formed by countries that are formally categorized as high-income and upper middle-income. The group that received financial assistance was formed by countries that are formally categorized lower middle-income and low-income countries.

The policy developed by Covax, made available in June 2020 and labeled as promoting "equitable access," placed different conditions on vaccine allocation depending on whether a participant was self-funded or had received financial support.[143] As they received their proportional share of vaccine doses, self-funded

[142] Gavi, "Covax Explained," (2020), www.gavi.org/vaccineswork/covax-explained.
[143] Gavi, "COVID-19 Vaccine Global Access (Covax) Facility, Preliminary Technical Design: Discussion Document" (June 11, 2020), https://perma.cc/HD4D-V2WK, at 2.

countries were free to decide how and according to which principles to distribute them to their populations. By contrast, countries who had received financial support were asked to distribute their proportional shares according to allocative criteria established through "guidance from the global allocation frame work under development by WHO."[144] While tied to a distinction in the financing of vaccine procurement, this disparate treatment bears no connection to matters of procurement. It constitutes an intrusion on the setting of public health policies at the national level – one that was not explained by Covax for any reasons other than the differences in the economic means through which orders were paid for.

In addition to this conditioning of the establishment of domestic allocative priorities in lower-income countries, Covax policy made yet another surprising distinction between self-funded countries and those that had received financial support. If countries in the latter group were able to negotiate the purchase of additional doses of vaccines from sources other than Covax and received enough doses to cover 20 percent of their domestic population, the partnership asked them to wait for their share of Covax-funded vaccines until all other countries participating in Covax – self-funded or not – had received their Covax allocation:

> If a country in this group successfully concludes a bilateral deal and receives enough doses to cover e.g. 20% of their population, the Facility [COVAX] requests that these countries delay receipt of any additional doses from the Facility until all other Facility country participants have received enough supply to also cover their highest priority populations.[145]

The policy, however, did not apply to self-funded countries. From a public health perspective, this made little sense. Self-funded countries tended to be higher-income countries and hence more likely to be able to bolster their vaccine supply through bilateral channels. This group of countries also included the major actors in vaccine nationalism, who had already captured most of the global vaccine supply before joining Covax. Restricting the ability of lower-income countries of acquiring the much-needed doses in a playing field that is already skewing vaccine allocation toward higher-income countries is at odds with the geographical contours of the pandemic, as well as its socioeconomic impact.

A final limitation of the Covax model is that it did not require countries that came to possess excedentary vaccine doses to share them with countries still struggling to obtain enough vaccine. In a reference to doses obtained through bilateral agreements, the policy did state that self-funded countries were "encouraged (but not required) to donate vaccines if they have more than they need."[146] The final section of this chapter will argue that this limitation, and the ones described earlier, can and should be corrected ahead of future vaccine races.

---

[144] Gavi, "COVID-19 Vaccine Global Access," note 143, at 11.
[145] Gavi, "COVID-19 Vaccine Global Access," note 143, at 11.
[146] Gavi, "COVID-19 Vaccine Global Access," note 143, at 4.

Even though these limitations are significant, the formation of Covax marks an important moment in the development of strategies against inequitable distribution of vaccines during large transnational public health crises. The discussion on vaccine nationalism in Chapter 4 had made the case that collaborative modes of allocation of scarce vaccine supply are preferable to nationalistic ones – Covax provided an example of how such collaborative modes can be implemented in practice. In so doing, it created a blueprint that can be adapted for future pandemics and epidemics.

Admittedly, that blueprint incorporates several flawed policies, some of which are hardly justifiable even when taking into account the extreme urgency and pressures created by the pandemic, and against which Covax was developed. That these flaws need remedying does not mean that a fairer and more robust global procurement of vaccines cannot be built by expanding the features of Covax's architecture that were successful, and correcting those that were not.

5.5.4 *The Case for Expanding International Vaccine Procurement*

The book here proposes the creation of a permanent structure dedicated to the procurement of vaccines needed for pandemic and epidemic preparedness. This structure could evolve organically out of Covax, or be developed to substitute it, should Covax come to an end after the COVID-19 pandemic. Irrespective of its formation, institutional permanency is critical to move vaccine procurement past remedial, short-lived responses to large-scale public health crises.

A permanent structure is also in a better position to navigate the time-consuming and politically fraught bargaining processes necessary to enable greater centralization and internationalization of vaccine procurement *ahead* of future outbreaks. The hasty negotiations that led to the formation of Covax also exposed the challenges faced by emerging international organizations as multilateral venues: Early in the COVID-19 pandemic, the United States, Russia, India, Brazil, and Argentina decided not to join the negotiations for the formation of Covax.[147] Long-term diplomacy and other persuasive efforts will likely be required to create a truly global vaccine procurement structure, tasks that temporary institutional actors in the international arena are ill-equipped to perform.

In a similar vein, permanency is instrumental for the development of funding strategies that will allow a centralizing entity to have a bigger footprint in international vaccine procurement when outbreak-induced vaccine races occur. As market-driven models of vaccine production and distribution are poised to remain the norm, contractual bilateralism and vaccine nationalism are unlikely to disappear. However, by expanding the relative purchasing power of a large player, the

---

[147] Richard Milne & David Crow, "Why Vaccine 'Nationalism' Could Slow Coronavirus Fight" (May 13, 2020) *Financial Times*, www.ft.com/content/6d542894-6483-446c-87b0-96c65e89bb2c.

international community can begin to lessen the inequalities in the allocation of vaccine doses obtained under conditions of scarcity. This can be achieved by incrementally raising quantitative procurement targets, which necessarily entails increasing financial commitments in support of greater acquisition of vaccine doses – for instance, by going beyond the mark established by Covax of procuring doses that would cover up to 20 percent of the population of each participating country. While consistent with global public health needs, this is by no means a small ask: Even at smaller scale and against the background of a devastating public health crisis, Covax has remained underfunded throughout most of the COVID-19 pandemic.[148]

In addition to permanency and enhanced funding, it is imperative that a global vaccine procurement structure improve upon Covax's allocative model. To act as a true driver of equitable vaccine allocation, such a structure should not make allocative distinctions based on financing mechanisms. The restrictions that Covax policy imposed on lower-income countries curtailed their already-limited ability to maneuver in markets disproportionately dominated by high-income purchasers of health goods.

Complementarily, this structure should impose a binding contractual obligation *on all countries* to share excedentary doses of vaccines. Current paradigms for sharing vaccine surplus rely on donation models that are not subject to any triggering mechanisms that can be counted upon. Instead, they rely on the goodwill of individual countries, which are often the same countries that have resorted to bilateralism to capture vaccine doses through a nationalistic approach. Activist Akin Olla has described the current dynamics of vaccine donation – and the fact that many countries delay donations or outright choose not to donate excedentary doses – as a "new colonialism."[149]

Moving forward, international procurement should incorporate mechanisms containing some type of trigger for mandatory vaccine-sharing obligations for countries with a vaccine surplus. This trigger should be based on measurable criteria – for instance, when a country acquires sufficient doses to vaccinate its population, or a set percentage thereof, depending on the characteristics of the underlying disease and on projections related to herd immunity. Several studies conducted during the COVID-19 pandemic showed that several high-income countries bought vaccine doses that greatly exceeded their domestic needs (even when a buffer was factored in to account for unforeseen needs) and did not share surplus doses with countries struggling to acquire doses for their

[148]   See e.g. Sigal Samuel, "Why COVAX, the Fund to Vaccinate the World, Is Struggling" (May 20, 2021) *Vox*, www.vox.com/future-perfect/22440986/covax-challenges-covid-19-vaccines-global-inequity.

[149]   Akin Olla, "Welcome to the New Colonialism: Rich Countries Sitting on Surplus Vaccines" (April 14, 2021) *Guardian*, www.theguardian.com/commentisfree/2021/apr/14/rich-countries-surplus-covid-vaccines.

own populations.[150] This phenomenon, often described as "vaccine hoarding," illustrates the need for a mandatory model of vaccine-sharing. Alone, such a trigger will not end vaccine colonialism, but it would constitute a first step toward lessening some of the most acute effects of the inequitable geopolitics of vaccine allocation.

---

[150] Duke Global Health Institute, "Will Low-Income Countries," note 27.

6

Vaccines of the Future

Present and Emerging Challenges

In previous chapters, the book considered instances of the lack of access to vaccines, attributable to supra-competitive pricing or skewed allocation of limited doses. This chapter shifts the narrative toward emerging scenarios in which different types of barriers stand in the way of the ultimate goal of having robust vaccine distribution and uptake among all populations in need.

The chapter first examines instances in which these barriers take the form of rejection of available vaccines by some indicated populations – a phenomenon that can be contemporaneous with scarcity faced by populations elsewhere, as illustrated by the COVID-19 pandemic, during which some individuals to whom a vaccine was available at no cost have chosen not to receive it.[1] In particular, the chapter explores the role of a particular set of technologies in the spread of vaccine misinformation and disinformation, which have been shown to contribute to hesitancy toward vaccination. The word *misinformation* is most commonly associated with the propagation of "false or misleading content."[2] Many commentators reserve the term for cases in which this propagation is done without intent to deceive, using the word *disinformation* to refer to cases in which false or misleading content is spread with the purpose of deceiving or confusing others.[3] This section of the book uses *misinformation* as an umbrella for inaccurate information, reserving *disinformation* for cases in which the existence of intent to deceive is relevant.

The chapter then turns to examples of other types of technologies that are progressively shaping ways in which vaccines are discovered, produced, and distributed. First, it explores the application of emerging health technologies to vaccinology – a process that may soon complicate the distinction between

---

[1] See e.g. Lisa Rosenbaum, "Escaping Catch-22 – Overcoming Covid Vaccine Hesitancy" (2021) 384 *New England Journal of Medicine* 1367–71 (noting that, as of April 2021, "vaccine confidence seems to be rising, but recent polling suggests that about 31% of Americans wish to take a wait-and-see approach, and about 20% remain quite reluctant").

[2] See e.g. Gordon Pennycook et al., "Understanding and Reducing the Spread of Misinformation Online" (2019) *PsyArXiv*, https://psyarxiv.com/3n9u8/.

[3] Claire Wardle & Hossein Derakhshan, "Information Disorder: Toward an Interdisciplinary Framework for Research and Policy Making" (2017) Council of Europe Report DGI 09, at 16.

vaccine and non-vaccine products. Second, the chapter considers how the use of emerging non-health technologies is also pushing vaccinology in new directions. Collectively, these examples provide a brief overview of how areas beyond drug regulation and intellectual property, and the laws and policies that govern those areas, will increasingly intersect with the vaccine ecosystem, and how they are likely to have practical effects on which vaccines are developed and how, as well as the conditions under which they are made available to those in need.

6.1 (RE)EMERGING CHALLENGES TO THE ADOPTION OF VACCINE TECHNOLOGY: VACCINE MISINFORMATION AND DISINFORMATION

As noted in the introduction, the use of vaccines may trigger the occurrence of certain side effects, which are generally mild, although in extremely rare cases serious effects do occur. While the existence of some degree of risk is inherent to the use of virtually any pharmaceutical product, vaccines have long been among the most polarizing biotechnologies made available to patients.

Historically, this polarization has been linked to discourses and movements that challenge the public health value of vaccines, by placing hyperbolic emphasis on the side effects of vaccination, questioning the safety or efficacy of approved vaccines, or implying a connection between the endorsement of vaccines by public health authorities and the furtherance of political or otherwise ideologically motivated agendas.

These recurring challenges are one contributing factor – although not the only factor – of vaccine hesitancy. The WHO defines this concept as "the reluctance or refusal to vaccinate despite the availability of vaccines."[4] These are therefore cases in which hurdles to the production of vaccine technology, or to its distribution, have been overcome. However, problems arise at the level of the reception of the technology, as the would-be recipient of a vaccine elects not to take it.

In several instances, the existence of a trust deficit surrounding vaccination or a given vaccine is understandable. Recall the case of racial and ethnic minorities that have been consistently underrepresented in vaccine clinical trials and, more broadly, neglected and exploited in medical research.[5] In other cases, hesitancy is connected to the uncertainty an individual may reasonably experience when faced with a complex technology – particularly when the technology is designed to interact with the human body. Moreover, a subset of individuals called to accept or reject a recommended vaccine are parents deciding on behalf of children, who are generally indicated for the administration of a larger number of vaccines over a concentrated period of time than older individuals.

---

[4]   World Health Organization, "Ten Threats to Global Health in 2019," (2019), www.who.int/news-room/spotlight/ten-threats-to-global-health-in-2019.
[5]   See Chapter 2, Section 2.2. See also Washington, *Medical Apartheid*, note 66.

While there are several reasons behind vaccine hesitancy, high levels of hesitancy are problematic from a public health perspective.[6] Studies correlate increases in vaccine hesitancy with the resurgence of vaccine-preventable infectious diseases in many countries. For instance, there were multiple measles outbreaks across the United States in 2019, which have now been linked to increasing hesitancy toward childhood vaccination.[7] The resurgence of vaccine-preventable diseases in multiple parts of the world led the WHO to declare vaccine hesitancy one of the "ten threats to global health" in 2019, alongside pollution, antimicrobial resistance, noncommunicable disease, and disease caused by emergency infectious disease pathogens, among others.

The tension between the unencumbered availability of a vaccine and low uptake poses a technological and public health paradox: While the technology necessary to prevent or lessen the burden of a given disease has been developed and is available to an indicated population, hesitancy toward these technologies opens the door to the return of the disease these technologies were designed to prevent or mitigate in the first place.

In recent decades, the popularization of a completely different type of technologies – Internet-based communication tools – has catalyzed the spread of substantial amounts of information about vaccines and vaccination that is incorrect, either inadvertently or on purpose. Social media in particular have become a hotbed for the promotion of vaccine misinformation and disinformation. Most recently, actors that traditionally did not operate in vaccine-related areas have started to spread content about vaccines as a way to increase social and political divergences among users of social media.

This section describes this new and growing problem in the vaccine innovation ecosystem: As players in the R&D space come together to create valuable public health technologies, players in areas that may be entirely unrelated to vaccines now have the ability to contribute to the erosion of trust in vaccines in unprecedented ways.

6.1.1 *Recent Events in the History of Vaccine Misinformation*

The most well-known episode in the recent history of vaccine misinformation is linked to the publication of an article in one of the most reputable and historied medical journals, *The Lancet*. Founded in 1823, the journal is peer-reviewed, with every article accepted for publication undergoing evaluation by experts in the underlying medical field. In 1998, *The Lancet* published an article whose lead

---

[6] See e.g. Denis G. Gill, "Vaccine Refusal and the Risks of Vaccine-Preventable Diseases" (2009) 360 *New England Journal of Medicine* 723.

[7] See David A. Broniatowski et al., "Facebook Pages, the 'Disneyland' Measles Outbreak, and Promotion of Vaccine Refusal as a Civil Right, 2009–2019" (2020) 110 *American Journal of Public Health* S312–18.

author was Andrew Wakefield, then a doctor practicing and lecturing at the Royal Free Hospital in London.[8] He had previously been the lead author of an article claiming a possible link between the measles virus and Crohn's disease, published in 1993 in another peer-reviewed publication, the *Journal of Medical Virology*. The article in *The Lancet* linked the MMR vaccine (targeting the measles, mumps, and rubella viruses) to cases of autism in children.[9]

Research performed by experts shortly after the article was published refuted these claims and revealed that the research had been methodologically flawed and fraudulently presented.[10] However, the 1998 article attracted enormous attention outside the medical community and, by 1999, vaccination rates for MMR had begun to decrease due to parental concerns about the vaccine.[11]

Even though criticism within the medical community arose quickly after publication of the article, it took *The Lancet* until 2010 to retract it. That same year, the body that oversees the licensure of physicians in the United Kingdom, the General Medical Council, found Wakefield guilty of more than thirty charges of misconduct and barred him from the practice of medicine.[12]

The now-discredited article has remained influential to this day.[13] Although scientifically disproven, Wakefield continues to divulge his claims, which in turn have been echoed by public figures with large followings. One of the most notable cases is that of actress and talk-show host Jenny McCarthy, who wrote the preface to a book Wakefield wrote and that perpetuates his claims of a causal link between the MMR vaccine and autism.[14] The book was published in 2011 in the United States and remains in print and widely accessible.

The popularization of online platforms – and the corresponding migration of many debates to the online environment – has also triggered a shift of many conversations about pharmaceutical products to these platforms. As seen in Section 6.1.2, social media have played an especially prominent role in the amplification of these debates.

---

[8] See Brian Deer, *The Doctor Who Fooled the World: Science, Deception, and the War on Vaccines* (Johns Hopkins University Press, 2020).

[9] See Fiona Godlee & Jane Smith, "Wakefield's Article Linking MMR Vaccine and Autism Was Fraudulent" (2011) 342 *British Medical Journal* c7452, www.bmj.com/content/342/bmj.c7452.

[10] T. S. Sathyanarayana Rao & Chittaranjan Andrade, "The MMR Vaccine and Autism: Sensation, Refutation, Retraction, and Fraud" (April–June 2011) 53(2) *Indian Journal of Psychiatry* 95–96.

[11] Sathyanarayana Rao, "MMR Vaccine and Autism," note 10; F. DeStefano and R. T. Chen, "Negative Association between MMR and Autism" (June 12, 1999) 353(9169) *Lancet* 1987–88, https://doi.org/10 .1016/S0140-6736(99)00160-9.

[12] See Clare Dyer, "Wakefield Was Dishonest and Irresponsible over MMR Research, Says GMC" (2010) 340 *British Medical Journal* c593.

[13] See e.g. Clyde Haberman, "A Discredited Vaccine Study's Continuing Impact on Public Health" (February 1, 2015) *New York Times*, www.nytimes.com/2015/02/02/us/a-discredited-vaccine-studys-continuing-impact-on-public-health.html.

[14] Michael Specter, "Jenny McCarthy's Dangerous Views" (July 16, 2013) *New Yorker*, https://www .newyorker.com/tech/annals-of-technology/jenny-mccarthys-dangerous-views.

6.1.2 *Vaccine Misinformation in the Online Environment: The Role of Social Media*

The use of social media grew exponentially during the 2010s. For instance, the first time the Pew Research Center gathered data on social media usage in the United States, in 2005, only 5 percent of adults in the United States used at least one of the leading social media platforms.[15] By 2011, almost 50 percent of Americans were using at least one major social media, and by 2019 that number had climbed to almost three quarters. As of 2019, according to data from the Pew Research Center, the largest social media in the United States by number of users were Facebook, Instagram, LinkedIn, Twitter, Pinterest, Snapchat, YouTube, WhatsApp, and Reddit. In 2020, TikTok, the international version of the popular Chinese video-sharing social media Douyin, also achieved leading status in the United States and across other Western countries. By August 2020, it had approximately 100 million users in the United States and had surpassed the 2.3 billion mark in all-time downloads.[16] As seen later, many of these mainstream social media also constitute the primary venues for the dissemination of inaccurate content about vaccines in the online environment.

The popularization of social media has opened up new pathways for the promotion of accurate information about health goods and emerging medical research.[17] It has created new fora for professional and patient communities to come together, and to share information both internally and externally. And it has also provided public health authorities with new channels that can be used to reach wide audiences quickly when an emergency occurs. During the COVID-19 pandemic, for instance, social media – and other online platforms – played an important role in propagating messages from domestic and international public health organizations, including updated numbers about the pandemic, recommendations about safe and unsafe practices, and the location of testing centers.[18]

As the first COVID-19 vaccines came close to entering the market, public health-oriented institutions like the WHO and the Centers for Disease Control and Prevention in the United States adopted communication strategies that made intensive use of social media as avenues for the promotion of their content about these new vaccines, as well as about vaccination in general. In addition to overarching educational purposes, these strategies were also deployed in direct response to

[15] Pew Research Center, "Social Media Fact Sheet" (June 12, 2019), www.pewresearch.org/internet/fact-sheet/social-media/.
[16] Paige Leskin, "Inside the Rise of TikTok, the Viral Video-Sharing App Wildly Popular with Teens and Loathed by the Trump Administration" (August 7, 2020) *Business Insider*, https://www.businessinsider.com/tiktok-app-online-website-video-sharing-2019-7.
[17] Jessica Y. Breland et al., "Social Media as a Tool to Increase the Impact of Public Health Research" (2017) 107 *American Journal of Public Health* 1890–91.
[18] See e.g. Jon Porter, "Google Search Panels Launch to Counter Vaccine Misinformation" (December 10, 2020) *Verge*, https://www.theverge.com/2020/12/10/22167185/google-vaccine-information-search-results-youtube-information-panels.

the significant growth of vaccine misinformation and disinformation circulating online.[19]

Much in the same way that they can be used as vehicles for the amplification of accurate content, social media can also serve as conduits for the dissemination of inaccurate information – and in recent years they have become prime territory for the spread of vaccine misinformation.[20]

One characteristic of vaccine-specific misinformation circulating in social media is that it actually represents the views (or agenda) of a very limited number of actors. These actors, however, exert disproportionate influence in online debates related to vaccines. They are both more connected with vaccine-centric networks and more efficient at populating social media networks with their own content.[21]

Studies focusing on parental exposure to vaccine content exemplify the skewed dynamics of vaccine misinformation circulating on social media.[22] Parents of young children using social media make up an especially relevant category because the majority of vaccines that most individuals will receive during their lifetime are administered during childhood. A substantial amount of effort to promote vaccine-questioning content is thus often geared toward those in decision-making positions about the administration of vaccines. Moreover, parents with vaccination-age children are also more likely to actively search for information about vaccines, and therefore more likely to encounter online content qualifying as misinformation.

A study published in the United Kingdom in 2019 by the Royal Society for Public Health provided a glimpse into how even vaccine-trusting parents are likely to be exposed to vaccine misinformation.[23] The study found that 91 percent of parents held favorable views about vaccines, agreeing that they were "important." Among parents using social media, 41 percent reported having encountered "negative messages" about vaccines or vaccination. When the study surveyed parents of children under five years old who were social media users, it found that percentage to be even higher, at 50 percent.

6.1.3 *The Automatization and Weaponization of Vaccine Misinformation*

While social media can be used to promote both accurate and inaccurate vaccine information, the circulation of the latter has been bolstered in recent years by the use of automated programs.

---

[19]   Mark Dredze et al., "Understanding Vaccine Refusal: Why We Need Social Media Now" (2016) 50 *American Journal of Preventative Medicine* 550–52.

[20]   Anna Kata, "Anti-vaccine Activists, Web 2.0, and the Postmodern Paradigm–An Overview of Tactics and Tropes Used Online by the Anti-vaccination Movement" (2012) 30 *Vaccine* 3778–89.

[21]   Neil F. Johnson et al., "The Online Competition between Pro- and Anti-Vaccination Views" (2020) 582 *Nature* 230–33 (describing this phenomenon on Facebook).

[22]   Royal Society for Public Health, "Moving the Needle: Promoting Vaccination Uptake across the Life Course" (2018), www.rsph.org.uk/static/uploaded/3b82db00-a7ef-494c-85451e78ce18a779.pdf, at 3.

[23]   Royal Society for Public Health, "Moving the Needle," note 22.

Online vaccine debates are by no means the only ones now being affected by the use of automated programs. Throughout the 2010s, internet traffic became increasingly populated by these types of programs, also known as bots. In 2017, the magazine *The Atlantic* published an article entitled *The Internet Is Mostly Bots*, in which journalist Adrienne LaFrance colorfully noted, "Look around you, people of the internet. The bots. *They're everywhere.*"[24]

Many bots perform valuable tasks, eliminating drudgery and helping make the Internet the marketplace we know today. These tasks range from reviewing and indexing content that is made available when somebody performs an online search, to monitoring and alerting tasks such as spotting system outages. However, there are also several types of automated programs that have become known as "bad bots." These programs are deployed for malicious purposes, which range from harvesting content made publicly available through a website to cracking passwords, collecting personal or financial information, or providing clickbait as part of a strategy to generate revenue.

Bad bots became increasingly sophisticated in the 2010s[25] and were soon deployed to aid in the dissemination of vaccine-related content. When the US Defense Advanced Research Projects Agency (DARPA) launched a bot-detecting competition in 2015, it chose to focus on bots operating on Twitter and specifically contributing to, or otherwise affecting, ongoing vaccine debates, or vaccine-related content sharing.[26] The Twitter Bot Detection Challenge lasted four weeks, during which participants were asked to examine tweets about vaccines and identify different types of automated programs. In particular, the Challenge was designed to prompt the development of better tools to recognize and eliminate "influence bots," a category encompassing "realistic, automated identities that illicitly shape discussion on sites like Twitter and Facebook."[27] The Challenge also called attention to the need to curb the use of these particular types of bot "before they get too influential."

Bad bots play a particular role in the spread of vaccine *disinformation*. In 2018, David Broniatowski, a researcher in the field of decision-making and systems architecture, published an article with colleagues in related fields charting the proliferation of online disinformation specific to vaccines, using Twitter as a case study.[28] The study analyzed vaccine-related tweets shared through Twitter between July 2014 and September 2017, and characterized the sources of these

24   Adrienne Lafrance, "The Internet Is Mostly Bots" (January 31, 2017) *Atlantic*, https://www.theatlantic.com/technology/archive/2017/01/bots-bots-bots/515043/.

25   Vedran Bozicevic, "Industry Report: Bad Bot Landscape 2019 – The Bot Arms Race Continues" (May 12, 2019) *Global Dots*, https://www.globaldots.com/resources/blog/industry-report-bad-bot-landscape-2019-the-bot-arms-race-continues/.

26   V. S. Subrahmanian et al., "The DARPA Twitter Bot Challenge," (2016), https://arxiv.org/abs/1601.05140.

27   Subrahmanian et al., "DARPA," note 26, at 2.

28   David A. Broniatowski et al., "Weaponized Health Communication: Twitter Bots and Russian Trolls Amplify the Vaccine Debate" (2018) 108 *American Journal of Public Health* 1378–1384.

communications. First, they noted that vaccine content was being shared by both automated and human-operated programs that nonetheless engaged in malicious behaviors. Within the category of automated programs, the study distinguished between "bots" proper and "content polluters." Bots were defined as Twitter "accounts that automate content promotion," whereas content polluters were defined as "malicious accounts identified as promoting commercial content and malware." Turning to programs operated by humans, the study labeled Twitter accounts "exhibiting malicious behaviors yet operated by humans" as "trolls."

The study found that both automated and human-operated programs were propagating vaccine-related content in sophisticated ways. Trolls identified as originating in Russia were especially active, sharing both pro- and anti-vaccine content. This is part of a strategy that was adopted with increasing frequency in the mid- to late-2010s by individuals or institutions targeting areas of social debate known for being particularly divisive, including political and electoral themes. With topics surrounding vaccines long bearing visible marks of discord, trolls furthering geopolitical strategies to increase social dissonance in countries like the United States were quick to tap into vaccine themes to accomplish this goal. By increasing the amount of pro- and anti-vaccine content at the same time, these players sought to increase the prominence of vaccine debates on Twitter. Their goals were not to persuade users of the merits of a particular set of views about vaccines, but rather to prompt increased discussion between parties likely to disagree with one another, thus contributing to escalating levels of divisiveness in Western societies. As they were spreading vaccine content through Twitter, Russian trolls specifically tried to politicize the underlying messages.

Although the study identified a large quantity of Russia-based trolls adopting this type of strategy, it also noted that some of the most sophisticated automated programs – and bots in particular – also employed a similar approach and that these programs had been traced back to several regions outside Russia and the post-Soviet world.

The study also found that sophisticated automated programs – those relying on more complex technology and harder to detect – shared vaccine-related content at significantly higher rates than human-operated ones. Content polluters were the prime spreaders of anti-vaccine tweets, outpacing accounts operated by humans at a rate of 75 percent.

Two other strategies linked to the promotion of disinformation in several other fields were observed in connection with vaccine disinformation circulating on Twitter during the period covered by the study. The first one, called "flooding the discourse," is used to artificially direct social media traffic toward a chosen topic.[29] Several programs will start sharing content on the same topic over a concentrated

---

[29]   Broniatowski study. See also Jeanette Sutton, "Health Communication Trolls and Bots versus Public Health Agencies' Trusted Voices" (2018) 108 *American Journal of Public Health* 1281–82.

period of time, falsely conveying the impression that many users of a particular social media are sharing or discussing it. Both Twitter bots and trolls resorted to this technique, synchronizing tweets to create spikes in the circulation of vaccine disinformation.

A complementary strategy used to spread vaccine disinformation through Twitter was "astroturfing," the feigning of the existence of grassroots support for a particular cause.[30] Developed well before the emergence of the Internet, astroturfing strategies are used by individuals or organizations trying to fabricate support for their product or agenda – for instance, by paying others to publicly consume or endorse their products seemingly of their own volition, while they themselves appear not to be linked to those actions. In the digital environment, the strategy can be deployed with relative ease, such as by creating a social media account that appears to be unconnected with the astroturfer orchestrating the move, and giving it a name and look that imply support by a community of users.[31] In the case of vaccine disinformation, Twitter accounts engaging in astroturfing feigned grassroots support for content that was predominantly anti-vaccine. The idea here is to magnify the Twitter presence of groups and ideologies that remain a minority in both online and offline environments.

As the supply of COVID-19 vaccines began to expand in 2021, Russian online platforms started spreading disinformation specifically about the Pfizer and Moderna vaccines.[32] On the one hand, this strategy was part of a larger plan to increase polarization of public discourse in the United States. On the other, it was also meant to cast doubts about the safety and efficacy of the two vaccines then most widely available across the United States as a way to increase demand for the COVID-19 vaccine developed and manufactured in Russia, Sputnik V.

6.1.4 *Responses to Vaccine Misinformation: Social Media Self-Regulation*

Toward the end of the 2010s, several mainstream social media began taking steps to specifically address the challenges posed by the growing footprint taken up by vaccine misinformation across their platforms. These responses were adopted largely on a voluntary basis and differed among social media, both in scope and time of implementation.

The most stringent form of content moderation is through suppression or "zero tolerance" approaches. Adopters of these approaches first screen for content that

---

[30] See e.g. Daniel Kliman et al., "Dangerous Synergies: Countering Chinese and Russian Digital Influence Operations" (May 1, 2020) *Center for a New American Security*, https://www.cnas.org /publications/reports/dangerous-synergies.

[31] Marko Kovic et al., "Digital Astroturfing in Politics: Definition, Typology, and Countermeasures" (2018) 18(1) *Studies in Communication Sciences* 69–85.

[32] Jennifer Hansler et al., "Russian Disinformation Campaign Working to Undermine Confidence in COVID-19 Vaccines Used in US" (March 8, 2021) *CNN Politics*, https://www.cnn.com/2021/03/07/ politics/russian-disinformation-pfizer-vaccines/index.html.

qualifies as vaccine misinformation or, more broadly, as vaccine-related. This screening, or at least a significant part thereof, is often performed by algorithms programmed to detect certain words, expressions, or other language-based clues that a user is sharing a specific type of content. Content can be further triaged through human interventions, performed by one or more people affiliated with a particular social media, or by third-party fact checkers.

Under a suppression approach, content falling into a predetermined prohibited category is removed. This may happen automatically: for instance, once a program recognizes a particular message or post as qualifying as prohibited under the policy, it deletes or otherwise blocks the content. Alternatively, content may be flagged for further analysis and suppressed only after it is confirmed as violating the policy in place.

The first mainstream social media to moderate vaccine-specific content was Pinterest, which took a broad suppression approach in early 2019, as news of outbreaks of vaccine-preventable diseases like measles started to surface. In response to data indicating that most vaccine-related pins and boards shared through its platform disputed or contradicted current scientific views on vaccines, Pinterest implemented a policy blocking the sharing of content related to vaccines.[33] The policy allowed users to pin vaccine content to their personal boards but, unlike what happens with other content, that content was then blocked from showing on searches about vaccines or vaccination-related themes. Later on, Pinterest began pairing this suppression approach with educational steps – namely, by allowing some vaccine-related content to appear in response to searches about vaccines, but publishing only content from organizations operating in the public health space, including the US Centers for Disease Control and Prevention, the American Academy of Pediatrics, and the WHO.

The use of blanket suppression approaches – the removal or blocking of *all types* of content related to vaccines, as Pinterest initially did – is rare. As they were called on to respond to the growth of vaccine misinformation, some social media argued that the need to maintain robust discussions in the "marketplace of ideas," allowing users to express competing views on vaccine-related topics, superseded other motivations for implementing strong forms of content moderation. This was, for instance, one argument Facebook leadership made on several polarizing topics, including vaccines.

Most social media adopting vaccine-specific content moderation practices eventually opted for downgrading or limiting approaches. Under this type of policy, a social media still allows users to share vaccine-related content – and, specifically, content known to be anti-vaccine or vaccine-questioning – but implements

---

[33]   See e.g. Taylor Telford, "Pinterest Is Blocking Search Results about Vaccines to Protect Users from Misinformation" (February 21, 2020) *Washington Post*, https://www.washingtonpost.com/busi ness/2019/02/21/pinterest-is-blocking-all-vaccine-related-searches-all-or-nothing-approach-policing -health-misinformation/.

technical measures that will render vaccine misinformation less prominent to other users.

This was Facebook's initial approach. In early 2019, shortly after Pinterest publicized its suppression policy, Facebook announced that it would continue to allow users to share content qualifying as anti-vaccine, both on Facebook and on Instagram, which it also owns.[34] However, according to the new policy, it would no longer promote anti-vaccine content through its recommendation and ad features, and it would downgrade it in search results. These limiting and downgrading steps were also paired with educational measures, with Facebook promoting informative vaccine content provided by many of the same organizations Pinterest (and other social media) relied on for scientifically accurate content about vaccines.

In addition to taking steps to manage vaccine misinformation, most social media also implemented an informational or educational approach by promoting vaccine-related content from credible science-driven organizations.

Even though these approaches work in ways that are far from perfect, as noted later, they are effective in capturing the attention of users with no particular investment in the vaccine-related topics. For instance, on February 16, 2021, I entered the word "vaccine" in Facebook's search function from a Saint Louis, Missouri-based Facebook account that does not follow, post, or click on any vaccine-related content. The top result was a link to the US Centers for Disease Control website on "Vaccines and Immunizations." In addition to being placed at the top of the list, the link also occupied a larger footprint than any other results. The second and third results were links to the Facebook pages for different groups: "Vaccines Save Lives," a public group with 8,100 members; and "Pro-Vaccine Parenting in Santa Cruz County," a private group with sixty-nine members. The fourth result was a link to the Facebook group of the American Academy of Pediatrics, after which links to three other private groups appeared, with seemingly disparate geographical connections, ranging from Ohio to Maine. The eighth result was a link to the Facebook page maintained by the WHO.

I then entered the word "vaccine" into Twitter's search function from a similarly Missouri-based Twitter account that does not follow, post, or click on any vaccine-related content. The first result was a message telling the user that "to make sure you get the best information on vaccinations, resources are available from the US Department of Health & Human Services," and providing the link to vaccines.gov, an informational website dedicated to vaccines maintained by the same government institution. Results for Twitter accounts having recently shared pro-vaccine content followed, with a tweet from the White House Press Secretary account displayed at the top, even though it was not the most recent account to have tweeted on this subject.

---

[34]   Louise Matsakis, "Facebook Will Crack Down on Anti-vaccine Content" (March 7, 2019) *Wired*, https://www.wired.com/story/facebook-anti-vaccine-crack-down/.

6.1.5 *Limitations of Current Modes of Self-Regulation*

Downgrading and limiting approaches can yield considerable results. For instance, when Facebook downgraded results associated with a popular Facebook-based anti-vaccine group – called "Stop Mandatory Vaccination"– monthly views went down from two million to 100,000.[35] Similarly, educational or informational approaches increase the visibility of accurate vaccine content. Nevertheless, current responses to the spread of vaccine misinformation are still far from sufficiently addressing the underlying problems in this area.

Response modes relying predominantly on educational approaches face significant limitations. A growing body of research has shown that the mere availability of accurate information about vaccines does not necessarily lead to behavioral changes among vaccine-hesitant individuals, nor is it enough to offset the spread of anti-vaccine content disseminated through social media and other online actors.[36]

The relative size and prominence of sources of pro-vaccine content on social media masks their inability to match the levels of message amplification achieved by sources of vaccine misinformation, even though sources providing scientifically accurate information about vaccines in social media draw considerably larger followings than those promoting anti-vaccine content. A 2020 study published in *Nature* analyzed the performance of these sources on Facebook, noting that a large anti-vaccine Facebook page might hope to draw around 40,000 followers.[37] By contrast, the Facebook page for the US Centers for Disease Control and Prevention – the top result for searches about vaccines conducted during the pandemic[38] – registered approximately two million followers at the time the study was published.

However, this asymmetry in number of followers must be understood in a dynamic context. First, social media pages maintained by governmental public health agencies or international bodies like the WHO must develop and share content in multiple health-related areas, as well as catering to highly diverse audiences. By contrast, anti-vaccine groups or pages on social media are much more focused, both content-wise and in terms of the audiences they plan to reach.

Moreover, producing accurate content about vaccines, treating it for educational purposes and packaging it for the online environment requires significantly more time, resources and coordination between players than generating vaccine misinformation.[39] In addition to not having to conduct field investigations or

---

[35] Tim Dickinson, "How the Anti-vaxxers Got Red-Pilled" (February 10, 2021) *Rolling Stone*, https://www.rollingstone.com/culture/culture-features/qanon-anti-vax-covid-vaccine-conspiracy-theory-1125197/.

[36] Terry Connolly & Jochen Reb, "Toward Interactive, Internet-Based Decision Aid for Vaccination Decisions: Better Information Alone Is Not Enough" (2012) 30 *Vaccine* 3813–18.

[37] Johnson et al., "Online Competition," note 21.

[38] See author's search described in Section 6.1.4.

[39] Renée DiResta, "Virus Experts Aren't Getting the Message Out" (May 6, 2020) *Atlantic*, https://www.theatlantic.com/ideas/archive/2020/05/health-experts-dont-understand-how-information-moves/611218/.

other types of research, anti-vaccine groups on social media can and do often recycle content used in a different context – for example, in connection with a different disease outbreak or health claim – and are thus able to quickly repurpose it to respond to emerging events. The WHO and the US Centers for Disease Control and Prevention need to first gather data on a novel pathogen like the coronavirus causing COVID-19, interpret it and then decide how best to convey it to the general public. Anti-vaccine groups with strong social media presence can circulate messages about the emerging pathogen or vaccines in development within minutes of the decision to intervene in a given area. And, as opposed to scientifically accurate content, much of the vaccine misinformation propagated through social media is expressed through inflammatory and attention-grabbing form and substance.

The second and more crucial difference is that anti-vaccine groups are much more skilled at using social media as vehicles to amplify their message. As a result, they disseminate their minority views at rates that pro-vaccine groups are unable to match. The 2020 *Nature* study shed light on this phenomenon within Facebook – an important reference point, since Facebook was and remains both the most widely used social media platform in the Western world and the largest social media venue for the dissemination of vaccine misinformation by number of users.[40]

The study mapped the dissemination of vaccine content within Facebook by identifying users expressing views on vaccines without initially differentiating between messages conveying favorable, questioning, or unfavorable views on the topic. Performed at a time when Facebook was fast approaching three billion users, the study identified almost 100 million individuals, communicating in both the dominant language on Facebook (English) and other languages.

Researchers concluded that Facebook users engaging with vaccine content were becoming more connected with one another, irrespective of their leanings in vaccine debates. However, while a majority of users held positive views on vaccines, users expressing anti-vaccine views were building much denser networks. They did so by forming highly connected clusters, which the study defined as the units formed by a Facebook page and its followers. Clusters labeled as sharing anti-vaccine content outnumbered clusters sharing pro-vaccine views by a factor of two. Anti-vaccine clusters were also more effective than pro-vaccine clusters in connecting with the estimated fifty million Facebook users who appeared to be undecided on issues related to vaccines. These users, in turn, were found to

---

[40]   Johnson et al., "Online Competition," note 21. See also Andrew Hutchinson, "Facebook Closes in on New Milestone of 3 Billion Total Users Across Its Platforms" (April 29, 2020) *Social Media Today* (reporting that Facebook had over 2.6 billion users at the time the *Nature* study was published), www .socialmediatoday.com/news/facebook-closes-in-on-new-milestone-of-3-billion-total-users-across-its-pla/577048/; Statista, "Number of Monthly Active Facebook Users Worldwide as of 4th Quarter 2020" (February 2, 2021) (reporting an increase of 0.2 billion in the number of Facebook users between the publication of the study and the end of 2020), www.statista.com/statistics/346167/facebook-global-dau/.

search for vaccine-related content and to interact with anti-vaccine clusters at much higher rates than previously thought.

In light of these dynamics, the researchers in the *Nature* study thus characterized anti-vaccine clusters as "robust and resilient." In spite of their limitations in relative size, these clusters were more effective at spreading vaccine-related content than most pro-vaccine sources on Facebook.

The social media presence of individuals or organizations promoting anti-vaccine content grew quickly during the early stages of the COVID-19 pandemic. A study by the Center for Countering Digital Hate found that during the first half of 2020, Facebook anti-vaccine clusters added 854,000 followers to their twenty-eight million user base.[41] YouTube added 5.8 million to its 21.3 million users following vaccine misinformation. Facebook-owned Instagram added one million to its 7.3 million-base.

Because self-regulation allows for heterogeneity of responses among different social media, it also allows for content migration and the possibility of time gaps. For instance, in 2019, Pinterest blocked the account of one of the most well-known anti-vaccine activists, Larry Cook. Cook has long been especially active on social media, using them to spread anti-vaccine content. While blocked on Pinterest, he continued his activity through other social media channels, including Facebook and Twitter. The anti-vaccine content shared by Cook remained available on these social media for eight months after COVID-19 was declared a pandemic. By the time Facebook deleted his account in November 2020 – as the first COVID-19 vaccines were weeks away from coming to market – his Facebook group had over 195,000 members.[42]

Self-regulation poses further problems by easily allowing for large time gaps to occur between the emergence of a problem and the moment in which a given social media decides to intervene. This gap is relevant outside the context of a pandemic or other large-scale public health crisis during which new vaccines are developed. Consider the following timeline.

A study by epidemiologist Amelia Jamison and colleagues, published in the journal *Vaccine* in early 2020 – but widely publicized in November 2019 through news media – revealed that most anti-vaccine content circulating online was promoted and paid for by a very limited number of players.[43] The study found that, in the case of Facebook, two individuals linked to groups or organizations focusing on anti-vaccine

[41] Center for Countering Digital Hate, "The Anti-Vaxx Industry: How Big Tech Powers and Profits from Vaccine Misinformation" (2020), at 14, https://www.counterhate.com/_files/ugd/f4d9b9_fddbfb2a0c05461cb4bdce2892f3cad0.pdf.

[42] Aatif Sulleyman, "Facebook Bans One of the Anti-vaccine Movement's Biggest Groups for Violating QAnon Rules" (November 18, 2020) *NewsWeek*, https://www.newsweek.com/facebook-bans-anti-vaccine-group-violating-qanon-rules-1548408.

[43] Amelia M. Jamison et al., "Vaccine-related Advertising in the Facebook Ad Archive" (16 January 2020) 38(3) *Vaccine* 512–20; Lena H. Sun, "Majority of Anti-vaccine Ads on Facebook were Funded by Two Groups" (November 15, 2019) *Washington Post*, www.washingtonpost.com/health/2019/11/15/majority-anti-vaccine-ads-facebook-were-funded-by-two-groups/.

activism originated most of the anti-vaccine content available through Facebook. The first one was Larry Cook, through the "Stop Mandatory Vaccination" group, and the second was Robert F. Kennedy, Jr., through World Mercury Project (now called Children's Health Defense), an organization he created in 2016 to "change government policies that injure children."[44] The study found that "Stop Mandatory Vaccination" and World Mercury Project had bought more than half of all anti-vaccine ads on Facebook.[45]

Cook's anti-vaccine activism relied significantly on online crowdfunding to support Facebook-based advertising campaigns, which he often directed at women over the age of twenty-five, thus targeting mothers of young children.[46] An investigation published by the news publication *The Daily Beast* in February 2019 reported that Mr. Cook had conducted four fundraising campaigns on GoFundMe, garnering $79,900.[47] These funds were transferred directly to Mr. Cook's personal account, and his website stated a "policy" according to which they could be used to pay Mr. Cook's "personal bills." The funds were nonetheless instrumental in supporting the purchase of anti-vaccine ads on Facebook.

Cook's Facebook group, "Stop Mandatory Vaccination," came under closer scrutiny in February 2020, when the four-year old child of a member of the group died of the flu.[48] The child had been diagnosed by a doctor and prescribed Tamiflu, an antiviral drug commonly used in flu treatments. The child's mother, who had posted messages in "Stop Mandatory Vaccination" since at least 2017 indicating that she would not have her children vaccinated against the flu, posted in the group after the diagnosis, indicating that she had not picked up the Tamiflu prescription, and expressing concern that the "natural remedies" (peppermint oil, lavender, and vitamin C) she was using did not seem to produce any effects. In response, members of the group suggested trying other non-pharmaceutical products, including thyme, elderberry, and breast milk. In her last known posts, the mother indicated that she would try administering these products. Presenting worsening symptoms, the child was eventually hospitalized but did not survive. At that point, the group had over 139,000 members.[49] In the nine months between this episode and Facebook's decision to block "Stop Mandatory Vaccination," the group added 56,000 followers.

44 World Mercury Project, "Robert F. Kennedy, Jr. Launches the World Mercury Project" (November 16, 2016), www.prnewswire.com/news-releases/robert-f-kennedy-jr-launches-the-world-mercury-project-300364404.html.
45 Sun, "Majority of Anti-vaccine Ads," note 43.
46 Dickinson, "How the Anti-vaxxers," note 35.
47 Julia Arciga, "Anti-vaxxer Larry Cook Has Weaponized Facebook Ads in War against Science" (January 19, 2021) *Daily Beast*, https://www.thedailybeast.com/anti-vaxxer-larry-cook-has-weaponized-facebook-ads-in-war-against-science.
48 K. Thor Jensen, "Colorado Boy Dies of Flu after Mom Tries Anti-vaccine Facebook Group Suggestions to Use Elderberries and Thyme Instead of Doctor's Flu Medicine" (February 10, 2020) *NewsWeek*, https://www.newsweek.com/boy-dies-flu-anti-vaccine-facebook-group-1486303.
49 Jensen, "Colorado Boy," note 48.

Time gap problems further intersect with weak regulatory frameworks applicable to the moderation of vaccine-specific content in the online environment. In the case described earlier, Facebook did not remove "Stop Mandatory Vaccination" due to concerns related to vaccine or health-related misinformation. Rather, the company acted because Cook's promotion of anti-vaccine content had become increasingly intertwined with the spread of content reflective of QAnon's ideology. QAnon is a network dedicated to the propagation of extremist messages and conspiracy theories, considered by the FBI as a potential domestic terrorism threat since 2019.[50] During the early stages of the COVID-19 pandemic, QAnon became more active in the anti-vaccine space. Cook played an instrumental role in the progressive overlapping of QAnon and segments of the anti-vaccine activism community. He publicized having espoused QAnon's deep state and other conspiracy theories in early 2020, and then started to actively promote QAnon content through social media.[51]

Facebook refined its policy toward "movements and organizations tied to violence" several times during the COVID-19 pandemic.[52] In August 2020, the category of "dangerous individuals and organizations" was expanded to include QAnon, and Facebook proceeded to remove accounts and groups representing or otherwise disseminating the views of "militarized social movements and violence-inducing conspiracy networks." Between August and mid-January 2021, Facebook removed 3,300 pages, 10,500 groups, 510 events, and 18,300 profiles for sharing QAnon content or being otherwise affiliated with the QAnon network. During that period, the company also removed 27,300 Instagram accounts for the same reason. Cook's Facebook group was thus removed pursuant to this policy and not specifically for the anti-vaccine content he had long disseminated through Facebook.

Finally, ongoing responses face yet another type of shortcoming – technical limitations. Given the sheer size of content traffic on mainstream social media, automated or partially automated techniques are often used to detect potentially problematic messages, and either remove them automatically or flag them for follow-up analysis. These techniques consist of using algorithms programed to sift through massive amounts of content and screen for trigger words, expressions, or even contextual constructions that may indicate the presence of content deemed undesirable (or in need of verification) by a given social media. Over time, these algorithms have become rather efficient at performing this type of screening and flagging tasks. However, the emergence of new areas or modes of discussion – including the onset of a public health crisis like a pandemic or epidemic, for

---

[50] Zack Budryk, "FBI Memo Warns QAnon Poses Potential Terror Threat: Report" (August 1, 2019) *Hill*, https://thehill.com/policy/national-security/fbi/455770-fbi-memo-warns-qanon-poses-a-potential-terror-threat-report.

[51] Dickinson, "How the Anti-vaxxers," note 35.

[52] Facebook, "An Update to How We Address Movements and Organizations Tied to Violence" (August 19, 2020; October 7, 2020 update), https://about.fb.com/news/2020/08/addressing-movements-and-organizations-tied-to-violence/.

example – can quickly upend many of the technical frameworks in place to triage content.

Consider, once again, the case of Facebook. The platform uses algorithms to identify content falling under the brackets of misinformation and hate speech.[53] Content labeled by these algorithms as presenting a high probability of infringing Facebook's policies in either area is automatically removed, whereas other flagged content is subject to further screening, this time performed by human reviewers at fact-checking organizations.[54] Data from early 2020 showed that Facebook's algorithms were becoming increasingly accurate at detecting content qualifying as problematic under the applicable Facebook policy.[55] For instance, the Community Standards Enforcement Report released by Facebook in May 2020 indicated that these screening algorithms had detected 88.8 percent of all hate speech found and removed by the platform. This constituted a nontrivial improvement over the previous reporting period (the preceding quarter), in which the rate was 80.2 percent.

Nevertheless, as the circulation of misinformation related to the COVID-19 pandemic began escalating, Facebook had to switch its screening approach to deal with the emergence of thematically new misinformation. It was forced to rely predominantly on human fact checkers rather than on automated programs because the screening algorithms had not been trained to identify forms of misinformation specific to COVID-19 and the pandemic.[56] From a technical perspective, algorithms have so far proved useful in long-term approaches to misinformation or other types of problematic content, as their accuracy depends on being trained on large and increasingly granular data. This process is time- and resource-consuming. A spike in misinformation linked to a disruptive event, accompanied by the emergence of data on which the algorithms have not been trained, leads to scenarios in which the most effective technical tools to spot misinformation in social media are largely unavailable – or perform with substantially less accuracy – at the time they are arguably most needed. Karen Hao, the senior AI reporter for the *MIT Technology Review*, summed up this problem in an article entitled "Facebook's AI is Still Largely Baffled by Covid Misinformation."

Another type of technical limitation relates to disparities between the dominant language on most of these social media (English) and languages that, albeit nondominant, are spoken by large segments of active social media users. For example, in October 2020, a group of researchers published the results of a study on vaccine-related content expressed in Portuguese and circulating through

---

53 See Karen Hao, "Facebook's AI Is Still Largely Baffled by Covid Misinformation" (May 12, 2020) *MIT Technology Review*, https://www.technologyreview.com/2020/05/12/1001633/ai-is-still-largely-baffled-by-covid-misinformation/.

54 Guy Rosen, "Community Standards Enforcement Report November 2019 Edition" (November 13, 2019) *Facebook*, https://about.fb.com/news/2019/11/community-standards-enforcement-report-nov -2019/.

55 Hao, "Facebook's AI," note 53.

56 Hao, "Facebook's AI," note 53.

YouTube in Brazil.[57] The researchers found that, although YouTube had formally committed to removing vaccine misinformation and disinformation about vaccines, anti-vaccine and vaccine-questioning videos in Portuguese continued to be shared and accessed on the platform, where they reached large audiences.

From a content perspective, the inaccurate claims and associations being made with regard to vaccines were very similar to the ones encountered in English-based vaccine misinformation and disinformation. Journalist Dayane Fumiyo Tokojima Machado and colleagues reported in their study that the main themes "were the claim of dangerous ingredients in vaccines, the defense of self-direction – freedom of choice, independent research – the promotion of alternative health services, the myth that vaccines cause diseases, conspiracy theories, and the allegation of vaccine's severe collateral effects."[58]

Technical limitations like those described here do not affect solely self-regulatory responses to the spread of inaccurate vaccine content. Even if a more stringent form of content moderation were externally imposed (and assuming *arguendo* that such imposition would pass muster), it would not automatically cure the gaps in the development and training of programs screening vaccine-related content in emerging contexts and the many non-English languages in which vaccine misinformation and disinformation is expressed.

Taken together, the different types of limitations outlined earlier in the text illustrate some of the challenges that the post-market for vaccines is now facing – and how non-health technologies can nonetheless influence the vaccine ecosystem and, more generally, public health outcomes. They also underscore the idea that bodies of law and policy areas that are (at best) tangential to health and intellectual property will likely become progressively more intertwined with vaccine-related matters.

6.2 PAVING THE WAY FOR THE VACCINES OF THE FUTURE: INTERDEPENDENCY OF LEGAL REGIMES

The majority of the book has focused on how long-established legal regimes related to current innovation policies affect the development and distribution of new vaccines. However, ongoing developments across multiple fields of technology are changing current approaches to vaccine R&D and enlarging the boundaries of what might be regarded as vaccine technology. This expansion of the vaccine ecosystem, and the progressive blurring of some of its edges, is likely to increase in the years to

---

[57] See Dayane Fumiyo Tokojima Machado et al., "Natural Stings: Selling Distrust about Vaccines on Brazilian YouTube" (October 26, 2020) *Frontiers in Communication*; Fernanda Ferreira, "Antivaccine Videos Slip through YouTube's Advertising Policies, New Study Finds" (November 2, 2020) *Science*, www.science.org/content/article/antivaccine-videos-slip-through-youtube-s-advertising-policies-new-study-finds.
[58] Machado et al., "Natural Stings," note 57.

come. This section provides a glimpse into what tomorrow's vaccines may look like and lays out some of the emerging challenges to law, policy, and equity brought about by this evolution.

As with online vaccine misinformation, these new frontiers of vaccine R&D tap into legal domains that traditionally had little or no connection to vaccine policy. The interdependency of multiple legal regimes – and the ways in which areas traditionally extraneous to health law, drug regulation, and intellectual property bear significant influence on vaccine development and distribution – is bound to become increasingly more salient. The purpose of this section is not to offer an exhaustive treatment of the legal regimes now emerging as being in connection with vaccine-related matter, but simply to foreshadow the magnitude of changes to come in the vaccine ecosystem, and to highlight the point that "general-purpose" regulation of technology – law- and policymaking outside the boundaries of the regulation of health technologies – is poised to have a growing impact on the vaccine ecosystem.

6.2.1 *Expanding the Concept of Vaccine Technology: New Frontiers in Vaccinology*

While the commercialization of the first mRNA vaccines in history made headlines during the COVID-19 pandemic, many other types of emerging vaccine technology are on the cusp of becoming available to indicated patients.

mRNA technology alone is considered a key platform technology holding great promise in the development of vaccines against emerging infectious disease pathogens in the near future. In a study published in *Nature Reviews Drug Discovery* in 2018, biochemist Norbert Pardi and colleagues echoed the growing scientific consensus that this emerging form of vaccine technology – which in decades prior, together with the leading researcher in the field, biochemist Katalin Karikó, had been largely dismissed[59] – would soon enable the production of new vaccines against emerging pathogens:

> Development of prophylactic or therapeutic vaccines against infectious pathogens is the most efficient means to contain and prevent epidemics. However, conventional vaccine approaches have largely failed to produce effective vaccines against challenging viruses that cause chronic or repeated infections, such as HIV-1, herpes simplex virus and respiratory syncytial virus (RSV). Additionally, the slow pace of commercial vaccine development and approval is inadequate to respond to the rapid emergence of acute viral diseases, as illustrated by the 2014–2016 outbreaks of the Ebola and Zika viruses. Therefore, the development of more potent and versatile vaccine platforms is crucial. Preclinical studies have created hope that

---

59   Damian Garde, "The Story of mRNA: How a Once-Dismissed Idea Became a Leading Technology in the Covid Vaccine Race" (November 10, 2020) *Stat*, https://www.statnews.com/2020/11/10/the-story-of-mrna-how-a-once-dismissed-idea-became-a-leading-technology-in-the-covid-vaccine-race/.

mRNA vaccines will fulfil many aspects of an ideal clinical vaccine: they have shown a favourable safety profile in animals, are versatile and rapid to design for emerging infectious diseases, and are amenable to scalable good manufacturing practice (GMP) production (already under way by several companies).[60]

Shortly after scientists expressed this hope, the promise of successful application of mRNA technology to the field of vaccinology materialized, as the first commercially available mRNA vaccines were given emergency authorization during the COVID-19 pandemic.

Scientists now predict that mRNA technology will lead to the development of vaccines against diseases that have long eluded the efforts of vaccine R&D players, and testing is ongoing in areas including HIV/AIDS and universal flu vaccines.[61] But mRNA technology is also being tested for purposes other than preventing disease. For instance, several applications of mRNA technology being tested at the time of writing relate to the field of oncology and seek to treat, rather than prevent, certain types of tumors – bringing vaccine development and administration potentially close to the realm of personalized medicine.[62] The technological platform being used in multiple projects in vaccine R&D is thus also relevant in non-vaccine fields. Many of these fields, such as cancer immunotherapy, occupy a different corner in public health and obey very different market dynamics from those that typically inform vaccine research and development. This, in turn, will affect many economic and strategic considerations surrounding the development of vaccine technology – the evaluation of intellectual property portfolios, the willingness of R&D players to enter into voluntary licensing or other technology-sharing agreements, and their propensity to channel R&D results toward secrecy models.

Against this backdrop, the distinction between older and newer vaccine technology, as well as the distinction between platform and non-platform vaccine technology, are likely to become increasingly relevant. Proposals for the adoption of new technology-sharing agreements, or for the formalization of temporary collaborative frameworks, may face difficulties if designed broadly as potentially encompassing all types of vaccine technology. From the perspective of practical implementation, they may stand better chances if designed to work around platform technology deemed to be highly monetizable in non-vaccine contexts; or policymakers may need to consider the awarding of mega prizes, or other trade-offs, when seeking to promote the sharing of platform technology.

---

[60] Norbert Pardi et al., "mRNA Vaccines – A New Era in Vaccinology" (2018) 17 *Nature Reviews Drug Discovery* 261–79.

[61] See e.g. Antonio Regalado, "The Next Act for Messenger RNA Could Be Bigger than Covid Vaccines" (February 5, 2021) *MIT Technology Review*, https://www.technologyreview.com/2021/02/05/1017366/messenger-rna-vaccines-covid-hiv/.

[62] Regalado, "The Next Act," note 61; Kelly Servick, "Messenger RNA Gave Us a COVID-19 Vaccine. Will It Treat Diseases, Too?" (December 16, 2020) *Science*; Lei Miao et al., "mRNA Vaccine for Cancer Immunotherapy" (February 25, 2021) 40 *Molecular Cancer* 21, www.science.org/content/article/messenger-rna-gave-us-covid-19-vaccine-will-it-treat-diseases-too.

Another blurring of technology divides stems from the fact that some health goods entering the market in the near future may be predominantly geared toward disease prevention and yet not qualify as vaccines per current regulatory standards. The Pardi article excerpted earlier references the potential of mRNA technology in the development of vaccines against respiratory syncytial virus (RSV) infection. RSV is a common virus that normally causes mild symptoms, resembling those of a common cold.[63] In some cases, though, RSV may trigger serious respiratory symptoms, including pneumonia, and worsens chronic medical problems, such as asthma. Infants, young children, and older adults are at a heightened risk for developing these more concerning symptoms. On average, 58,000 children under the age of five are hospitalized each year in the United States due to a severe case of RSV infection.[64] Globally, the WHO considers RSV infection a "leading cause of hospitalization" in infants and young children.[65] To date, there is no approved vaccine against RSV, although multiple RSV vaccine candidates have reached clinical trial stages.[66]

Alongside vaccines, the RSV pipeline also contains late-stage monoclonal antibody (mAb) candidates. Monoclonal antibodies are laboratory-engineered proteins that bind to a specific target, such as a bacterium or virus, and which are now often used in oncology treatments. The FDA has defined monoclonal antibodies as "laboratory-made proteins that mimic the immune system's ability to fight off harmful pathogens such as viruses."[67]

While monoclonal antibodies function predominantly as treatments, they have also been used for preventative purposes. For instance, during the COVID-19 pandemic, several monoclonal antibodies received emergency use authorization and were administered in the United States to individuals at heightened risk for COVID-19, as well as patients in the early stages of COVID-19.[68] In the field of RSV, monoclonal antibodies are also being explored for preventative purposes, with some R&D projects in late-stage clinical trials at the time of writing.[69] While final outcomes associated with these R&D projects remain inconclusive at the time of writing, this illustrates the

---

[63]   US Centers for Disease Control and Prevention, "Respiratory Syncytial Virus Infection (RSV)," (2020), www.cdc.gov/rsv/index.html.

[64]   US Centers for Disease Control and Prevention, "RSV in Infants and Young Children," (2020), www .cdc.gov/rsv/high-risk/infants-young-children.html.

[65]   World Health Organization, "WHO Global Respiratory Syncytial Virus Surveillance," (2021), www .who.int/influenza/rsv/en/.

[66]   Path, "RSV Vaccine and mAb Snapshot," (2021), https://path.azureedge.net/media/documents/RSV-snapshot-07APR2021_HighResolution_NonEditable_PDF_3KgK9PB.pdf.

[67]   US Food & Drug Administration, "FDA Authorizes Revisions to Fact Sheets To Address SARS-CoV -2 Variants for Monoclonal Antibody Products under Emergency Use Authorization" (2021), https:// www.fda.gov/drugs/drug-safety-and-availability/fda-authorizes-revisions-fact-sheets-address-sars-cov -2-variants-monoclonal-antibody-products-under.

[68]   Jon Cohen, "Monoclonal Antibodies Can Prevent COVID-19 – but Successful Vaccines Complicate Their Future" (January 22, 2021) *Science*, https://www.science.org/content/article/monoclonal-antibodies-can-prevent-covid-19-successful-vaccines-complicate-their-future.

[69]   Path, "RSV Vaccine and mAb Snapshot," note 66.

case of a non-vaccine product that may be used for purposes that overlap with those achieved through the use of a vaccine.

Importantly, monoclonal antibodies are also expensive. Recent calculations indicate that the median annual cost of a monoclonal antibody treatment in the United States ranges from USD 15,000 to USD 200,000.[70] Gavi has noted that, as a result of the steep price tag, nearly "80 per cent of monoclonal antibodies are sold in the US, Canada and Europe."[71] If and when monoclonal antibodies are used to prevent infection caused by infectious disease pathogens, this will raise questions about access to an emerging technology that will mimic, and likely exacerbate, concerns with the affordability of health goods. And, as with vaccines, populations in lower-income countries are poised to be the most affected by pricing issues and skewed allocation of newly developed health technologies.

In an era of hope for vaccinology, many of the market-driven dynamics and allocative inequalities that permeate the vaccine ecosystem may thus extend, or be exacerbated, as R&D on preventative technologies straddles the boundaries between vaccines and other products.

6.2.2 Tech on Tech: From 3D-Printed Vaccine Delivery to Artificial Intelligence

The development, distribution, and administration of vaccines has progressively come to rely on the use of technologies from multiple fields, several of them largely extraneous to vaccine or pharmaceutical R&D – and some relatively new as scientific disciplines. Consider the case of 3D printing and artificial intelligence, two disparate areas of technology that each encompass an increasing number of heterogeneous subfields.

The expression "3D printing" refers to the process of generating three-dimensional goods through the use of a printer-like machine that follows instructions contained in a digital file. Although increasingly diversified, 3D printing typically works through additive layering, with the printer depositing layer upon layer of a chosen material. For instance, products commonly used include various types of plastics and materials in powdered form, which are melted and layered according to the instructions.

Some early applications of 3D printing involved the production of health goods. For instance, one of the fields that grew the fastest as the cost of 3D-printing technologies started decreasing was that of prosthetics, allowing engineers to produce certain types of customized prosthetics at relatively low cost for patients[72] – and which led to the formation of networks where participants freely shared models of prosthetics for customization at no cost for others.[73]

[70] Gavi, "What Are Monoclonal Antibodies – and Can They Treat COVID-19?" (2020), www.gavi.org /vaccineswork/what-are-monoclonal-antibodies-and-can-they-treat-covid-19.
[71] Gavi, "What Are Monoclonal Antibodies," note 70.
[72] Albert Manero et al., "Implementation of 3D Printing Technology in the Field of Prosthetics: Past, Present, and Future" (2019) 16(9) *International Journal of Environmental Research and Public Health* 1641.
[73] US National Institutes of Health, "3D-Printable Prosthetic Devices," (2021), https://3dprint.nih.gov /collections/prosthetics.

Although the field of vaccines has not yet seen comparable levels of activity, recent R&D projects have tested the use of 3D-printing technology in vaccine delivery. In September 2017, MIT engineers were able to 3D-print microstructures in the shape of cups that can be used to deliver vaccine doses at different rates.[74] They created silicone molds for the cups, which were then filled with PLGA (poly lactic-co-glycolic acid), a material approved by the FDA that has long been used in drug delivery applications, particularly when there is a need for the slow release of a drug or other product.[75] PLGA is biocompatible: it does not interact with the human body in any harmful way. It is also biodegradable: the human body eventually breaks down and metabolizes PLGA using the same mechanisms it uses to turn food into energy. The FDA approved the first PLGA delivery system in 1989, and since then has green lighted the use of PLGA technology for the delivery of drugs over periods ranging from one week to six months.[76] The European Medicines Agency has similarly approved PLGA-based products.

In the case of the MIT project, doses of vaccine were placed into the cups, which were then fused with lids to prevent them from leaking before the intended delivery date. Different cups were set to release their vaccine content at different rates. In studies with mice, these 3D-printed cups successfully released their content on schedule, at nine, twenty, and forty-one days.[77]

One possible application of this technology is to deliver vaccine doses to populations in low-income countries, as well as in remote or impoverished areas of higher-income countries. In these contexts, it is often difficult – and sometimes prohibitively expensive or overly burdensome – for patients to make multiple visits to health-care providers. This technology would concentrate administration of vaccine doses while preserving release times, saving patients at least some of the costs and logistical problems associated with multiple visits to a vaccine administration site. It would also help with compliance problems attributable to other causes, such as forgetfulness. In the long run, the technology may also be used to customize vaccines to the needs of specific patients.[78]

Another set of technologies once absent from vaccine development and distribution but now beginning to permeate these areas relates to the field of artificial intelligence. Although no universal definition of artificial intelligence exists, legal

---

[74]   Clare Scott, "New 3D Printing Method Combines Multiple Vaccines into One Shot" (September 17, 2017) *3Dprint.com*, https://3dprint.com/187945/3d-printing-vaccines/.

[75]   Hirenkumar K. Makadia & Steven J. Siegel, "Poly Lactic-co-Glycolic Acid (PLGA) as Biodegradable Controlled Drug Delivery Carrier" (September 1, 2011) 3(3) *Polymers* 1377–97.

[76]   Kinam Park et al., "Injectable, Long-Acting PLGA Formulations: Analyzing PLGA and Understanding Microparticle Formation" (2019) 304 *Journal of Controlled Release* 125–34, at 126.

[77]   Kevin J. McHugh et al., "Fabrication of Fillable Microparticles and Other Complex 3D Microstructures" (September 15, 2017) 357(6356) *Science* 1138–42.

[78]   3D Adept Media, "'Advances in Vaccines': 3D Printed Vaccinations would Improve Administration of Drugs" (December 26, 2017), https://3dadept.com/advances-in-vaccines-3d-printed-vaccinations-would-improve-administration-of-drugs/.

scholar Ryan Calo notes that "AI is best understood as a set of techniques aimed at approximating some aspect of human or animal cognition using machines."[79]

One of the earliest applications of artificial intelligence in the field of vaccines involved flu vaccines. As seen in Chapter 3, the development of new flu vaccines remains problematic, based on the collection of influenza samples and predictive selection of quickly mutating pathogens. In 2019, Berg, a Boston start-up, announced that it was working in partnership with French pharmaceutical company Sanofi to use machine learning algorithms to analyze data on patients who had received a flu vaccine.[80] The algorithms processed different types of information, such as measurements on proteins and metabolite levels, with the goal of providing researchers with a clearer picture of the biological mechanisms that induce the body to trigger an immune response to flu viruses.

Artificial intelligence has also been used in projects exploring more effective ways of promoting vaccination, particularly among populations deemed at high risk for a disease. For instance, in 2020, Geisinger, a large health-care organization started testing different types of interventions designed to promote flu vaccination among high-risk populations. High-risk individuals were identified through the use of a machine learning algorithm, which sifted through large numbers of electronic health records.[81]

During COVID-19, Pfizer employed artificial intelligence to speed up analysis of vaccine clinical trial data.[82] AdventHealth, a hospital system operating in nine US states, used artificial intelligence to analyze data on COVID-19 vaccine hesitancy.[83] Scientists used Vaxign, a system that predicts and analyzes vaccine targets, to identify possible COVID-19 vaccine candidates.[84]

These are but a few examples from two burgeoning fields that have only begun to be explored in connection with vaccine R&D and other vaccine-related areas. While they hold great scientific promise and seem poised to have democratizing effects in access to health-related technologies, the policies that govern their development and increasing adoption far from guarantee that emerging advancements in vaccinology will benefit everyone.

---

[79] Ryan Calo, "Artificial Intelligence Policy: A Primer and Roadmap" (2017) 51 *U.C. Davis Law Review* 399, at 404.

[80] Alejandro de la Garza, "These Researchers Are Using Artificial Intelligence to Make a Better Flu Vaccine" (March 5, 2019) *Time*, https://time.com/5535186/flu-vaccine-artificial-intelligence/.

[81] Christopher F. Chabris, "Encouraging Flu Vaccination among High-Risk Patients Identified by ML," (2020), https://clinicaltrials.gov/ct2/show/NCT04323137.

[82] Sara Castellanos, "How AI Played a Role in Pfizer's COVID-19 Vaccine Rollout" (April 1, 2021) *Wall Street Journal*, https://www.wsj.com/articles/how-ai-played-a-role-in-pfizers-covid-19-vaccine-rollout-11617313126.

[83] Anuja Vaidya, "How AdventHealth Is Using AI to Fight Covid Vaccine Hesitancy" (April 6, 2021) *MedCity News*, https://medcitynews.com/2021/04/how-adventhealth-is-using-ai-to-fight-covid-vaccine-hesitancy/.

[84] Edison Ong et al., "COVID-19 Coronavirus Vaccine Design Using Reverse Vaccinology and Machine Learning" (July 3, 2020) 11 *Frontiers in Immunology* 1581.

For instance, in the case of artificial intelligence, some of the advancements it will bring to the field of vaccinology might not benefit lower-income populations to the same extent as they will benefit higher-income ones. For instance, legal scholar Nicholson Price has noted that many health-related applications of artificial intelligence are prone to "contextual bias," as the entities that have the means to employ or develop artificial intelligence typically operate in wealthy contexts, which might not capture data representative of all types of populations:

> Medical AI is typically trained in high-resource settings: academic medical centers or state of-the-art hospitals or hospital systems. (. . .) low-resource contexts have different patient populations and different resources available for treatment than high-resource contexts, and disparities in available data make it hard for AI to account for those differences. The translational disconnect between high-resource training environments and low-resource deployment environments will likely result in predictable decreases in the quality of algorithmic recommendations for care, limiting the promise of medical AI to actually democratize excellence.[85]

The laws and policies that inform the development of artificial intelligence and its applications are largely unrelated to vaccine law and policy, and even to the segments of intellectual property that help shape investment, technology transfer, and allocation of vaccine technology. Yet, systemic lacunas and biases in data, as well as other practices ingrained in the use of artificial intelligence technologies in the development of health goods are likely to affect the development and use of future vaccine technology – especially as vaccine technology itself expands and some of its subfields start allowing for greater customization of vaccines according to patient populations, or even to individual patients.

The vaccine ecosystem is thus expanding, and with it the types of actors, laws, and policies that ultimately dictate whether populations indicated for a vaccine – and especially lower-income populations in the Global South and economically disadvantaged areas of the Global North – will see it developed and distributed affordably and equitably.

---

[85] W. Nicholson Price II, "Medical AI and Contextual Bias" (2019) 33 *Harvard Journal of Law & Technology* 65.

Conclusion

Broader Implications for Global Public Health

Although adopting a vaccine-centric viewpoint, the book has highlighted problems that are not exclusive to the field of vaccines. These issues affect the production and distribution of vaccines in particular ways, but also suggest the existence of broader, systemic flaws in the production and distribution of health goods – especially those that, albeit critically needed from a public health perspective, fare poorly under predominantly market-driven paradigms. The book concludes with a short reflection on how problems observed in the vaccine ecosystem feed into the larger backdrop of persistent shortcomings in the global public health system.

C.1 QUESTIONING THE DESIRABILITY OF EXCLUSIONARY MODES OF PRODUCTION OF HEALTH GOODS

In exploring potential solutions to mitigate the inequitable effects of continued reliance on these modes, the book has searched for solutions primarily within intellectual property or otherwise exclusionary frameworks – which, per current international and domestic legal architectures, are extremely hard to displace. Yet, a deeper question pervades any inquiry into how well current modes of R&D suit the production of socially valuable goods, and in particular health goods. These modes are market-driven in nature and rely on legal frameworks that incentivize siloed competition and the commercialization of goods under legally sanctioned monopoly-like conditions – but are they always necessary, and ultimately desirable, especially when public health needs are taken into account?

In her study of the global network formed for the sharing of influenza viruses, legal scholar Amy Kapczynski has argued that open science models offer a viable blueprint for the expansion of modes of knowledge-sharing that enable R&D beyond exclusionary molds.[1] As per the definition offered by UNESCO, "the idea behind Open Science is to allow scientific information, data and outputs to be more widely

---

[1] Amy Kapczynski, "Order without Intellectual Property Law: Open Science in Influenza" (2017) 102 *Cornell Law Review* 1539–648.

181

accessible (Open Access) and more reliably harnessed (Open Data) with the active engagement of all the stakeholders (Open to Society)."[2] Kapczynski studied the WHO's Flu Network, which plays a critical role in the surveillance of flu cases around the globe, the collection and analysis of data on emerging flu strains, and the sharing of knowledge and resources leading to the production of seasonal flu vaccines. Her work suggests that non-exclusionary modes of knowledge-sharing and R&D enabled by open science approaches need not remain as outliers, especially in the case of scientific work performed in connection with the development of health goods needed for epidemic and pandemic preparedness:

> Even where capital costs are high, creation without IP can be reasonably effective in social terms, if it can link sources of funding to reputational and evaluative feedback loops like those that characterize open science. It can also be sustained over time, even by loose-knit groups and where the stakes are high, because organizations and other forms of law can help to stabilize cooperation.[3]

This strand of legal thought has evolved within a larger doctrinal framework, which legal scholar Mario Biagioli has christened "intellectual property without intellectual property." A vast body of literature has surveyed instances in which goods deemed societally desirable are produced predominantly through cooperative (or at least permissive) norms. While this literature focuses on productive systems largely outside the context of the production of health goods – such as music, fashion, and culinary recipes[4] – it further brings into question the universality of intellectual property as a sine qua non incentive to innovation. A related strand of literature draws attention to the benefits arising out of collaborations made possible by the advent of networked digital technologies, through which commons-based modes of production – perhaps best exemplified by the open source software movement – thrive against the background of market-driven economies.[5]

Kapczynski's insight into an area related to the production and sharing of scientific knowledge in a segment of the pharmaceutical R&D universe further stresses the point that policymakers should be asking harder questions about our current defaulting to exclusionary modes of production and distribution of health goods.

[2] UNESCO, "Open Science," https://en.unesco.org/science-sustainable-future/open-science.
[3] Kapczynski, "Order without Intellectual Property Law," note 1.
[4] See e.g. Keith Aoki, "Distributive and Syncretic Motives in Intellectual Property Law (with Special Reference to Coercion, Agency, and Development)" (2007) 40 *U.C. Davis Law Review* 717–802; Kal Raustiala & Christopher Sprigman, "The Piracy Paradox: Innovation and Intellectual Property in Fashion Design" (2006) 92 *Virginia Law Review* 1687–777; Emmanuelle Fauchart & Eric A. von Hippel, "Norms-Based Intellectual Property Systems: The Case of French Chefs" (2008) 19 *Organization Science* 187–201.
[5] Yochai Benkler, *Wealth of Networks: How Social Production Transforms Markets and Freedom* (Yale University Press, 2006); Yochai Benkler, "Coase's Penguin, or, Linux and the Nature of the Firm" (2002) 112 *Yale Law Journal* 369–446.

The book has described the shortcomings of current paradigms as applied to vaccines. Yet, R&D in several pharmaceutical areas faces comparable problems.

C.2 BEYOND VACCINES: OTHER AREAS OF PHARMACEUTICAL R&D FALTERING UNDER MARKET-DRIVEN MODELS

Vaccines face distinctive problems because of their unique characteristics, but they are not alone in facing problems. Many other areas in pharmaceutical R&D reflect commodification problems, experiencing chronic underfunding problems and lack of prioritization of R&D. Diseases with limited markets, or markets predominantly located in the Global South, struggle to attract R&D funding. This group of diseases includes the so-called neglected diseases, as well as orphan diseases. This highly heterogeneous group of diseases is unified by the fact that they affect a very small number of people – as well as the fact that the majority of these diseases are thought to be caused by genetic factors. In the United States, for example, an orphan disease is currently defined as a condition affecting fewer than 200,000 people across the country.[6] Examples of these conditions include Lou Gehrig's disease (amyotrophic lateral sclerosis, a degenerative disorder) and cystic fibrosis (a progressive disease triggering persistent inflammation of the lungs and other organs). Collectively, orphan diseases affect twenty-five million Americans. In Europe, an orphan disease is defined as a condition affecting five or fewer people per 10,000 across the European Union.[7] Currently, around thirty million people in Europe are affected by an orphan disease. The WHO calculates that 400 million people across the globe are likely to suffer from one of these conditions.[8] This estimate means that one in fifteen people worldwide suffers from an orphan disease. Yet, in spite of this enormous burden on individual and public health, orphan diseases do not receive a lot of R&D attention and funding.[9]

There are also several cases of diseases or areas of biomedical research involving goods needed in the Global South and North alike for which longstanding models of R&D have proved lacking. For example, legal scholar Kevin Outterson has produced an extensive body of work documenting how R&D on antimicrobial resistance is insufficient.[10] The WHO defines antimicrobial resistance as occurring

---

[6] US Food & Drug Administration, "Orphan Products: Hope for People with Rare Diseases" (2018), www.fda.gov/drugs/information-consumers-and-patients-drugs/orphan-products-hope-people-rare-diseases.

[7] European Medicines Agency, "Orphan Designation: Overview," www.ema.europa.eu/en/human-regulatory/overview/orphan-designation-overview.

[8] World Health Organization, "Rare Diseases," (2013), www.who.int/medicines/areas/priority_medicines/Ch6_19Rare.pdf.

[9] See e.g. Carolyn Y. Johnson, "Why the Diseases That Cause the Most Harm Don't Always Get the Most Research Money" (July 17, 2015) *Washington Post*, www.washingtonpost.com/news/wonk/wp/2015/07/17/why-the-diseases-that-cause-the-most-harm-dont-always-get-the-most-research-money/.

[10] See e.g. Kevin Outterson, "The Vanishing Public Domain: Antibiotic Resistance, Pharmaceutical Innovation and Intellectual Property Law" (2005) 67 *University of Pittsburgh Law Review* 67–123;

"when bacteria, viruses, fungi and parasites change over time and no longer respond to medicines making infections harder to treat and increasing the risk of disease spread, severe illness and death. As a result of drug resistance, antibiotics and other antimicrobial medicines become ineffective and infections become increasingly difficult or impossible to treat."[11] According to 2019 data, antimicrobial resistance accounts for 2.8 million infections and over 35,000 deaths per year in the United States alone.[12] Globally, it accounts for 700,000 deaths each year, a number the United Nations project will soar to several million a year absent a forceful intervention in this area to bolster R&D.[13] Yet, in 2020 the WHO noted that the "clinical pipeline of new antimicrobials is dry."[14]

Even within areas of biomedical R&D considered as a whole as more mainstream, there are problems. The example of cancer R&D may be instructive here. Cancer R&D has long been characterized by considerably more robust activity targeting products for late-stage cancers than the development of preventative products, or products targeting early-stage cancers.[15] While there are contributing scientific reasons for this disparity, researchers Eric Budish, Benjamin Roin, and Heidi Williams, working in the fields of economics and law, have shown that the problem of underinvestment in early-stage cancer R&D also relates to economic considerations: Private-sector companies tend to direct resources toward products that they can bring to market quickly.[16] Clinical trials for products targeting late-stage cancers are shorter – and consequently less costly to run – than clinical trials for products targeting early-stage cancers and for preventative products. Budish and colleagues concluded that companies underinvest in preventative and early-stage cancer R&D "because late-stage cancer drugs can be brought to market comparatively quickly, whereas drugs to treat early-stage cancer and to prevent cancer require a much longer time to bring to market."[17] Health economist Austin Frakt summarized these findings by noting that "preventing cancer is not the priority in drug development."[18]

As with vaccines, which operate primarily as preventatives, an approach to cancer R&D driven primarily by public health imperatives would prioritize the allocation of

Kevin Outterson, "The Legal Ecology of Resistance: The Role of Antibiotic Resistance in Pharmaceutical Innovation" (2010) 31 *Cardozo Law Review* 613–78.

[11] World Health Organization, "Antimicrobial Resistance," chapter 1, note 18.

[12] US Centers for Disease Control and Prevention, "Biggest Threats and Data " (2021), https://www.cdc.gov/drugresistance/biggest-threats.html.

[13] World Health Organization, "No Time to Wait: Securing the Future from Drug-Resistant Infections" (2019) Report to the Secretary-General of the United Nations, www.who.int/antimicrobial-resistance/interagency-coordination-group/IACG_final_report_EN.pdf.

[14] World Health Organization, "Antimicrobial Resistance," chapter 1, note 18.

[15] Eric Budish, Benjamin N. Roin, & Heidi Williams, "Do Firms Underinvest in Long-Term Research? Evidence from Cancer Clinical Trials" (2015) 105(7) *American Economic Review* 2044–85.

[16] Budish, Roin, & Williams, "Do Firms Underinvest," note 15.

[17] Budish, Roin, & Williams, "Do Firms Underinvest," note 15, at 2045.

[18] Austin Frakt, "Why Preventing Cancer Is Not the Priority in Drug Development" (December 28, 2015) *New York Times*, www.nytimes.com/2015/12/29/upshot/why-preventing-cancer-is-not-the-priority-in-drug-development.html.

resources to research on products to prevent the onset of disease or curb its burden as early as possible, thereby saving lives and reducing costs to health-care systems. A predominantly market-driven approach, by contrast, leads to the current scenario: Even though public health places a premium on preventative approaches and early interventions, products targeting late-stage disease are more immediately monetizable.

C.3 A FRAUGHT RELATIONSHIP BETWEEN PUBLIC HEALTH AND SOVEREIGNTY-ASSERTING BEHAVIORS

The gulf between public health imperatives and many of the ways in which health goods are produced and allocated is further accentuated when exclusionary behaviors rooted in property rights intersect with exclusionary behaviors anchored in notions of sovereignty.

The book discussed the phenomenon of vaccine nationalism in Chapter 4, emphasizing the inequitable allocation of R&D outputs in the vaccine ecosystem. Nationalistic practices, however, extend well beyond the allocative realm. Legal scholar Sam Halabi has explored the problem of "viral sovereignty" in the context of the transfer of samples of biological resources, which includes the exchange of pathogens within the scientific community at large.[19] One longstanding problem identified by researchers in connection with the transfer of biological materials is that a significant amount of these materials is generated in, or provided by, lower-income countries, but often used to the benefit of populations predominantly located in higher-income countries.[20] This discrepancy, with its ties to much more profound and exploitative discrepancies between higher and lower income countries, has on occasion prompted some countries to refuse to share viral matter needed to develop and manufacture vaccines. For example, in late 2006 Indonesia announced that it would withhold samples of the influenza A (H5N1) virus from the network overseen by the WHO for the surveillance and management of influenza viruses – the same described in Kapczynski's study.[21] Indonesia framed its refusal by resorting to notions of sovereignty that, as legal scholar David Fidler has observed, technically did not violate any laws or binding precepts:

> Indonesia claimed that the samples are its sovereign property and do not constitute resources that other countries or the international community can access and use

---

[19] Sam F. Halabi, "Viral Sovereignty, Intellectual Property, and the Changing Global System for Sharing Pathogens for Infectious Disease Research" (2019) 28 *Annals of Health Law* 101–26. See also Sam F. Halabi & Rebecca Katz, eds., *Viral Sovereignty and Technology Transfer: The Changing Global System for Sharing Pathogens for Public Health Research* (Cambridge University Press, 2020).

[20] See e.g. Ciara Staunton & Keymanthri Moodley, "Data Mining and Biological Sample Exportation from South Africa: A New Wave of Bioexploitation under the Guise of Clinical Care?" (2016) 106 *South African Medical Journal* 136–38, at 138; Halabi, "Viral Sovereignty," note 19, at 108–09.

[21] Kapczynski, "Order without Intellectual Property Law," note 1.

without Indonesia's consent. This claim cut against the ethos and practice of sample sharing (...). Indonesia did not equate this ethos with an international legal obligation to engage in sharing that limited its sovereign rights over the samples. From a legal perspective, Indonesia's arguments were plausible [as the obligation to share] was not organized under treaty law, so no countries had treaty obligations to share samples. In addition, international law on infectious diseases applicable to Indonesia when this controversy began contained no obligations to share samples with WHO.[22]

Indonesia's motivations to withhold the samples were an understandable reaction against centuries of exploitation of the resources of lower-income countries – an exploitation that includes the appropriation of resources for both medical and nonmedical purposes. In this particular case, Indonesia's stance was a reaction to the fact that samples it had provided to the WHO had been used by scientists in a wealthier country (Australia) to develop a vaccine against avian influenza for which patent applications were now pending. The refusal was therefore also a protest against a longstanding practice of higher-income countries, which by patenting health goods developed with materials shared by lower-income countries, drive the price of these goods up, often preventing populations in the Global South from accessing them.[23]

At the same time, the position taken by Indonesia highlights the fragility of international forms of cooperation in the development of health goods. While international intellectual property emanates from a body of hard law, global public health is regulated predominantly through weaker normative frameworks. Breach of these norms may sometimes be remedied through diplomacy and similar bargaining processes, but in many cases there are no legal pathways to force noncooperative players to change their behavior. While Indonesia eventually changed its stance through intermediation of the World Health Assembly,[24] the many higher-income countries that engage in vaccine nationalism have yet to abandon or temper their practice of reserving disproportionately large doses of vaccine earlier in a pandemic or epidemic. Global procurement of health goods through an international body such as Covax may constitute a first step in the right direction – but one that so far remains structurally limited, as there is no mechanism in place to bind sovereign actors to collaborative frameworks for the allocation of vaccines.

The constraints to which the development and the allocation of vaccines are subject from the perspective of international relations illustrate the need for reinforced structures in international law and policy for the creation and

---

22 David P. Fidler, "Influenza Virus Samples, International Law, and Global Health Diplomacy" (2008) 14 *Emerging Infectious Diseases* 22–94.
23 Fidler, "Influenza Virus Samples," note 22.
24 The World Health Assembly is the forum for decision-making at the World Health Organization. See World Health Organization, "World Health Assembly," www.who.int/about/governance/world-health-assembly.

management of health goods – at both the institutional and procedural levels, enabling swift responses to nationalistic or sovereignty-asserting practices that are detrimental to global public health.

In much the same way that market constructs are poor drivers of socially valuable R&D on technologies needed to prevent and respond to the spread of emerging pathogens, sovereignty-asserting behaviors – which may be appropriate in many other contexts – fit poorly into global public health frameworks. Countries draw and take advantage of artificial lines that bear no resemblance to the borderless progression of disease and the toll it takes on human health.

At the time the writing of this book drew to an end, the European Union announced its support of a "pandemic treaty," noting that "the international community needs to be much better prepared and better aligned in responding to possible future pandemics across the entire cycle of detection, alarm and response."[25] While the effectiveness of such a treaty will largely depend on the substantive content that is successfully incorporated into binding provisions, it is significant that the treaty proponents recognized the need for the international community to adopt legally binding frameworks in this area of public health. The European Union justified its support of beginning treaty negotiations through the World Health Assembly precisely in these terms:

> A treaty is a legally binding instrument under international law. An international treaty on pandemics adopted under the World Health Organization (WHO) would enable countries around the globe to strengthen national, regional and global capacities and resilience to future pandemics.[26]

One goal of the treaty would be to "ensure universal and equitable access to medical solutions, such as vaccines, medicines and diagnostics."[27] For now, this goal remains largely aspirational. The book has highlighted non-treaty avenues that are available to actors in the vaccine ecosystem – and, by adaptation, to players in ecosystems suffering from comparable problems in the production and allocation of health goods – to mitigate some of the longstanding problems faced by global public health. Whether through a treaty or incremental interventions across interdependent fields of law and policy, the time for change is overdue. As we wait, the next pandemic is around the corner.

---

[25] Council of the European Union, "An International Treaty on Pandemic Prevention and Preparedness," (2021), www.consilium.europa.eu/en/policies/coronavirus/pandemic-treaty/.

[26] Council of the European Union, "An International Treaty," note 25.

[27] Council of the European Union, "An International Treaty," note 25.

Index

3D printing, 177–78

Affordable Care Act, 31, 112
algorithms, 165, 171, 172, 179
An Act to Encourage Vaccination (1813), 27
antimicrobial resistance, 11, 25, 141, 158, 183
Army, 51–52, 64, 86, 95–96
artificial intelligence, 178–80
    bias, 6, 180
AstraZeneca, 53, 103, 119, 150
astroturfing, 164

Babington Macaulay, Thomas, 68
BARDA. *See* US Biomedical Advanced Research
    and Development Authority (BARDA)
Belmont Report, 42
biologics, 6, 28–29, 30–31, 61, 90, 134–35
Biologics Control Act (1902), 28
Biologics License Application (BLA), 33
biosimilar drugs, 31
bioterrorism, 15, 52, 53

CEPI. *See* Coalition for Epidemic Preparedness
    Innovations (CEPI)
clinical trials, 32–33, 37–47
    non-publication of results, 47
    publication delays, 46–47
    racial and ethnic disparities, 42–47
Coalition for Epidemic Preparedness Innovations
    (CEPI), 144–48
Combating Antibiotic-Resistant Bacteria
    Biopharmaceutical Accelerator (CARB-X),
    140, 141
Common Rule, 42
compulsory licenses, 130, 131
coronaviruses, 3, 14, 64–66
COVID-19, 3, 7, 35, 79, 94, 102–4

COVID-19 Prevention Trials Network
    (COVPN), 43–44
COVID-19 Technology Access Pool (C-TAP),
    117–18, 120
COVID-19 Vaccines Global Access (COVAX),
    51, 148–53

Declaration of Helsinki, 46
Diamond v. Chakrabarty, 74
disinformation, 156, 162–64, 167–71
Doha Declaration on the TRIPS Agreement and
    Public Health (2001), 71, 131
Drugs for Neglected Diseases Initiative
    (DNDi), 140

Ebola, 7, 14, 54, 55, 66, 79–81, 85, 144
emergency use authorization (EUA), 35, 122, 150, 176
European Medicines Agency, 35, 178

Facebook, 160, 166–72
Fauci, Anthony, 45, 46, 79
FDA. *See* US Food and Drug
    Administration (FDA)
Federal Food, Drug and Cosmetic Act (1938), 39
flu, 100–2, 185–86
    influenza A, 185–86
    Spanish flu, 101
    swine flu, 100–2

Gates Foundation, 49, 143, 145, 149
Gavi. *See* Global Alliance for Vaccines and
    Immunizations (Gavi)
generic drugs, 31
GlaxoSmithKline, 82–84
Global Alliance for Vaccines and Immunizations
    (Gavi), 51, 148–49
grants, 107–8

hepatitis C, 140
HIV/AIDS, 14, 50, 52, 136
Horstmann, Dorothy, 74

incentives to innovation, 68, 94
    limitations, 79–83
    non-intellectual property incentives, 106–14
Innovative Medicines Initiative (IMI), 139, 140
Instagram, 160, 166, 169, 171
insurance, 111, 112
intellectual property, 4, 67–89, 115–16, 147
    harmonization, 8, 70
    instrumentalization, 84–86
    "intellectual property without intellectual prop-
        erty", 182
    limitations of proprietary models, 79
    vaccines, 73–78
    waivers, 91–92
internationally displaced people, 104
    See also refugees
Investigational New Drug application (IND),
    32, 33

Jenner, Edward, 17–18, 71–72
Johnson & Johnson, 24, 53, 119

Karikó, Katalina, 174
Kelsey, Frances, 39

licenses, 124–25
    Apache 2.0 license, 125
    General Public License, 125
    MIT license, 125
LinkedIn, 160
Lyme disease, 82, 83, 84

Machlup, Fritz, 69, 107
malaria, 12, 49, 50
March of Dimes, 38, 75
measles, 13, 19–20, 21–22, 23
Merck, 85, 86
Middle East Respiratory Syndrome (MERS), 14,
    65, 146
military, 13, 51, 52
misinformation, 156, 158–73
    automatization, 161–64
    Russia, 163–64
    weaponization, 162–63
Moderna, 44–45, 50, 53, 96, 119, 122
Morse, Stephen, 14
mRNA, 24, 119, 174–75 *See also* Karikó, Katalin

National Foundation for Infantile Paralysis.
    See March of Dimes

National Institutes of Health (NIH), 29, 42, 107
neglected diseases, 48, 49, 50, 183
NewLink Genetics, 81, 84, 85, 86, 115
NIH Revitalization Act (1993), 42

Open COVID-19 Pledge, 124–27
open science, 181, 182

patent, 4, 8, 68–71, 73–78, 134–36
    Medicines Patent Pool, 116, 118
    pledges, 121–29
Pfizer, 44, 50, 53, 119, 150, 179
pharmaceutical drugs, 29, 61–62
Pinterest, 160, 165, 166, 169
polio, 1, 19, 38, 73–75
prizes, 109, 110, 119, 120, 128
Public Health Emergency of International
    Concern, 63, 120, 129
Public Health Service Act (1944), 29, 30, 32, 34
public–private partnerships, 137–55
    access partnerships, 139
    Coalition for Epidemic Preparedness
        Innovations (CEPI), 144–48
    Combating Antibiotic-Resistant Bacteria
        Biopharmaceutical Accelerator (CARB-X),
        140–41
    COVID-19 Vaccines Global Access (COVAX),
        148–53
    definition and taxonomy of, 138–41
    Drugs for Neglected Diseases Initiative
        (DNDi), 140
    Global Alliance for Vaccines and
        Immunizations (Gavi), 51, 148–49
    health-focused partnerships, 139–41
    Innovative Medicines Initiative (IMI), 139–40
    limitations, 141–43
    product development partnerships, 139
    vaccine-specific partnerships, 143–53
Pure Food and Drugs Act (1906), 28

QAnon, 171

Reddit, 160
refugees, 104 *See also* internationally displaced
    people
Regulatory exclusivities, 111
respirators, 126, 132, 134

Salk, Jonas, 38, 74, 75
Sanofi Pasteur, 83–84, 86–89, 95–97, 179
Serum Institute of India, 8, 150
Severe Acute Respiratory Syndrome (SARS), 14,
    64–66
smallpox, 16, 27–28, 71

Snapchat, 160
social media, 160–73
 Facebook, 160, 166–72
 Instagram, 160, 166
 LinkedIn, 160
 Pinterest, 160, 165–66, 169
 Reddit, 160
 self-regulation, 164–73
 Snapchat, 160
 TikTok (Douyin), 160
 Twitter, 160, 162–64, 166
 WhatsApp, 160
 YouTube, 160, 169
sovereignty, 105, 185–87
 "viral sovereignty", 185–86

Tesla (car company), 121, 122, 123
thalidomide, 39
The Lancet (medical journal), 158, 159
TikTok, 160
trade secrecy, 90–92, 134–35, 175
Trade-Related Aspects of Intellectual Property
 Rights (TRIPS), 69–71, 130–31
tuberculosis, 15, 50, 116
Tuskegee Study, 40, 41
Twitter, 160, 162–64, 166
 Twitter Bot Detection Challenge, 162

US Biomedical Advanced Research and
 Development Authority (BARDA), 87, 88,
 89, 97
US Defense Advanced Research Projects Agency
 (DARPA), 52, 162
US Food and Drug Administration (FDA), 8, 26,
 29–31, 37
 Biologics Effectiveness and Safety System (FDA
 BEST), 37
 Center for Biologics Evaluation and Research
 (CBER), 33
 Food and Drug Administration Amendments
 Act (2007), 46
 Food and Drug Administration Modernization
 Act (1997), 46
 Kefauver-Harris Amendments, 39
 Sentinel Program, 37
US National Institute of Allergy and Infectious
 Diseases (NIAID), 43, 45, 87, 107
US Trade Representative, 132–33,
 136–37
US Uniform Trade Secrets Act, 90

vaccine
 3D printing, 177–78
 access to, 93
  advance orders for, 99–103
  affordability, 93–99
  allocation of, 4, 100, 186
  anti-vaccine groups, 167–71
  artificial intelligence, 6, 178–80
  clinical trials, 36, 37–47, 59
  colonialism, 154
  commodification of, 56–57
  COVID-19, 64–66, 79, 102–4, 160–61
  definition of, 18
  disinformation, 156, 162–64, 167–72
  Ebola, 54, 66, 79–81, 84–86
  equity, 98–105, 133, 151
  exclusive licensing, 86–89
  farms, 27
  flu, 59, 175, 179
  hesitancy, 15, 19, 21, 156, 157–58, 179
  history of, 16–18
  HIV/AIDS, 52, 57, 116, 175
  hoarding, 155
  Human papillomavirus (HPV), 78,
   97–98
  inequitable access to, 20
  intellectual property of, 73–78
  licensure, 35
  Lyme disease, 81–84
  mandates, 27
  measles, mumps, and rubella, 21, 23,
   159
  misinformation, 156, 158–73
  monitoring, 35–37
  nationalism, 99–105
  patent applications, 75–76
  patent pools, 118–20
  polio, 19, 38–39, 73, 148
  preclinical development, 32
  pricing considerations, 93–95
  procurement, 50–51, 148–52
  projected savings associated with administration
   of, 20–21
  public health value of, 18–20
  regulation, 26–37
  Severe Acute Respiratory Syndrome (SARS),
   64–66
  side effects, 9, 37, 157
  smallpox, 27, 73
  swine flu (H1N1), 101–2
  technology pledge, 126–29
  trust, 43, 46–47, 157, 158–59
  Types of (US Department of Health and
   Human Services 2021 classification), 23–25
  Vaccine Adverse Event Reporting System
   (VAERS), 36–37
  Vaccine Safety Datalink, 37

whooping cough, 77–78
Zika, 50, 62–64, 86–89, 95–97

Wakefield, Andrew, 159
Waterhouse, Benjamin, 72
WhatsApp, 160
Willowbrook State School "experiment", 41, 42

World Health Organization, 2, 7, 13, 14, 63, 110, 138, 143, 149, 165, 168, 176

YouTube, 160, 169, 173

Zika, 7, 14, 50, 54, 62–64, 86–89, 95–97, 147, 174

Lightning Source UK Ltd.
Milton Keynes UK
UKHW022243120422
401492UK00013B/430

9 781009 125765